The Ch
A Muslim Parent's Handbook

The Child in Islam
A Muslim Parent's Handbook

BY

NORMA TARAZI

With contributions by Zeba Siddiqui

American Trust Publications

American Trust Publications
2622 East Main Street
Plainfield, Indiana 46168-2703

Library of Congress cataloging in publication data
Tarazi, Norma.
   The Child In Islam/Norma Tarazi; with contributions
   by Zeba Siddiqui.
      p.   cm.
   Includes bibliographical references and index.
   ISBN 0-89259-158-7
   1. Child rearing—Religious aspects—Islam.
   2. Parenting—Religious aspects—Islam.
   3. Muslim children—Religious life.
   4. Muslim children—United States.   I. Siddiqui, Zeba. II. Title.
HQ769.3.T37 1995   95-19619
649' . 1'0882971—dc20   CIP

Contents

Introduction

This book is a mothers' book—not that it can't be read by fathers as well—the outgrowth of a mothers' study group which met in Kuwait before the Gulf War, focused on rearing children in an Islamic way. The mothers were mostly American and British converts to Islam, although in cosmopolitan Kuwait there were women from many other backgrounds. The group was an offshoot of meetings for English-speaking Muslim women, held weekly in the home of Sister Zainab Ashry in Kuwait for more than ten years prior to the Gulf War.

From their knowledge of Islam, the women involved wanted to study the implications of their faith on their child-rearing practices. The first step was to collect information—any Qur'anic verse or *hadith*—that a participant found relevant. Other information was collected from such knowledgeable people and books as were available. Monthly discussions were organized on different topics.

Since the war, some of the participating sisters have returned to Kuwait, but many of our group are now scattered all over the world. All the notes and papers collected by the study group were in my home in Kuwait when the invasion occurred; fortunately my husband was able to salvage them and bring them here to our new home in the States. I felt an obligation to compile this collected information to share with other Muslims, especially converts like myself. My deepest thanks must go to my husband, whose support and cooperation gave me the means to carry out this task.

This book begins with the birth of a child to Muslim parents, and the traditional Islamic response to the birth, following the example of Prophet Muhammad (S). Very few specific actions are defined, and these mostly relate to practices at the time of birth. All of these fall into the category of *sunnah* (following the Prophet's example or what he approved of in others), and though highly recommended, they are not *fard* (obligatory) actions.

Aside from these few simple practices carried out when a baby comes into the world, Islam has no ceremonies devoted exclusively to children—no first communion, no coming-of-age celebrations. Children are not segregated into a special world separate from that of adults; they are members of families in the great, embracing cycle of human life. The family supports them when they are young; they support the family in their productive years, and in old age they are again supported by the family. They grow and develop gradually in a system that encourages growth and learning, but places little emphasis on milestones and anniversaries.

A large portion of this book is given to defining relationships from the Qur'an and *hadith*. To understand the significance of the child in Muslim society, it is necessary to recognize the total number and value of his or her relationships within it, which are different from the relationships defined by other societies. Chapter 1 includes some of the traditions of the Prophet Muhammad that apply to the newborn. Chapter 2 describes the nature of the child's relationship with Allah and the spiritual world, with some suggestions for encouraging spiritual awareness. Chapter 3 contains Qur'anic verses and *ahadith* relevant to the child's relationship with his or her parents.

In light of these definitions, and with reference to the Islamic teachings concerning morals, manners, and the purpose of life, an attempt is made in chapters 4, 5, and 6 to present an organized structure dealing with the practical how-to of rearing a child in an Islamic way, from a parent's viewpoint. Chapters

7 and 8 progressively broaden out the child's world by adding brothers and sisters, extended family, and community relationships. The practical suggestions for improving relationships among adult family members, in order to pave the way for improving the child's relations with his or her extended family, are an important aspect of chapter 8.

The only relationship which really changes for the child as he or she grows up is that of accountability to Allah, since no child is accountable for his or her actions before reaching the age of understanding. All other relationships develop and deepen as the child grows but remain basically the same, for the general commands to honor parents, show respect to elders, be gentle with younger ones, and honor family ties continue for a Muslim throughout his or her life.

I pray to Allah that this book may bring only good to mothers and their children, and that He protect them from any mistakes or misunderstandings. I have done my best to prepare the material contained within it in a suitable manner and hope to see other literature published on this important subject, expanding and enriching it. While I alone am responsible for the contents, I am deeply indebted to the many sisters who helped collect references and discussed the practical implications of our findings. I have no list to prompt me and consequently may have unwittingly forgotten some names, but I well remember Terry, Lianna, Salma, Noura, Mia, Khadijah, Sandra, Hicleir, Debbie, Sara, Maryam, Aneesah, Dianne, Karen, Kauthar and Nawal from Kuwait, all of us working together on this project. My friend Daaiyah Saleem in Ohio has also been very helpful, offering many suggestions for improvement and clarification as she aided in proofreading. My sister-in-law Ghada, of course, has helped along the way.

In the course of preparing this book for publication, sister Zeba Siddiqui was chosen by the publisher to edit the text. I have known Zeba, a mother of four and a grandmother, and author of several excellent childrens' books as well as the

Parent's Manual: A Guide for Muslim Parents Living in North America, for several years. When I heard she had taken on this task, I asked her to add anything she felt was missing, from her years of experience and knowledge of the subject. She has supplied all of the hadith reference numbers in the text, in itself an enormous task. In addition to editing, she has filled out and amplified several topics, checking and adding material where needed. The sections on the Hereafter, *tahara*, respect for religion, and hospitality are prepared and written by her. It was only fair therefore that her name should appear on the title page of this book in recognition of her valuable contribution. I am deeply grateful to her for her help and input.

I also need to thank my children, who suffered through my learning experience and projects for self-improvement in parenting skills, and my mother, whose life-long interest in the growth and development of children helped me understand the importance of the matter and the need for a book such as this.

A final note, to the book's non-Muslim readers: I have chosen to use the word *Allah* throughout the book instead of the word *God*. The words are interchangable in English for Muslims, but all of the women involved in this project have the habit, indeed, they have the love of refering to God, the God of Abraham, Moses, Jesus, and Muhammad, by His Arabic name, Allah.

Chapter One

THE NEWBORN

The creation of a child is something very special and wonderful, a time for us to marvel at the immense creative power of Allah. As He says,

> And We surely created man in the best of molds. (Qur'an 95:4)

> It is He Who fashioned you in the wombs as He pleases. There is no deity except Him, the All-Mighty, the All-Wise. (Qur'an 3:6)

> O mankind, if you are in doubt about the Resurrection, then (consider) that We created you out of dust, then out of sperm, then out of a clot, then out of a morsel of flesh, partly formed and partly unformed, in order to make (matters) clear to you. And We cause whom We will to remain in the wombs for an appointed term; then We bring you forth as babies, then (cause you to grow) so that you reach your full strength. (Qur'an 22:05; 40:67)

Each child is born different from every other. Even identical twins exhibit some minor differences. A sense of wonder comes over us as we gaze at a newborn, coming into this world from its Creator's hand, so perfectly formed, down to its minuscule fingernails. For all the preoccupations and worry that children may cause their parents, each one also has something special and endearing about him. There is something about a child's or a baby's face that tugs at our heart strings. When their faces glow with a smile, they bring pleasure to all who see them. When their faces are sad in fear or hurt, only the hardest of hearts can resist the desire to respond to them and help.

Allah speaks about the creation of mankind, and of the human individual, in moving and eloquent verses of the Qur'an:

> And We surely created man from an extract of clay.
> Then We placed him as a drop (of sperm) in a firmly
> fixed place of rest. Then We made the sperm into a
> clot of congealed blood; then We made the clot into
> a (fetus) lump; then out of that lump We created
> bones; then We clothed the bones with flesh; then
> from it We produced another creation. So blessed be
> Allah, the Best of Creators! (Qur'an 23:12-14)

> Such is the Knower of the Unseen and the Visible,
> the All-Mighty, the All-Wise, Who made all things
> He created good, and He began the creation of Man
> from clay. Then He made his progeny from an
> extract of despised fluid. Then He fashioned him
> and breathed into him from His Divine Spirit, and
> made for you hearing and sight and feeling. How lit-
> tle you are thankful! (Qur'an 32:6-9)

> And that it is He Who gives life and death, and that
> He created the two pairs, the male and the female,
> from a drop when it pours forth. (Qur'an 53:44-46)
> Does Man think that he will be left aimless? Was
> he not a drop of gushing fluid? Then he was a clot;

then He created and fashioned, and made of him a pair, the male and the female. Is not that One able to give life to the dead? (Qur'an 75:36-40)

Then let Man consider of what he is created. He is created from a gushing fluid, coming from between the loins and the arch of bones. Surely He is able to return him (to life). (Qur'an 86:5-8)

And Allah created you from dust, then from a drop; then He made you into pairs. And no female carries or gives birth without His knowledge. And no one grows old among those who become old, nor is anything lessened of his term, without its being in a Book (of decrees). Truly, that is easy for Allah. (Qur'an 35:11)

Did We not create you from a despised fluid? Then We put it in a secure abode for a known term, and thus We decreed. Then how excellent is Our decreeing! (Qur'an 77:20-23)

These, then, are our origins—the origin of every descendant of Adam (S). Created out of the lowliest of materials, the human being nonetheless is the carrier of an immortal soul, which comes from Allah and will return to Him.

And so the new baby comes. It is launched into the ship of existence in this world. It carries with it the personality which its Creator gave it, its own bit of individuality and uniqueness within its species. Boy or girl, it is a cause for deep thankfulness and rejoicing. If it is healthy, we are deeply grateful and pray that this favor will be continued; if it is not, we ask Allah for patience and help with the test He has seen fit to send us, and begin our life with him or her.

The beginning of life for a Muslim, like its middle and its end, has a strong Islamic color. Following the *sunnah* of the blessed Prophet of Islam (S) in regard to a new baby is at once our duty and our pride, for it marks us and our newborn as members of the *ummah* (the community) of Muhammad (S), the best and noblest of mankind.

THE SUNNAHS OF THE PROPHET (S) AT THE BIRTH OF A BABY

Five events which are sunnah—that is, according to the practice or recommendations of the Prophet (S)—are associated with the newborn baby. These sunnahs are not *fard*, or obligatory for Muslims. They are, however, highly recommended. There is no punishment for noncompliance, and the form or detailed "how to" is reasonably flexible for the parents' specific situation. These events are: reciting the *adhan* in the baby's ears, *tahneek, tasmaya, aqiqah,* and *khitan.* These are carried out as follows.

Adhan (call to prayer)

According to the Prophet's *hadith,* if the new human being begins its life in this world by being called to the worship of the one true God, it is protected from Satan. He said,

> If one has a baby and makes the adhan in its right ear
> and the iqamah in its left ear, Satan will not disturb
> the child, Allah willing. (Baihaqi)

This should be done as soon after birth as possible, according to the instructions of the Prophet (S). It is reported in the hadith collection of Abu Dawud that the Prophet (S) made the adhan in the ear of his grandson, Hasan bin 'Ali (R), immediately after Fatima (R) gave birth to him (Abu Dawud,

5086). This may be done by either parent or by any Muslim. However, according to the Shafi'yyah school of thought, it is disliked for anyone to recited the adhan if they are in a state of impurity. Therefore, according to that school, the mother should refrain from reciting the adhan while experiencing postpartum bleeding.

Tahneek (masticatory feeding)

Tahneek refers to the sunnah of softening a date by any ordinary means and rubbing a small amount in the baby's mouth. Anyone can do this, following it with *du'a* (supplication) for the child, according to the example of the Prophet (s), who chewed dates to soften them before feeding.

> Abu Musa (R) said: A son was born to me and I took him to the Prophet (S), who named him Ibrahim, did tahneek for him with a date, invoked Allah to bless him, and returned him to me. *(Bukhari, 7.376)*

The idea of tahneek may seem strange to anyone not familiar with it. However, dates are a wonderfully wholesome, nutritious food, sweet and delicious. Thus, on a physical level, tahneek may be thought of as resembling the practice of many hospitals in giving newborns a little sugar water as sustenance before the mother's milk comes in. The deeper spiritual meaning and benefit of this is known only to Allah and to His Messenger (S), who instituted the practice for his *ummah* (community).

Tasmiya (naming)

In the hadith cited above, the Prophet (S) gave infants names following the tahneek. Several *ahadith* relate to naming a child. The Prophet (S) said,

On the Day of Resurrection, you will be called by
your names and by your fathers' names, so give
yourselves good names. *(Abu Dawud, 4930)*

Allah's Messenger (S) favored names reflecting servant-
hood to Allah Most High, such as Abdullah and Abdur-
Rahman, and advised calling boys by the names of prophets
(Abu Dawud, 4932). Some other general considerations concerning the giving of a name can be summarized as follows:

1) Muslims should not use names that overly glorify the
   individual being named, such as Malik al-Mulk (the
   King of Kings). Many ahadith record the fact that the
   Prophet (S) changed the names of individuals that he
   did not consider appropriate for one reason or another
   (Muslim, 5329; Abu Dawud, 4932, 4938, 4942).

2) Names that are specifically identified with other reli-
   gions are forbidden, just as wearing priestly garments,
   following non-Islamic religious customs, and eating
   food offered in unIslamic religious rites are all forbidden. Names like Martin Luther (the Protestant
   reformer) or Siva (a Hindu god) should not be used by
   Muslims. The names of prophets, including the name
   Jesus, are allowed and were even favored by Prophet
   Muhammad, who named his third son Ibrahim.

3) As a matter of common sense, it is better to avoid giving
   a name that might subject a child to ridicule in any particular social group, or calling him by a nickname that
   might embarrass him. For example, "Bunny" may
   sound like a cute name for a baby, but an older child
   might cringe at the sound. Children as well as adults
   have a sense of dignity and it is good to encourage it,
   for a feeling of dignity gives children a sense of high
   self-esteem and self-worth, a sense of certainty and
   confidence about themselves and their direction.

Ibn al-Qayyim, in his book on children, *Tehfet Al Moudood* (The Gift of the Newborn), gives a reasonable argument in favor of the father's having the right to select the child's name. While giving the father the final say can certainly prevent disputes, at the same time, it is certainly recommended that he consult the child's mother, and perhaps the grandparents as well.

Aqiqah (sacrifice for the newborn)

To celebrate the birth of a child, the family slaughters a sheep or other animal and serves the meat at a party for friends and family. The formal announcement of the name may be made at this time. The Prophet (S) said,

> Every child . . . is ransomed by his aqiqah, which is done on the seventh day. (Tirmidhi, al-Nasa'i and Ibn Majah)

Ransoming (or being in pledge for, or depending on), is explained as meaning that the parents are doing something that will protect the child from growing up a nonbeliever. It is reported that the Messenger of Allah (S) sacrificed a sheep on the seventh day for his grandson Hasan (R) and instructed the boy's mother, his daughter Fatimah (R), to shave the baby's head and give the weight of his hair in silver as *sadaqah* (charity). *(Mishkat,* 4154; *Muwatta*; Abu Dawud, 2835). He said,

> A boy is ransomed by his aqiqah. Sacrifice is made for him on the seventh day, his head is shaved, and he is given a name. *(Abu Dawud, 2832)*

> If anyone has a child born to him and wishes to offer a sacrifice on its behalf, he may offer two sheep resembling each other for a boy and one for a girl. *(Abu Dawud, 2836, 2829 and 2830)*

People today ask, why two for a boy and one for a girl. Actually, though this one, often quoted hadith makes this statement, there are other ahadith, and reported examples from the companions, of people doing the same for both sons and daughters (See Muwatta, for example). In fact, hadith have minor differences in details of these sunnah events.

Shaving the baby's head and weighing the hair to calculate money for charity is not a "ceremony" done at the party but a simple, unconnected act carried out at about the same time with similar significance. It is normal for babies to lose their initial hair and new hair grows in, gradually thickening. Shaving the head at this early state can avoid the cleaning problem of normal hair shedding. The shaving can be done by anyone, in any normal manner. The practice of shaving only part of the baby's hair is not acceptable, as is made clear by the following *hadith:*

> The Prophet (S) saw a boy with part of his head shaved and part left unshaven. He forbade them to do that, saying: Shave it all or leave it all. *(Abu Dawud, 4182)*[1]

Tahneek and naming can be done at the same time or in conjunction with the aqiqah.

Khitan (circumcision)
The Prophet (S) said,

> The (practices related to) *fitrahh* (that is, the pure, correct human nature) are five: circumcision, shaving the pubic hair, trimming the mustache, cutting the nails, and removing the underarm hair. *(Bukhari, 7.77; Muwatta)*

---

[1] This hadith is not specific to babies, but discourages odd hair styles for Muslims of any age .

In the time of the Prophet (S), khitan was done for boys at about the time of their aqiqah, as reported in al-Baihaqi. Other ahadith mention it being done later. The details here are not critical. It goes without saying that this minor operation is easier on a small baby than it is on an older boy. If necessary, circumcision can be delayed for practical reasons, but it should be done before the boy starts praying regularly if only for the practical reason of simplifying *taharah*, or being clean.

Unlike in the Judaic tradition, in Islam circumcision is not a symbol of Allah's covenant with man. In fact, it is not mentioned anywhere in the Qur'an; the references to it occur in hadith. Circumcision was first practiced by the prophet Abraham (S), the spiritual ancestor of Muslims; a hadith cited in Bukhari mentions that he was circumcised at the age of eighty. Muslim commentators, however, have never emphasized this aspect.

Circumcision is an important aspect of *taharah* (purity and cleanliness), which is so strongly emphasized in Islam, for when the foreskin is not removed, or, as is done by some non-Muslim physicians, only partially removed, urine and other secretions can collect under the folded skin. In Islamic hygiene, all Muslims regularly wash with water at the toilet to remove what is impure *(najas)*; otherwise *wudu* (washing for prayer) is not acceptable. This area can become the site of very painful infections from bacterial growth. The minor operation of circumcision greatly simplifies basic hygiene for men and boys.

Chapter Two

DEVELOPING THE CHILD'S AWARENESS OF ISLAM

ALLAH TA'ALA

Every child is born possessing two innate qualities: his or her own individual nature and characteristics, and the basic, innate God-given nature common to every human being.

> Our Lord is the One Who gave each thing its natural disposition, then gave (it) guidance. (20:50)

Islam gives the word fitrah to this basic nature. The word fitrahis very important in understanding the Islamic view of Allah's creation. The fitrah of a thing is the innate nature, disposition, and characteristics which have been given to all the members of its species and to it individually by its Creator.

Islam teaches that the human being's original fitrah or nature, is pure and uncorrupted. Consequently, each newborn baby comes into this world in an absolutely pure state, untainted by anything such as "original sin," which is an alien concept in Islam. Its emotions and temperament are given to it by Allah, an inseparable part of its being. Like every other thing created by Allah, it is *muslim* with a small "m" in the sense that its original nature submits to its Lord.

And whatever is in the heavens and whatever is on
the earth, of moving creatures or the angels, pros-
trates to Allah, and they are not arrogant (before
their Lord). They fear their Lord above them, and
they do whatever they are commanded. (Qur'an
16:49-50)

And whoever are in the heavens and the earth prostrate to Allah, whether willingly or unwillingly, as
well as their shadows, in the mornings and evenings.
(Qur'an 13:15)

Later, as it grows up, it is brought up in the faith of its parents, whatever that may happen to be. The true faith which
corresponds with the basic fitrah of the human being is Islam—
that is, to be connected with and responsible to God Almighty.
The Prophet (S) said,

No child is born except on the fitrah (of connectedness to Allah), as the animal gives birth to a perfect
offspring. Do you find it mutilated? Then his parents
Judaize or Christianize or Magianize (referring to
the religion of the Zoroasterians or Parsees) him.
(Bukhari, 2:440 and 2.441)

The narrator of the hadith, Abu Hurayrah (R), then recited
the verse:

The fitrah of Allah, upon which He created mankind.
(Qur'an 30:30)

We are all aware of the variations among human beings.
Often this is very evident in the children of a family, for each
child is born with a unique temperament and characteristics—
its own special, individual Allah-given fitrah. One child may

be so slow and deliberate in his actions that he exasperates his mother. It takes him an hour to eat a meal, and he rarely runs, preferring to stroll calmly. This is his own inner timing, perhaps different from that of others around him, but it is how he has been created. Another child cannot sit still; his mother feeds him a bite here and a bite there as he runs around playing. One baby has a particularly grating sound to his cry. Another baby cries with a soft whimper, while still another howls like a police siren. Some babies seem to have come into the world fighting and angry, with irritable temperaments. Others are serene and contented from the start.

Obviously a small baby is incapable of intending to aggravate his parent on purpose, but toddlers and older children often do this. They deliberately test their parents now and then—or even most of the time—to see how far they can push them. But we must recognize the fact that this is not a sign of innate wickedness in children; it does not mean that they are bad or little devils or anything else evil. This is simply a part of their human nature: to cry and demand, to search for limits, to explore and define the world around them. They respond to their environment with the emotions of love, hate, fear, humor, jealousy, and wonder that Allah created in them.

As parents, we can make some elements of our child's nature more dominant by emphasizing them. We can likewise make them less noticeable by ignoring them. What we cannot do is to change our child into something incompatible with his true nature, for it is Allah Who created him as he is—not only his physical body but also his unique, individual characteristics and qualities.

The most important point to understand concerning fitrah is that it is the means by which we are connected to Allah. It is through Allah-given nature that the child can recognize his Creator and his connectedness with the world around him, and through which he is led to receive His guidance; it is also the source of his feeling of connectedness with the world around him. This is why we experience such peace while taking a walk in the woods or watching the sunset. A part of this sense is also the basic understanding of good and evil, truth and falsehood, which is part of the child's pure nature. When this is relatively uncorrupted, the child will have no difficulty in recognizing the truth of the prophets' message.

It is the task of the parents (more specifically of the mother, as she is the main guide for the child) to work with this pure nature. When a parent guides a child to recognize his Creator and teaches him a correct understanding of the world around him, the child's mind and understanding develop in a clear, straight manner, without distortions and complications. There is all the difference in the world between a child who has been guided by a sound Muslim parent's understanding, and a child whose understandings of life come primarily from non-directive parent substitutes, from the interaction he sees in the streets, or from watching television. The mind and understanding of the one are clear, straight, correct, and undistorted, corresponding to his fitrah, while the other's have almost no relation to any higher reality. This is why day care providers or babysitters simply cannot take the place of a mother, especially of a wise, understanding Muslim mother.

TRIALS

As much as we would like to avoid pain, distress, troubles, calamities, the pains of illness, disability and old age, it is Allah Who is in control of our destinies, and it is inevitable that we must bear our allotted portion of problems. Concerning this, the Holy Prophet (S) said,

> No weariness nor illness nor sorrow nor sadness nor hurt nor distress befalls a Muslim, even to the pricking of a thorn, without Allah's expiating some of his

sins by it. (In another version it is worded: "No calamity befalls. . . .") *(Bukhari, 7.545 and 7.544)*

Be moderate and stand firm in trouble that falls to the lot of a Muslim, for it is an expiation for him, even to stumbling on the path or the pricking of a thorn. *(Muslim, 6243)*

When a Muslim is afflicted by some trouble in his body, the angel is told to record for him his good deeds which he was accustomed to do. Then, if Allah cures him He washes and purifies him (from sins), and if He takes him in death, He forgives him and shows mercy to him. *(Mishkat, 1560)*

Our minds are often puzzled by the question of why, since a child is sinless, Allah allows some children to suffer illness or pain. How can a merciful and compassionate God permit this? This is truly a test for the child, his parents, and society.

Part of growing up is learning how to live in this world, in a life which may include millions of possibilities, including such hard tests. As there is pleasure, so there is also pain; as there is happiness and joy, there is also trouble and suffering. And each experience we have is meant to teach us something, to bear some constructive fruit.

The pain of falling down teaches the child something about carefulness in handling his body. Coping with the sorrow of losing a friend makes him aware of his dependence on others, and also how to go out and make new friends. Any pain or suffering is recorded, and Allah will surely reward him for it on the Day of Judgment. The suffering and loss he is experiencing will bring him, and his parents as well, to a high station in Paradise, especially if he bears it with patience and trust in Allah. And if death should take him as a young child, he enters Paradise without accounting.

The Prophet (S) was asked, "Who are in Paradise?"
He said, "Prophets are in Paradise, martyrs are in
Paradise, infants are in Paradise, and children buried
alive are in Paradise." *(Abu Dawud, 2515)*

It may be helpful to remind children, when they pass
through periods of difficulty, of how much suffering the
prophets bore from their people, even though prophets are sinless, the best of mankind. In particular, mention of the Prophet
Muhammad's repeated bereavements as a child, and all the suffering and troubles he bore in later life, may be helpful. If the
child is old enough, it may be explained to him that suffering
and troubles are the forge in which characters are developed,
strengthened and perfected. Helplessness and pain drive us to
call upon Allah, to depend on Him, and to trust Him for the
outcome. They are the means of securing His forgiveness and
of coming closer to Him.

The one for whom Allah intends good encounters
afflictions to get it. *(Bukhari)*

When Allah has decreed for a servant a rank which
he has not attained by his action, He afflicts him in
his body or his property or his children. *(Abu
Dawud, 3084)*

ANGELS

Like all people, children have angels around them who
record their acts.

And indeed there are guardians over you, noble
scribes, knowing whatever you do. (Qur'an 82:10-12)

Allah says, (addressing the angels), "If My slave intends to do a bad deed, do not write it down unless he does it. If he does it, then write it down as it is. But if he refrains from doing it for My sake, then write it as a good deed. If he intends to do a good deed but does not do it, write a good deed (in his account), and if he does it, then write it for him as ten good deeds up to seven hundred times." (Bukhari, 9.592 and 8.498; Muslim, 0233 and 0235)

Several ahadith make it clear that the bad deeds of children under the age of puberty are not recorded. Until they reach the age of reason, the sign of which is physical maturity, young people are not held accountable for their bad deeds, according to the saying of the Prophet (S):

There are three (kinds of people) whose actions are not recorded: a sleeper until he awakens, a boy until he reaches puberty, and a lunatic (in other versions it is "a mentally defective one") until he comes to reason. *(Abu Dawud, 4389; also 4384, 4385, 4387 and 4388)*

The understanding of this fact is so important. Too often a child is seen doing bad things: he hits his brother; he lies; he tries to steal a neighbor's toy. Adults and other children may label him a "bad boy." But we must remember that Allah does not hold him responsible for these actions because he is not old enough to know the difference between right and wrong. His *deeds* are bad, not the child.

However, being born in fitrah does not mean being perfect. Our fitrah prepares us to receive the guidance of Allah (S) and to search for it, but we need that knowledge from outside ourselves in order to live in the best way. Guidance in this comes through the prophets, and above all through the Seal of the Prophets, Muhammad (S). For a child, this guidance is first transmitted by his parents, who have learned it from the Prophet (S), internalized it, and are now in a position to pass it on to the child by both example and teaching, aided by the use of a lot of common sense and wisdom.

Though the bad deeds are not recorded, good deeds are never lost.

> The Messenger of Allah (S) met some riders at (a place called) ar-Rawha and asked who they were. They replied that they were Muslims. They said, "Who are you?" He said, "The Messenger of Allah." A woman lifted up a boy to him and said,"Will this child be credited with having performed the hajj?" At that, he said,"Yes, and you will have a reward." (Muslim, 3091)

Although the child will need to repeat it as an adult though, to fulfill his requirement of at least once in his life, performing *hajj* (pilgrimage) as a child is rewarded. We have numerous other ahadith that show children participating fully in religious acts, like prayer, in a regular way that would not be necessary if there was no blessing in it. And of course in the Qur'an, we have the promise:

> Allah suffers not the reward of the faithful to be lost (in the least). (Qur'an 3:171)

> Never will I suffer to be lost the work of any of you, be he male or female. You are members one of another. (Qur'an 3:195)

> For Allah suffers not the reward to be lost of those who do good. (Qur'an 9:120)

> As to those who believe and work righteousness,

verily We shall not suffer to perish the reward of any
who do a (single) righteous deed. (Qur'an 18:30)

Let us share the knowledge we have of the angels with our
children, and encourage them to make the search for doing
good deeds a habit. Even a small child can learn to do some
good deeds. (see chapter 4, Practices, Manners, and Values).

In the Islamic understanding, the age of consciousness and
reason, which occurs at puberty, marks the endpoint of childhood's freedom from responsibility. This is traditionally considered the onset of menses in a girl, but for a boy there is no con-
sensus on a date. Allah knows the time exactly. From that time
on, a young person is considered responsible for his or her
actions in front of Allah—in other words, he or she is considered an adult and accountable.

Today, angels have become a quite common theme, even
among non-Muslims, just as dinosaurs and fairies were in the
recent past. However, this popular "belief" in angels is based
upon guesswork and speculation. As Muslims we do not have
to guess. Belief in angels is one of the six main articles of faith
in Islam. Angels are mentioned repeatedly in the Qur'an; the
collections of hadith currently available in English contain
about 220 sayings of the Prophet (S) in which angels are mentioned. He himself saw them, conversed with them, and found
them present in an endless variety of situations. He said,

Angels come to you in succession by night and day,
and all of them assemble together at the time of the
Fajr and Asr prayers. Those (angels) who have spent
the night with you ascend (to Heaven). Allah asks
them, although He knows everything about you, "In
what state did you leave my slaves?" The angels
reply, "When we left them they were praying and
when we reached them they were praying."
(Bukhari, 1.530)

Satan exercises his influence upon the son of Adam, and likewise the angel exercise his influence (upon him). The influence of Satan is that he holds the promise of evil and denial of truth. And the influence of the angel is that he holds the promise of good and the affirmation of truth. Then the one who sees this (the truth of this promise of good) should praise Allah, and the one who finds the opposite of it should seek refuge with Allah from Satan the Accursed. (Mishkat, 0074, transmitted by Tirmidhi)

He then recited the verse,

Satan threatens you with the prospect of poverty and orders you to indecency (2:268).

When a servant of Allah's is accustomed to worshipping Him in a good manner and then he becomes ill, the angel entrusted with him is told to record for him actions equivalent to what he did when he was well, until Allah frees him from his illness or takes him in death. (Mishkat, 1559 and 1560)

If a Muslim recites a surah from the Book of Allah when he goes to bed, Allah will put an angel in charge of him, and nothing which can harm him will come near him until he awakens. (Mishkat, 2396, transmitted by Tirmidhi)

When a man lies, the angel moves a mile from him because of the bad odor of what he has produced. (Mishkat, 4844, transmitted by Tirmidhi).

A man abused Abu Bakr (R), and (meanwhile) the Prophet (S) was sitting, showing pleasure and smiling, but when the man went on at length and Abu Bakr (R) replied to some of what he said, the Prophet (S) became angry and got up and left. Abu Bakr (R) caught up with him and said, "O Messenger of Allah, he was abusing me while you were sitting, but when I replied to some of what he said you became angry and got up and went away." He replied, "There was an angel with you, replying to him, but when you replied to him, a devil came down." In Abu Dawud's version, it is: "I was not going to sit when the Devil came down." (Mishkat, 5102; Abu Dawud, 4878)

A child may feel comfort in knowing that he has such beneficent, friendly beings at hand; this helps him feel that he is not alone in the world, even if his parents are out of sight. Allah says,

There is no soul without a guardian over it. (Qur'an 86:4)

We can send him to bed, as A'isha bint Abu Bakr is reported to have done with a member of her family after the evening prayer, saying, "Won't you let the recording angel rest?" (Malik)

Many of the fanciful descriptions of angels and jinn, featuring tales and descriptions not mentioned in the Qur'an, ahadith, or sound traditions coming from early traditionists, however, constitute a form of falsehood, and it is very undesirable to encourage our children to believe in such make-believe. Children remember these stories very well. Often they are not able to clearly separate fact from fiction until around the age of six or seven, and they easily mix fanciful stories with the truth. With a similar interweaving of myths and stories, Christians slowly turned their main religious observances—Christmas, the celebration of Jesus's birth, and Easter, the time of his supposed resurrection—into secular festivals centered around celebrations of Santa Claus and eggs. Christian depictions of angels as lovely blonde ladies with birds' wings have corrupted the imaginations of children the world over. The ultimate invention in religion is, of course, the depiction of the Lord God Almighty, Creator of the heavens and earth, as a grandfatherly old man with a long white beard, sitting in the clouds. To avoid innovation in our religion, changing the revealed information about the world of the unseen into fables, we must be wary of cute fairy tales of all sorts, and especially about angels and jinn.

> They ask you (Muhammad) about the soul. Say: the soul proceeds from the command of my Lord, and only a little of knowledge has been given to you (mankind). (Qur'an 17:85)

> Woe to him who tells things, speaking falsely, to make people laugh thereby. Woe to him! Woe to him! (Abu Dawud, 4972)

The pagans of Makkah were reproved several times in the Qur'an for associating jinn with Allah and calling the angels the daughters of Allah. These were attacks on *tawheed* (the oneness of Allah Most High) and symptoms of *shirk* (associating others with His divinity), infringements on the supremacy and uniqueness of the Creator.

THE HEREAFTER

As the child grows, the awareness of death will sooner or later become part of his world-view. People get sick, become old, have accidents and die. His cat gets run over, his great aunt has a terminal illness, his friend's father is killed in a plane crash.

What is death like to a small child? One day a person (or a pet) is here, the next day he or she (or it) isn't. The child may be aware that there is a funeral service and that the dead body is put into the ground. He may be aware, to a lesser or greater degree, of the loss of a person who is significant to himself or to someone else he knows.

Here the wise parent does not make light of the subject (generally out of a feeling of embarrassment or inadequacy in speaking about it), try to hush it up, or neglect to address the child's concerns. It is to be talked about, questions asked and answered, openly and freely, like any other subject which comes up in the course of life. Allah Almighty, in His Holy Book, mentions death, dying, and the future Life hundreds of times. From this extreme emphasis on the subject, how can it possibly be one which we do not bring up and discuss with our children?

How can you disbelieve in Allah when you were dead and He gave you life? Then He will cause you to die, then bring you to life (again); then unto Him you will return. (Qur'an 2:28; 22:06; 30:19, 50; 36:12; 42:9; 46:33; 75:40)

Say: "(Even) if you had been in your houses, those who were decreed to be killed would have gone forth to their places of (final) rest, and this is in order that Allah might try what is in your breasts and prove what is in your hearts. And Allah is Knower of what is in the breasts." (Qur'an 3:154; 4:78; 39:42; 59:60)

And He is the Omnipotent over His slaves, and He sends guardians over you; until, when death comes to one of you, Our messengers receive him, and they are not neglectful. (Qur'an 6:61)

Each soul tastes death. And We try you by evil and

good as a test, and to Us you will return. (Qur'an
21:35; 3:185; 29:57)

The Prophet (S), too, mentioned death innumerable times.
He said,

Allah, the Exalted and Glorious, has decreed for
each servant among His creation five things: his
death, his actions, his abode, the places of his moving about, and his means of provision. (Mishkat,
0113, transmitted by Ahmad)

The Prophet (S) said, "These hearts become rusty,
just as iron does when water affects it." On being
asked what could clear them, he replied, "Much
remembrance of death and recitation of the Qur'an."
(Mishkat, 2168, transmitted by Bayhaqi).

Adults often suppose that death is a very hard concept for
a young child to grasp, and this may be true. However, when
the subject comes up—say, when a grandparent dies or a pet is
run over—we should not shy away from it as if it were something too painful for a child to have to deal with or beyond his
ability to grasp. He or she will grasp it, as with many other
matters, with a young child's partial and incomplete understanding, but with *some* understanding nonetheless. Simple
explanations suffice.

When the child is a little older, the conceptsof the Day of
Judgment and Heaven and Hell can be introduced. But a word
of caution needs to be said here. Many parents use the threat of
Hell, as it were, like the threat of a boogeyman or menacing
policeman: "If you do that, you'll end up in Hell!" Such an
approach leads a child—or an adult who has grown up with
such an understanding—to imagine that Allah is a terrible,
threatening monster who is just sitting there waiting for him to

commit mistakes or sins so He can zap him and throw him into Hell; in short, that Allah's ultimate purpose is to punish people. What could be further from the truth, and further from the kind of Islamic understanding we want our children to have, than this? Nonetheless, many Muslims give precisely such an understanding to their children.

Dwelling excessively on guilt, shame, and fear presents a distorted vision of Allah (S). Allah does punish, but He also rewards, and His reward system is so generous. He is the Compassionate and the Merciful and the vast majority of the ninety-nine attributes used by the Qur'an to describe Him are not fearful: The Holy, The Source of Peace, The Forgiver, The Provider, The Nourisher, etcetera. Remember again the hadith that describes His generous judgment of deeds and intentions:

> Allah says, (addressing the angels), "If My slave intends to do a bad deed, do not write it down unless he does it. If he does it, then write it down as it is. But if he refrains from doing it for My sake, then write it as a good deed. If he intends to do a good deed but does not do it, write a good deed (in his account), and if he does it, then write it for him as ten good deeds up to seven hundred times." (Bukhari, 9.592 and 8.498; Muslim, 0233 and 0235)

We do this and we don't do that, because we love Allah. We point out to our children His endless mercies and favors. Then Paradise is understood as the results of what we ourselves did, not something put upon us by the whim of a mean, nasty God whom a child fears but can never imagine loving.

Dhikr (Rememberance of Allah)

Allah Most High says,

> Then remember Me; I shall remember you. (Qur'an
> 2:152)
> Only those are (real) believers whose hearts tremble
> when they remember Allah. (Qur'an 8:2)
>
> And the remembrance of Allah is greatest. (Qur'an
> 29:45)
>
> And remember Allah much in order that you may be
> successful. (Qur'an 62:10)
>
> The Prophet (s) said: Allah Most High says, "I am
> to My slave as He thinks Me to be, and I am with
> him when He remembers Me. Then, if he remem-
> bers Me within himself, I remember him within
> Myself; and if he remembers Me in a group of peo-
> ple, I remember him in a group better than them; and
> if he comes near to Me one span, I go near to him
> one cubit; and if he comes near to Me one cubit, I go
> two outstretched arms' distance nearer to him; and if
> he comes walking to Me, I go running to him."
> (Bukhari, 9.502)

The life of a Muslim is based on maintaining his connection with Allah, and dhikris the chief means for this. Dhikr is a
word which means to make mention of, to recall, or to remember. Although it is most commonly associated in our minds
with sitting after prayers and saying *"subhanallah," "alhamdulillah,"* and *"Allahu akbar,"* it actually includes all forms of
mentioning, recalling, or remembering Allah Most High.

This remembrance is the basis of our doing good deeds, of refraining from bad ones, of keeping our path even when it is extremely difficult, of comforting our hearts in times of crisis, and stabilizing ourselves when the going gets too rough. And because this is the basis of our spiritual life, it is something which we can easily impart to our children from an early age.

Mentioning Allah, His greatness, omnipotence, wisdom, and creative power is a form of dhikr which can be used easily and naturally with young children. Teaching a child to recall Allah's endless favors and give thanks, to apologize and ask for forgiveness and guidance, forms the basis for a life-long habit of remembrance.

It is good to teach children to ask for all their needs from Allah, Who, according to a hadith, loves to be asked, even for the smallest needs. Children may be taught to make du'a after salah—and at other times as well—as soon as they are old enough to pray. They can also benefit from dhikr and du'a among a group of other people. This can be done quite informally—for example, as the family sits relaxing out on the back porch watching the sunset. It doesn't have to be a very high level of conversation as long as it is respectful. Let children talk *to* Allah and *about* Allah, and express their understanding in their own words. With their pure nature, they can sometimes express basic truths with surprising clarity, and adults can learn from them as well.

> He who treads the path in search of knowledge, Allah will make that path easy, leading to Paradise for him and those people who assemble in one of the houses of Allah (mosques), recite the Book of Allah, and learn and teach the Qur'an. There will descend upon them tranquillity, mercy will cover them, the angels will surround them, and Allah will mention them in the presence of those near Him. (Muslim, 6518)

Frequently, however, children confuse facts or information, and then they need gentle correction. Listening to them is the only way to find out what they have learned and what they need to know. A common example of children's mistakes might be heard by watching two children at play.

"You didn't finish your apple before you threw it away. You're going to Hell!" Sawsan, age five, taunts Selima, age four.

Six-year-old Mataz returns from school very upset and worried. His classmate swore to him, saying *"wal-Allahi"* (by Allah), that he has a real live pet dinosaur at home, a Tyrannosaurus Rex that eats people. "But he swore to me by Allah, Mommy!"

Another common error for children (and also for adults) is to pray for something and then lose faith in Allah or in prayer because it didn't happen. One mother found her child praying for a Saint Bernard dog like one he'd seen on television. Unfortunately, the family lived in a city apartment, and naturally there were some other considerations (the mother breathed a silent prayer of thanks that Allah had not granted that particular wish).

Assure children that, whether or not their particular prayer is answered in the way in which they asked it, Allah definitely knows all of their needs and hears all their prayers. Perhaps the thing that they asked for was not good for them, or Allah wanted something else for them, something that would be better in the long run. Remind them that He knows everything and that, compared to His knowledge, we know nothing at all. The Prophet (S) said,

> Prayers of all of you are granted provided you do not get impatient and start grumbling that, "I prayed to my Lord but He did not grant me." (Bukhari & Muslim in Riyadh-us-Saleheen, 1499)

You will be answered as long as you are not impatient and say, "I made a du'a and I was not answered." (Muwatta)

No one makes a du'a without one of three things happening. Either it is answered, or it is stored up for him, or wrong actions are atoned for by it. (Muwatta)

Whenever a Muslim supplicates Allah, Allah grants his supplication or averts some kind of evil from him, as long as he does not ask for something sinful or something that would cut off the ties of kinship. (Mishkat, 1506[R], transmitted by Tirmidhi)

A well-educated parent is generally better able to guide such learning experiences of children. It is therefore very important for Muslim parents to equip themselves with sufficient secular as well as Islamic knowledge. For example, an Islamic prescription for handling nightmares is to recite the two *surahs* of protection, *Surah al-Falaq* and *Surah al-Nas* (113 and 114). One mother did this with her child but the nightmares continued. She should search further. Scary cartoons, bad stories from playmates, or a heavy atmosphere of fear, or anger, prevailing in the home may be key factors, or there may be some hidden physical problem. Therefore, in addition to asking Allah for help, the root of the problem needs to be addressed. Allah will always help, but He wants us to make an effort, too. With this understanding, we ask Him for help when we are sick, but at the same time we also follow our physician's advice and take medication. Parents need vital information on child development as well as on their faith.

We know that Allah's guidance, help, and support *are* always there, but we must have the wisdom and understanding to see it. As an example, four-year-old Haroon was outdoors trying to learn to bowl with a little plastic bowling set. Time and time again he rolled his ball down toward the pins, only to see it curve off to the side. Then, in desperation, he called out *"Bismillah ar-Rahman ar-Raheem"* and rolled the ball again, with determination. The ball again veered off to the side, missing the pins, but a little gust of wind came up at that moment and knocked all the pins down. The child was jubilant. Allah had helped him! The next roll was less blessed. His mother gently nudged him into realizing that perhaps Allah had helped him in order to encourage him to practice and become skillful, but that it is not Allah's way to obey our every command. Later, she heard Haroon announcing that Allah must not want him to play Candyland (a board game for children that uses dice). Why? While he had been playing at a neighbor's and had asked Allah's help, Allah had not helped him win at all!

As with angels and jinn, it is important to be as truthful as possible when answering children's questions about Allah. Young children, particularly between the ages of three and six, are very curious about such matters as what Allah is like, where He is, what He does, and distinguishing between "Allah-made" and "man-made" things. They have quite vivid imaginations that may supply details which are incorrect, and a wise parent will check on a child's understanding by questions: "Where do you think Allah is?" "How do you think Allah made this?" "Do you suppose this car is an Allah-made or a man-made thing?" In the latter case, Mommy explains that a car—or any other man-made object—is both, because it consists of materials which Allah provides and is crafted by man. And if one doesn't know the answer to a question, it is better to admit not knowing than to invent false stories. The mother can always check on the answer and supply it to the child later. However, an invented lie contaminates the truth and can only lead the child astray.

When children ask about descriptions of Allah, it is usually easiest to describe what He is *not,* particularly that He is not like man or any other created thing. We can use His *siffat* (the ninety-nine attributes or Holy Names of Allah) to describe His power, mercy, kindness, love, and the like. And we can trace the forces that act in our world, such as wind, rain, ocean waves, electricity, and so on, back to His infinite power and creativity.

Children love these kinds of explanations, which resonate in their innate fitrah. Not only do they accept them easily and naturally, but they also build their world-view upon them. It is vitally important to remember that each child is a new creature on this planet. As such, he or she possesses no world-view whatsoever. The world-view that will be his is gradually built into him by environmental influences, which teach him directly or indirectly, and by what he himself deduces from this environment.

Any and all parts of this emerging world-view may be correct or incorrect, true or false. For example, if a baby were born in a mental hospital and grew up there, his world view would be shaped by the world-view of the people and environment around him—and this is true of any environment in which a child may grow, and the truths or falsehoods it teaches him.

When a parent sits with the child and talks about Allah and His glorious attributes, His creation and how we all fit into it— that is, about *Haqq,* the Ultimate Reality—he or she is both feeding his fitrah and building into him a correct world-view. That world-view will be part of him as long as he lives. Even if he should "misplace" it later in life, it is still built into his consciousness.

This is the wider meaning of the reported hadithof the Prophet (S), that a mother gives her child, when she nurses him, something more than milk, and that something is *wisdom.* For the very first and most important element in a child's world-view is that the world is a friendly, caring place, in which he is looked after and supported, and this is brought about by his warm, loving relationship with his mother (or mother substitute). Studies have shown that if an infant lacks this early bonding with the mother, it does not manage to grow or thrive, and ultimately may die due to lack of connection with any significant figure in its new sphere of life, this world. Thus it is correct to say that any child who does not have the "wisdom" of his mother (or a mother-substitute) poured into him is a child without a foundation, a crippled, unstable, deficient being. The foundation of a child's character is love, learned from a mother who loves him, as the Prophet (S) said:

> There are one hundred (parts of) the mercy of Allah, and out of these He has sent down one part of mercy upon the jinn and human beings and the insects, and it is because of this (one part) that they love one another, show kindness to one another, and even the animal treats its young with affection; and Allah has reserved ninety-nine parts of mercy (to Himself), with which He will treat His servants on the Day of Resurrection. (Muslim, 6631)

SATAN AND JINN

Satan or *Shaytan* and jinn are part of the unseen Reality which Allah, in His infinite wisdom, has seen fit to create. Satan's presence and his working among us cannot be denied, and our children grow in awareness of this, for it has a very direct effect upon their lives.

Now, how can we best deal with the subject of jinn? Many times children are told stories about jinn which can be a source of difficulty for them. We have to be quite careful with this subject because so many folk tales, with no basis in reality, are current in Muslim societies. In actuality, the subject of jinn does not need to be discussed with a young child unless he or she brings it up.

For an older child, the topic comes up in the study of the Qur'an. In that case, it is sufficient to say that jinn are another species of creatures, made by Allah from fire, as we are made from clay, who live among us, although they are normally invisible. Satan, or Iblis as he is also called, is the leader of the bad jinn, also called "little satans" in some texts. However, some jinn are Muslims, and Prophet Muhammad was sent to lead them as well as to lead mankind. A matter of fact approach to this topic is encouraged, because nothing happens except what Allah wills, and He is our protection from evil in every form.

The Qur'an contains numerous verses referring to Satan and the way in which he works. Among them, we cite the following,

> Do not follow the footsteps of Satan, for he is an open enemy to you. (Qur'an 2:168, 208; 6:142; 7:22; 12:5; 17:53; 24:21; 35:06; 36:60; 43:62)

> And for the one who has Satan as his close companion, an evil companion is he! (Qur'an 4:38; 43:36)

> And the one who takes Satan as a patron (or friend) instead of Allah has surely incurred a great loss. He makes promises to them and arouses desires in them, but Satan's promises are nothing but deception. (Qur'an 4:119-120; 17:64)

In the books of Hadithwhich are translated into English, we find more than 150 references to the same subject. The following put the matter into clear perspective for us:

> No child is born without Satan's touching it at its birth, whereupon it cries loudly from Satan's touching of it, excepting Mary and her son (Bukhari 6.71; slightly different versions are found in Bukhari, 4.506, and Muslim, 5839)

Truly, Satan reaches (into the depths of) the human being just as blood reaches. (Bukhari, 3.251; Muslim, 5404)

The Prophet (S) informed us that a satan accompanies each human being, saying: "There is no one among you with whom there is not an attache" (despatched) from among the jinn (i.e., a personal satan). (Muslim, 6757)

Once when his wife A'isha (R) was feeling jealous, the Prophet (S) noticedit and asked her about it. He then said, "It was your satan who came to you," and she said, "O messenger of Allah, is there a satan with me?" He said, "Yes." She said, "Is there a satan attached to everyone?" He said, "Yes." She said, "O Messenger of Allah, with you too?" He said, "Yes, but my Lord has helped me against him so that I am safe from his mischief." (Muslim, 6759)

The idea of Satan and his whispering is one that we can easily bring up with our children at an early age. What is the best way to do this? We can explain that there is an evil being called Satan who wants us to disobey Allah, and who tries to get us to do this by putting evil ideas in our heads—disobeying Mommy, forgetting to pray or say du'abefore sleeping, being mean to a sibling, lying, being rude, and the like. He whispers to us, making bad deeds sound like a good idea, and later encouraging us to fear attempting to set right what we have done wrong, but he cannot force us to do anything. We are responsible for what we do. We teach the child that Allah, Who created him and gave him everything he has, is the One whom he must obey and try to please, and that whatever displeases Him should not be done.

The child can be encouraged to disregard or disobey promptings that he knows are wrong (and people of any age, if they listen to their hearts, always know) by a simple inner act of negation: "No, I'm not going to do that! Allah doesn't like it," or, "You leave me alone, you bad old Satan! I'm not going to listen to you. Get out of here!" In other words, we give him some tools for fighting against Satan's promptings and his own undesirable impulses and desires. When he is old enough, we teach him to use the *surahs* of taking in refuge with Allah, *Surah al-Falaq* (113) and *Surah al-Nas* (114) as a means of protection against Satan and his works.

> And if an evil suggestion from Satan incites you, seek refuge with Allah. Surely He is All-Hearing, All-Knowing. Those who are mindful of Allah, whenever an instigation of Satan's touches them, bring (Allah) to mind, whereupon they see (with true vision). (7:200; 41:36)

> And say: "My Lord, I seek refuge with You from the suggestions of the satans, and I seek refuge with You, my Lord, from their being present with me." (23:97-98)

> The Prophet (S) used to seek protection against the jinn and the evil eye until Surah al-Falaq and Surah al-Nas were revealed. After they were revealed, he kept to them and left off all (ways of seeking refuge) besides them. (Mishkat, 1019[R], and Mishkat, 4563)

He recommended this practice to his companions, saying to a companion named Uqbah (R):

> Use them (Surah al-Falaq and Surah al-Nas) when seeking refuge in Allah, for no one can use anything for the purpose to compare with them. (Abu Dawud, 1458)

Various charms, amulets and talismans are available, surrounded by much folklore encouraging their use as a protection
from "the evil eye," jinn, and Satan. According to various
Islamic authorities, it is permissible to wear an amulet to ward
off evil if it contains verses of the Qu'ran or Allah's Holy
Names (see Ahmad al-Naqib al-Misri's *Reliance of the
Traveller,* translated by Noah HaMim Keller, or Muhammad
ibn 'Abd al-Wahhab's *Kitab al-Tawheed* on this subject).
Others reject the use of amulets altogether. Ibn Mas'ud was
among the many who considered them not to be prohibited
(haram) but discouraged *(makruh)*. If one does use an amulet,
it must be with the clear understanding that there is no power in
the object itself, but that all power is with the Lord of the Holy
Names or sacred verses inscribed on it.

The practice of the Prophet (S) in this regard is well-docu-
mented. His wife A'isha (R) reported,

> When the Prophet (S) went to bed each night, he
> would join his hands together and blow upon them,
> and he would recite over them (the surahs contain-
> ing) "Qul: Hua Allahu Ahad" and "Qul: A'udhu
> bi-Rabbi-l-Falaq" and "Qul: A'udhu bi-Rabbi-n-
> Nas," and then wipe them over whatever parts of his
> body he was able; he would begin with them on his
> head, face, and the front of his body, and he would
> do that three times (Bukhari, 6.536 and 6.636A).
> A'isha (R) also reported: Whenever Allah's
> Messenger (S) became sick, he would recite
> Mu'wwadithat (Falaq and Nas) and then blow his
> breath over his body. Then, when he became seri-
> ously ill, I would recite (the two surahs) over him
> and wipe his hands (on himself, as he used to do),
> hoping for the blessing of it. (Bukhari, 6.535; also
> Bukhari 7.644)

Among the practices of the Prophet (S) for healing is that he used to seek protection for some of his wives by wiping his right hand over the site of trouble and saying:

"O Allah, Lord of the people, remove the trouble and heal her. You are the Healer. There is no healing except Yours, healing that leaves behind no ailment." *(Bukhari, 7.639, 7.638)*

Or he would say,

"Wipe away the trouble, Lord of the people. The cure is in Your hands, and no one can remove it except You." (Bukhari, 7.640)

The Prophet (S) possessed a deep understanding of the causes of illness and the properties of various healing substances. Once, when he was asked, "Is there any good in medicine, O Messenger of Allah?" he is reported to have replied, "The One Who sent down the disease sent down the remedy." (Muwatta) He also said: "Allah has sent down both the disease and the cure, and He has appointed a cure for every disease; so treat yourselves medically but do not use anything unlawful." (Abu Dawud, 3865).

In fact, the classic books of *tibb nabawiyah* (the Prophet's medicine), which have been used for many hundreds of years, contain the Prophet's natural remedies and medicines for a variety of ailments.

What about bad dreams and nightmares? It is reported that the Prophet (S) said, "A good dream is from Allah and a bad dream is from Satan. So if one of you sees (in a dream) a thing he dislikes, when he gets up he should blow three times (on his left side) and seek refuge with Allah from its evil, for then it will not harm him." (Bukhari, 7.643 and 9.124; Muwatta). In another report he is said, "If one of you sees a dream which he likes, it is from Allah, so he should praise Allah for it and tell it; but if he sees otherwise of what he dislikes, it is only from Satan, and he should seek refuge from its evil and should not tell it to anyone, for it will not harm him. (Bukhari, 9.169).

There can be many causes for a child's having nightmares or fears, and other kinds of inner turmoil. A look at the atmosphere of the home may be the first place to start.

A little use of common sense, as well as the latest research findings, makes it clear that television has a powerful impact on children. Violence in cartoons, hideous, terrifying, vicious monsters in fantasy or sci-fi films, violence or fantasy-based video games or toys, can create all kinds of horrors in a child's imagination. Such unnatural phantoms can also produce a distorted and sick view of reality and human relationships in a child. It is essential to remember that his immature, inexperienced, developing mind has no ability to sort out things for itself but relies on information from outside to shape its view of reality.

The impact of such things as amusements for our children should never be underestimated: they *are* having an impact, and it cannot be a constructive one. As parents, let us do our best to see that our children have more wholesome forms of entertainment. And this means devoting time, effort, and other resources to finding alternatives.

It is also important to realize that because children have a very partial view of the world, their partial comprehension can create all sorts of problems for them. This can occur with conversations overheard between adults or with actions of adults that are not properly explained, as in the following.

One girl heard about the Gulf war on television and understood that there was a war occurring at the local miniature golf course. She developed nightmares worrying about the bombs falling there as she had seen on TV.

Another child overheard his parents arguing violently about how badly he was doing in school. He didn't know how much general disharmony existed between them and when they divorced, he thought it was his fault. As a result, he developed multiple behavioral problems.

Even very trivial experiences can sometimes bother a young child. A toddler was thrilled to see a cat from a safe distance at the neighbor's. He seemed quite happy at the time. Two nights later, he awoke from a bad dream, screaming, "Kittycat took my socks!"

To summarize: We don't neglect to search for the possible tangible causes of any trouble our child is having. At the same time, we continually pray for Allah's protection from all harm, especially from Satan and his whispering, and ask earnestly for guidance and divine support. And when we ask Allah for help and guidance, He will never turn us away.

Chapter Three

CHILDREN AND PARENTS

THE RIGHTS OF PARENTS

Islam places the strongest possible emphasis on both the respect and the obligations that a child owes to his parents. Several Qur'anic verses contain general injunctions to be kind to one's parents. Others are much more specific:

> Your Lord has decreed that you worship no one but Him and be good to your parents. Whether one or both of them reach old age at your side, do not say to them a rough word nor repulse them, but address them with respectful speech, and, out of compassion, lower to them the wing of humility and say, "My Lord, have mercy upon them, as they cared for me in childhood." (Qur'an 17:23-24)

> And We have enjoined man concerning his parents: his mother bore him in weakness upon weakness, and his weaning is in two years, in order that you may be thankful to Me and to your parents. To Me is the (final) return. But if they strive to make you associate with Me anything about which you have no knowledge, do not obey them; and keep company with them in this life with goodness, and follow the path of the one who turns to Me. (Qur'an 31:14)

And We have enjoined on man goodness to his parents. But if they strive to make you associate with
Me anything of which you have no knowledge, do
not obey them. To Me is the (final) return, where-
upon I shall inform you of what you used to do.
(Qur'an 29:8)

And We have enjoined on man goodness to his parents. His mother carried him in pain and gave birth
to him in pain, and his carrying and his weaning
(comprise) thirty months; until, when he attains his
full strength and reaches (the age of) forty years, he
says, "My Lord, inspire me to be thankful for the
favor which You have bestowed upon me and upon
my parents, and that I may do righteous deeds pleasing to You, and make sound for me my descendants.
Truly, have I turned to You, and, truly, I am among
the Muslims." (Qur'an 46:15)

These verses make it clear that we must honor our parents,
appreciate their sacrifices and efforts for us, and do our best for
them. This is required regardless of whether they are Muslims
or not. Allah knows the parents to whom He gave us and the
test we will find in living with them.

Disrespect and neglect of parents is a major sin, as reported
in the following ahadith:

The Prophet (S) said three times, "Shall I inform you
about the greatest of the major sins?" They said,
"Yes, O Messenger of Allah." He said, "To join others in worship with Allah and to be undutiful to parents. . ." *(Bukhari, 3.822)*

Abdullah ibn Mas'ood (R) asked the Prophet (S),
"What deed is dearest to Allah?" He said, "The prayer

at its proper time." Ibn Mas'ood (R) then asked, "Then what?" He said, "Goodness to parents. . ." *(Bukhari, 1.505)*

The Prophet (S) also said,

> The greatest of the major sins are to make others partners with Allah and to kill a human being and to be undutiful to parents and (to speak) the false word," or, he said, "to bear false witness." *(Bukhari 9:9, 9.10 and 9.55)*

In a hadith reported by Abu Hurayrah (R), the Prophet (S) three times evoked Allah's humiliation upon an unspecified individual. When he was asked to whom this referred, he replied,

> The one who sees his parents during their old age, either one or both of them, but does not enter Paradise (because he has been undutiful to them). *(Muslim, 6189-6191)*

It is also reported that a man came to the Prophet (S) and asked, "Messenger of Allah, is there any kindness left that I can do for my parents after their death?" The Prophet (S) replied,

> "Yes. You can invoke blessings on them and forgiveness for them, carry out their final instructions after their death, join ties of relationship which are dependent on them, and honor their friends." *(Abu Dawood, 5123)*

He also said,

> If anyone possesses these three characteristics, Allah will give him an easy death and bring him

into His Paradise: gentleness toward the weak,
affection toward parents, and kindness to slaves.
(Mishkat, 3364)

Once the Prophet (S) was asked, "What rights can parents
demand of their children?" He replied simply,

They are your Paradise and your Hell. (Mishkat,
4941)

In addition to these, there are other ahadith which order
respect and kindness for one's mother in particular, such as the
following:

Allah has forbidden you to be undutiful to your
mother. *(Bukhari, 8:6)*

A man came to the Prophet (S) and asked him for
permission to join a military expedition. The Prophet
(S) asked him if he had a mother, and when he
replied that he had, he said, "Stay with her, for
Paradise is at her feet." (Ahmad, al-Nasa'i and
Baihaqi, in Shu'ab al-iman)

Once a man came to the Prophet (S) and asked,
"Who among people has most right to good treat-
ment from me?" He (the Prophet (S) said, "Your
mother." He (the man) said, "Then who?" He said,
"Your mother." He said, "Then who?" He said,
"Your mother." He said, "Then who?" He said,
"Then your father." (In a version reported in
Muslim, "then your nearest relatives according to
order [of nearness]" is added after "Then your
father.") *(Bukhari, 8.2, and Muslim, 6180-6183)*

In Buhkari (8.9), we find two ahadith from Asma bint Abu Bakr (R) in which the Prophet (S) advised her to be kind to her non-Muslim mother.

Abdullah ibn Umar (R) saw a man carrying his mother on his shoulders while going around the K'aba. The man said, "O Ibn 'Umar, do you see me taking her around?" He replied, "Yes, but your effort is only equal to a single one of her labor pains. Nonetheless, you are doing (something) good, and Allah will give you a great reward for the little you are doing." (Cited in *The Major Sins*)

A similar story is told about a man who made a great sacrifice of time, effort, and money to help his mother in ill health during her old age. When she passed away, he went and asked a wise man, "Have I repaid all that I owed to my mother?" The wise man answered, "No. She gave birth to you and helped you grow, praying for you to live and thrive. You helped her knowing that she would die."

RESPECT

Respect and good treatment of parents and elders is one of the main elements of good manners or customary usages (*adab*, plural, *aadaab)* in Islam. Now, the order to respect parents is general. However, the specifics of what is respectful and what is not are culturally defined. It is reported that the Prophet's daughter Fatima (R) would stand up if her father came to see her, and he would kiss her on greeting her. Parents today may not want their children to stand when they enter the room, but they can legitimately set some standards of respectful behavior that they would like.

We are living in a time when children's speaking disrespectfully *to* adults and *about* adults, particularly parents and teachers, is the norm rather than the exception. Teenagers are especially noted for putting down and behaving disrespectfully to

their parents. And of course, another major teacher of this attitude is the "Shaytan-box." On television, the wise-guy kid is
portrayed as humorous and intelligent, while parents are frequently portrayed as stupid and bumbling. Even though it is all
done for laughs, the message is not lost on children: "I'm smart
and know all this stuff, and the old guys are dumb and outdated,
so why should I respect them?" Today's children repeatedly get
the message that the ones to be respected are the rich, the powerful, the beautiful, and the "cool." This influence carries over
into the conversation and actions of many children, and is only
one of the many reasons to control what they watch.

Another major influence on children that can teach them
disrespectful behavior toward parents is the behavior of their
friends. Children learn so much from imitating each other.
Who hasn't heard a child say, "But all the kids wear this" or
"say that" or "do that". Kids strongly desire to be like everyone else, so a Muslim parent needs to see that "everyone else"
contains as many well-mannered, respectful peopleas possible,
adults as well as children, to help encourage Islamic behavior
in our children.

A duty of Muslim parents and of the Muslim community is
to set consistent standards of respect due to the parents and to
train children from earliest childhood to follow some minimum
guidelines. A toddler is taught to speak to his parents in ways
that are polite and reprimanded or even punished mildly if he
deliberately transgresses this. If both parents are present, one
reinforces respect, politeness, and good behavior toward the
other in the child. Training is explanation, reinforcement, and
above all example. The simplest way to teach respect and
proper behavior is by behaving well with our own parents.
However, in a society that so strongly encourages disrespect,
some more direct efforts may be needed (see chapter 5).

When the ground rules are laid down about who is in
charge in a family—that is, whose rules are to be honored and
obeyed—parents are generally able to guide their children

without continuous conflict and rebellion. And when parents are respected just for their place in the family—for the fact that they *are* the parents—they feel more positive about themselves and can better respond to their children's needs in a warmer, more loving way.

Someone might protest, "But I want my child to love me on his own. I don't want to *oblige* him to do things for me." However, though love and respect are related, they are different. Love is a spontaneous emotion, part of our basic nature, a gift from Allah. It seems to be a natural part of virtually all parent-child relationships, no matter how deficient the parent may be. However, if a child loves his parent without respect, there will be some pity in that love. What parent wants to be pitied? Respect for a person can likewise come naturally, as part of our innate response to him, but it can also be a response to the role a person fills in society.

While we cannot order ourselves to love or to stop loving (although we can determine how we express that love), we *can* order ourselves to act with respect toward other people. And Islam places great emphasis on respectful, courteous behavior, even toward one's enemy or toward someone one does not consider an upright person. Disrespectful behavior is putting-down behavior; it breeds anger and resentment in the person insulted, and generates undesirable behavior in return. Respectful behavior, however, gives rise to good feelings and helps the other person carry out his proper role. It can provide a climate in which positive behavior or a positive relationship can grow. We place a great deal of emphasis on our children's respecting us, their parents. At the same time, we often observe harsh, thoughtless behavior toward children on the part of older Muslims (it sometimes seems as if some Muslims view young people as individuals to be automatically put down and despised). But this does not come from Islam. Islam encourages caring, compassionate behavior toward those who are younger.

> He is not one of us who has no affection for the
> young and no respect for the old, and who does not
> enjoin good and forbid wrong. *(Ahmed)*

American society today would wish us to require adults to respect children (even as it refuses to encourage children to respect adults), but the Prophet (S) didn't advise this. He requested adults to be loving and considerate, not respectful. There is a difference. We expect more knowledge and wisdom to come from those who are older. This expectation creates the difference in the relationship. Though the older person may not have more knowledge and wisdom, the expectation of the younger one encourages him or her to rise to the level of the expectation and seek that knowledge.

> A man saw the Prophet (S) kissing his grandson
> Husain (R). He said, "I have ten children and I never
> kiss any of them." The Prophet (S) said, "The one
> who does not show tenderness will not be shown
> tenderness." *(Abu Dawud, 5199)*

> When Fatimah (R), the Prophet's daughter, came to
> visit him, he got up for her, took her by the hand,
> kissed her and made her sit where he was sitting; and
> when he went to visit her, she got up for him, took
> him by the hand, kissed him, and made him sit where
> she was sitting. *(Abu Dawud, 5198)*

CHILDREN AS A TRUST

Islam makes it clear that children are, at one and the same time, a blessing, a trust, and a test from Allah Ta'ala.

> And know that your possessions and your children

are a test, and that with Allah is a mighty reward. (Qur'an 8:28)

Your wealth and your children are only a trial, while with Allah there is a tremendous reward. (Qur'an 64:15)

A Muslim male or female is tried in person and children and property until he or she faces Allah the Exalted (on the Day of Judgment) in such a state that of all of his or her sins have been forgiven (Mishkat, 0049[R], transmitted by *Tirmidhi)*

The believing man or woman continues to have affliction in person, property, and children so that he or she may meet Allah free from sin. (Mishkat, 1567, transmitted by *Tirmidhi)*

The Messenger of Allah (S) delivered a speech to us. Meanwhile, (his little grandsons) al-Hasan and al-Husayn arrived, stumbling and wearing red shirts. He came down from the pulpit, took them, and ascended it with them. Then he said, "Allah has said truly, 'Your property and your children are only a trial' " (64:15). . . Afterwards he resumed the speech. *(Abu Dawud, 1104)*

One day the Prophet (S) came out carrying his grandchild, and he said, "You (i.e., children) become the means of miserliness, cowardice, ignorance, and foolishness. And you are also the fragrance of Allah." *(Tirmidhi)*

The Prophet (S) was asked, "O Messenger of Allah, what rights can parents demand from their children?" He replied, "They are your Paradise and your Hell." *(Mishkat, 4941, transmitted by Ibn Majah)*

On another occasion, he said, concerning a poor woman's care for her daughters:

> "The one who is in charge of these girls and treats them well, they will be a shield for him from the Fire." *(Bukhari, 8.24)*

That we instinctively love our children and want to protect them and have the best for them, Allah knows. As a rule, children are greatly sought after among Muslims. Many Childless couples experience a great feeling of emptiness, and this is a severe test for them. The Qur'an compares children to wealth (Qur'an 64:15). While everyone wants to be wealthy, nonetheless wealth constitutes a test and a trust for us in using it wisely and responsibly. On the Day of Judgment, we will be held accountable and will be questioned concerning all these favors.

Sometimes we may feel overwhelmed by the seriousness of our responsibility toward our children, especially at this difficult time in history. But for all the care and concern that children may involve, we are also promised that the task will not be beyond us:

> No soul shall be taxed with more than its capacity.
> No mother shall be injured on account of her child,
> nor a father on account of his child. (Qur'an 2:233)

It is in light of this verse that if, at the time of birth, a doctor or midwife must chose between saving the life of the mother or the baby, the mother's life is chosen. Allah knows the task He sets before us in each child. We will surely find within ourselves the patience and love needed; we will find the wisdom, the resources, and all that is necessary to care for this child Allah has sent to us. This is part of faith.

GOALS OF THE MUSLIM PARENT

In general, the goals of many parents in the world today are probably something like this: to rear a child to be a contributing member of society, to have a "good" education and get a "good" job, and to eventually settle down to rear a family of his own. The "good" job and education are usually defined as those which lead to wealth and material comfort.

Practically all parents want these things for their children, and it would be ungracious and ungrateful to refuse any wealth and comfort Allah grants us in this world. But while these goals are reasonable, we find better goals mentioned in the Quran in the prayers and advice of the prophets and other great men of Allah for their children.

PRAYERS AND ADVICE OF THE PROPHETS FOR THEIR CHILDREN

The first prophet mentioned in the Qur'an to give advice to a child of his is the prophet Noah (S). His son rejected his message and joined with the disbelievers who persecuted his father, continuing his rebellion up to the very end, when his destruction through the flood was imminent. At that, his father, ever compassionate and forgiving, called out to him from aboard the Ark, saying, "O my dear son, come aboard with us and do not be with the deniers (of Allah)!" But his son replied, "I shall go to a mountain. It will save me from the water." But his prophet-father knew better. "There is no safety this day from Allah's command except for the one upon whom He has mercy ," he said urgently (11:42-43).

But, not heeding his father's advice or caring for his deep, loving concern for him, the son tried to save himself from the rising waters on his own. As a result, he was drowned with the others who denied Allah. And in spite of being a prophet and a beloved servant of Allah, his father could do nothing to save his son, from either a painful death or the Hellfire. In fact, later, when he pleaded with Allah on behalf of his son as being part of his family, Allah reprimanded him by saying that his son did not belong to his family because his deeds were so unrighteous (11:45).

After him came the prophet Abraham (S). When his wife Sarah proved to be barren, he prayed to Allah for a son and Allah granted his petition. The following supplication is one that Abraham (S) uttered for his descendants, particularly for his son Ishmael (S), whom he settled without any visible provision in the barren desert of Makkah at his Lord's command:

> My Lord, make this city safe, and turn me and my sons
> away from worshipping idols. . . Indeed, I have settled
> some of my descendants in a valley without vegetation,
> beside Your Sacred House (the Ka'ba), our Lord, so
> that they may establish the salah. Then make the hearts
> of the people be drawn toward them, and provide them
> with the fruits (of the earth) in order that they may be
> thankful. . . . Praise be to Allah who bestowed upon me
> in my old age Ishmael and Isaac; truly, my Lord is the
> Hearer of prayer. My Lord, make me establish the
> salah, and some among my descendants (also), our
> Lord, and accept my prayer. Our Lord, forgive me and
> my parents and the believers on the Day when the
> Reckoning takes place. (Qur'an 14:35-41)

In this du'a, we feel the utter devotion of a man for whom his Lord's business was his *only* business. He saw himself and his sons Ishmael and Isaac (S), and his grandson Jacob (S), as his Lord's agents, living only for His worship and service, and asked that at least some from among his later descendants might follow the same path. Years later Abraham and Ishmael (S) were to pray together,

> Our Lord, accept (this) from us; truly, You are the
> All-Hearing, the All-Knowing. Our Lord, and make
> us surrenderers to You, and, from among our descen-
> dants, a community surrendering to You; and show
> us our rites and turn to us; truly, You are the
> Relenting, the Most Compassionate. (Qur'an 2:128)

These noble prophets did not ask for worldly success for themselves and their descendants. Instead they asked, first, that Allah would accept their service, and then, that they and some of their descendants might be acceptable, surrendered servants, worshipping their Lord according to the rites of worship which He had revealed to them. What finer goals than these for one's children can we ever imagine for a Muslim parent?

A final word of advice was given by Abraham (S) to his sons, and it was later repeated by his grandson, the prophet Jacob (S):

> O my sons, Allah has chosen the faith for you.
> Therefore, do not die without your being Muslims.
> (Qur'an 2:132)

Here, the prophet did not advise his sons to work hard, to become wealthy, or to succeed in this life, as many of today's Muslims do. Instead, he emphasized to them that the primary, most essential goal of their lives was to be true to the faith that Allah, their Lord, had appointed for them, and not to die except in a state of surrender to Him. May Allah help us to follow his noble example when we give *our* children advice.

In the story of the prophet Jacob and his son Joseph (S), narrated in full in surah 12, we find the finest example of a prophet-father's relationship with his sons. In this surah, Jacob (S) repeatedly gives wise advice, first to his son Joseph (S) and later to his other sons. Although his ten rebellious sons have betrayed his trust, behaved treacherously, and separated him from the one he loved best in this life, he does not turn away from them, hate them, or speak to them harshly. Instead, he continues steadfastly on the path of "beautiful patience," treating them with undeserved kindness and forbearance. Finally, when they come to him repenting of their terrible misdeeds and asking him to beseech Allah for forgiveness, he turns to them in fatherly love, saying, "I shall ask forgiveness for you from my Lord. Truly, He is the Most Forgiving, Most Merciful" (Qur'an 12:98).

Another well-known father mentioned in the Qur'an is the sage Luqman, for whom a surah of the Qur'an (surah 31) is named. Luqman is considered the prototype of a wise, devoted father giving advice to his son concerning right conduct:

> O my dear son, do not associate (anything) with Allah; truly, associating (anything) with Allah is the most terrible wrong-doing. . . . O my son, establish the *salah*, enjoin what is good and forbid what is unlawful, and be patient in whatever befalls you; surely that pertains to fixed determination in (conducting) affairs. And do not turn your cheek away from people nor walk insolently upon the earth, for Allah does not love any arrogant boaster. And be moderate in your pace and lower your voice; indeed, the most disagreeable of sounds is the sound of the donkey. (Qur'an 31:13, 17-19)

Here the first piece of advice to the son is not to commit the worst of all sins—that is, to deny the One Who created him and accept a false reality by ascribing partners to the Lord of the universe. The next is to acknowledge Allah's lordship by establishing prayers, enjoining what is good and forbidding wrong-doing, and practicing patience and steadfastness in all matters. Luqman then counsels his son against behaving with arrogance and pride, and encourages him to be moderate in his bearing and manners, so that he is never associated with insolent, ill-behaved people. The end result of such advice, if heeded, will be an individual who is just, correct, and acceptable in his behavior, and who is respected and loved by people of sound understanding.

Also in want of a son, the childless prophet Zachariah (S) prayed, "O my Lord, grant me from Yourself a goodly child. Truly, You are the hearer of prayers!" (3:38). At that, his Lord answered his petition by giving him the news of the birth of a son, the prophet Yahya (John "the Baptist," S), who was sent as the fore-runner of one of the most honored of all prophets, Jesus (S).

Two general prayers for children are found in the Qur'an. In one of these, "Our Lord, grant us spouses and offspring who will be the comfort of our eyes" (25:74), Allah shows us to ask for a life partner and children who will bring happiness, peace, comfort, and satisfaction. In the second, "If You give us a goodly child, we vow we shall be grateful" (7:189), the aspiring parents promise gratitude to Allah if He blesses them with a sound, healthy child, according to their deepest desires.

The Prophet (S) said,

> Three supplications are answered, without doubt: that of a father, that of a traveller, and that of one who has been wronged. *(Abu Dawud, 1531)*

A Muslim parent should desire both the good of this world and the good of the life hereafter for his or her child. If a choice must be made between these two, the life-to-come is eternal and it is the most important goal for us. In practical terms, this may mean giving up or leaving off something that may be seen fine for the child in terms of this world's life but which will lead him to unhappiness Hereafter. If we ask Allah for guidance in all our affairs, we will be able to know the difference between what is good in the everlasting perspective and what is good only temporarily and materially.

THE RESPONSIBILITIES OF PARENTS

Allah Most High says,

> And the mothers shall breast-feed their children for
> two full years, for those desiring to complete the
> (limit of the term of) breast-feeding, and the feeding
> and clothing of them rests upon the father, in a suit-
> able manner. No soul is burdened beyond its means:
> a mother shall not be injured because of her child nor
> the father because of his child, and on the (father's)
> heir rests the like of that (which was an obligation for
> the father). Then, if they desire to wean the child by
> mutual consent and consultation, there is no sin upon
> them; and if you desire to give your children to a wet
> nurse, there is no sin upon you, provided that you pay
> (the wet nurse) what is due from you in a suitable
> manner. And be mindful of Allah, and know that
> Allah is Seer of whatever you do. (Qur'an 2:233)

This verse establishes several important principles in establishing the parents' responsibility for children:

1. Mothers are encouraged to nurse their children. Nursing
is then seen as an extension of the pregnancy, the means of the
child's secure and wholesome entry into the earthly world from
the world of the womb. From this we can deduce the divine
ordinance of the mother's being the primary caregiver of the
child whenever possible. That she is not positively obliged to
nurse the child herself can be understood from the permissibili-
ty of employing a wet nurse, who then takes on the status of a
foster mother.

Thus, a divinely ordained, permanent bond of *mahrem* relationship is established between the nursed infant and his "milk
mother" and her family, restricting marriage possibilities with
them, just as with one's own blood relatives. The Prophet (S)

himself had a milk mother, the Bedouin woman Haleema Saadia (R), whom he never ceased to treat with great respect. The Prophet's son Ibrahim is also reported to have been placed with a milk mother.

However, from the Qur'anic wording, "It is no sin for you" if a wet nurse is used, and from the mention of mother's nursing first, we can understand that Allah wishes and expects a mother to care for her children. And while man is definitely not simply a higher animal, this is in keeping with the fitrah or innate nature of all species of higher animals, with which mankind is linked, in which mothers provide nurturing and nourishment.

2. This verse clearly makes fathers responsible for providing for their children. A man is obliged, first, to take the final responsibility for the welfare of his family members and, second, to provide the means of obtaining food, clothing, shelter, and other needs, both for the wife for whom he has taken responsibility and for his children. In Islam, these are rights as well as responsibilities, giving the father a clearly-defined, vitally important task and a role: while the woman produces the family (with his help), he takes care of her and of it. And when Allah Ta'ala speaks of the "degree" which men have over women (2:228), it is the degree of responsibility and authority within the family that is meant. This responsibility allocates to the husband/father the headship of the family unit and the final word in decisions, since he is responsible for its welfare.

Thus the father occupies a vital role in the child's life from the very beginning. Not only is he the partner in giving that life but he is responsible for its care and maintenance. And this is only in keeping with the divine justice, which does not burden anyone with more than he or she can bear. Any woman who has ever been pregnant and given birth, nursed and tended to children, knows that if it is to be done properly, this task is enough, and much more than enough, for one individual, without adding the additional burden of having to be responsible for all decisions or earning the living for the family.

3. Consultation between the parents is advised for important decisions concerning the children. Fairness and reason-
ableness is expected; the obligations involved in rearing the
child are not to exceed the limits of bearabilty for anyone,
whether mother, father, or foster-mother. When there is a balanced effort among those responsible for the child, they become
a team and can coordinate their efforts so that all the child's
needs can be met. And while this verse refers specifically to
cases of divorce in which achieving harmony is the most difficult, it is certainly just as applicable in general cases as well.

The equity outlined in the foregoing Qur'anic verse
reminds us that all extremes in religion are discouraged in
Islam. A woman and children share in the wealth of the hus-
band/father, or in his poverty. Who can accept a wealthy man
who abandons his wife and children in a tiny cramped apartment, with cheap clothing and poor quality food, while he is
out engaged in business and social affairs eighteen hours of the
day? Who can accept a wife who spends her time visiting,
dragging her children from one adult social function to the
next, leaving her house a mess and no food in the kitchen,
while her husband works a sixty-hour week to just make ends
meet? It is by looking at the extremes that we can grasp the
desirability of the middle ground. And Islam is "the religion of
the middle path" (2:14)—the religion of balance and moderation in the conduct of all affairs.

THE MOTHER'S ROLE

Considering the high status given to the mother in Islam—
higher than the father's, and second only to Allah in deserving
respect— it is easy to see why Muslim women usually desire
children and why they are happy to stay home and care for
them. Few careers offer so great a reward as guiding little people as they grow up. However, when needed or wanted, foster

mothers or other relatives can substitute for the mother, either temporarily or over the long term.

There are three obvious cases in which a woman might choose to delegate the care of her children to someone else, or in which her right to care for the child might be taken away.

1. In case of her ill health.
2. In case of divorce, and specifically when she afterwards marries another man. This is so because the new husband has no right to usurp the position of the real father in relation to his children. Moreover, the wife's obligations to her new husband might create a conflict of interest.
3. In case of the importance, benefits or rewards of her career outweighing the importance of her caring for her child.

The question of women—especially mothers—working is quite controversial among Muslims (and even non-Muslims) today. People tend to view it in black-and-white terms and ignore any nuances. Many traditional Muslims insist that the woman's place is in the home, in keeping with the Qur'anic verse addressed to the wives of the Prophet (S), "And stay in your houses" (33:33). In any case, the effort involved in ministering to the needs of the family, in creating a warm, loving, peaceful atmosphere with all the conflicting personalities and temperaments a family can contain, is indeed a tremendous one. Without question, it really is a *jihad* (a striving) for a conscientious woman.

The time-honored model in Islam has been that of a respected, honored woman at home caring for her children and extended family, usually with spacious rooms in a home designed for a Muslim family. The home had plenty of light and air, and an enclosed courtyard and garden in which the women and children could enjoy complete privacy as the children played and the women worked and relaxed together—grandmothers, aunts, sisters, cousins, neighbors, in small towns and villages. In earlier times, a widow, divorcee, or other woman in financial distress was supported by the men of her extended family or by help from zakah or sadaqah, so there was no economic necessity for a woman to leave the home to work outside.

Today, such a structure is generally not available to Muslims living outside the Muslim world, nor does it even exist in many places in Muslim communities, unfortunately. The traditional conventions of family life and responsibility become a prison sentence for both mother and children, unhealthy in all respects, when families are packed into small modern apartments with little sunshine or fresh air, miles from friends and family.

On the other hand, although traditionally the majority of Muslim women have stayed home, and have surely earned the highest reward from Allah for their activities within it, there are some jobs in the community that require women, such as doctors, nurses, teachers, dressmakers, and sellers of women's clothing, etcetra. Allah knows best, but it may be that when the community has legitimate needs in these areas, some women who are qualified will get more reward for filling community needs than they would for staying home with their children.

This is understood under the Islamic principle of *fard kifiyah* (community obligation). When the community has needs, these take precedence over the other personal obligations of an individual if that person can fulfill the need. An example to illustrate is the draft for the army. If soldiers are needed, the community looks to all those with ability, the young healthy men. When few are needed, there are many exemptions because of personal circumstances, parents to support, weak ankles, poor eyesight, etcetra. When the need becomes greater, the list of exemptions is shortened. When the community is under siege, old men, women, and children may have to be called up to man the walls of defense.

The Muslim community obviously needs women teachers, for example. We can provide for this need by using qualified unmarried women, married women without children or those whose children are older. If more are needed then we can ask among those with children who have sisters and mothers who can help with child care. When a woman is leaving her children to fulfill important community service, other women should help her as their form of community assistance. This example is a simplification, of course, of a complex situation for many women. Some are more gifted at teaching than others. The experience of being a mother is very enriching for a teacher.

The needs of children are not all that may keep a woman home. She may have an elderly parent who needs constant care. Each person knows his or her situation and the situation of the community, and can analyze it and pray for guidance. Then we make decisions and act upon them, and we are held responsiblie for them.

Whether their efforts in business or the community are needed or not, women absolutely have full rights over their money and are no more restricted than men in managing their business affairs. Traditionally it has often proved desirable to act through agents; in other cases, they have needed or preferred to act directly, controlling their own enterprises. This discussion is not intended to put these rights into question, but rather to look at the choice of the mother with children, particularly young children, from the view point of maximizing her reward from Allah for her time, and how she spends it.

A woman who leaves her children to spend her time on a career in order to "find herself" or make a reputation as a "modern woman" has probably misunderstood and undervalued the importance of her role in the home and her relationship with her children. Self-glorification and ego gratification are forms of arrogance, excuses for following one's own will and desires instead of Allah's, which cannot be expected to bear good fruit. The Prophet (S) said,

> Each one of you is a guardian and is responsible for
> what is in his custody. The ruler is a guardian of his

subjects and is responsible for them; a husband is a guardian of his family and is responsible for it; a lady is a guardian of her husband's house and is responsible for it; and a servant is a guardian of his master's property and is responsible for it. *(Bukhari, 3.592)*

But while mothers are guardians and are responsible for their children, they are not slaves to them nor prisoners in their homes. Allah surely rewards a woman for the time and effort she devotes to her children, but she has her own personal needs, talents, and wishes as well, and she too needs to be fulfilled as a person.

Does a woman find childcare fulfilling? If not, maybe she can learn whatever she needs and create ways to make it so, spending as her husband's means allow on things that would make her work more enjoyable. Motherhood is a creative, flexible, versatile process, and if one approach doesn't produce fulfillment, others can be tried. Her husband, family, and community can help her with moral support and encouragement. How many women today have been discouraged from enjoying their mothering role because of the negative view of a stay-at-home woman in our society?

Besides this, a woman can do many things that she enjoys at home. Some women have mastered special skills, becoming writers, artists, expert seamstresses or craftspeople, and learning a myriad of other special skills, without leaving their children or their homes to pursue a career. And this is in keeping with the previously-mentioned injunction of Allah Ta'ala to the wives of the Prophet (S), "Stay in your houses" (33:33). A woman's house can be her palace, her special medium, the place where her soul can be at peace, in which she is the queen. The Prophet's advice to women to pray in the most private corner of their houses rather than going out to the mosque may well be related to a woman's inner nature and needs. Unlike a man, who must be involved in the outer world, she is the master of inner space, in keeping with the fitrah of her physiology and inner life.

To round out the discussion here, we need to mention the many women who sincerely wish to stay home with their children, but who cannot because of economic necessity. Too often we treat this subject as if women have the choice to stay home. Community leaders need to be more responsive to assisting mothers. Too often today, people criticize mothers for not staying home, but men do not step forward to marry divorced or widowed women with children. Extended families are not living up to their obligations to help needy members. Too many women are out in the work force because they and their children would starve otherwise! They will be rewarded for their sacrifices and the communities that ignored them will be answerable before Allah for their hard hearts.

We all agree that the highest of rewards is the pleasure of Allah Ta'ala. We also all know the critical importance of the family in Islam, and in society as a whole, with the tremendous emphasis in the Islamic teachings on ensuring its well-being. By looking at the society around us, we can easily see how it is being rapidly warped and destroyed by women's not giving the vital role of mother its due, by their not being there for their children because they have unnecessarily gone to work.

The condition of Western society today can be said to prove the correctness of the Islamic teachings concerning the diverse responsibilities of men and women, of the husband/father and the wife/mother, within the family. We see what happens if the foundation of security, and trust in the universe as a safe, nurturing place, is not laid down in early childhood by the efforts of a committed mother, who is supported and assisted in her role by a caring, committed father. When women fulfill their nurturing role and men their protective, maintaining role, society flourishes; when they do not, society falls apart. And a just society recognizes and supports this by making every sort of assistance available to parents in carrying out their vital roles.

A wise woman evaluates her situation seriously, weighing the fulfillment and reward possible from caring for children and home, versus the fulfillment and reward possible from other efforts. Her entire situation should be considered, weighed, and discussed responsibly with her husband, keeping in mind the needs of the individual family members and the total family group.

THE FATHER'S ROLE

The Muslim father's role in the lives his children is likewise of great importance. The Qur'an and hadith establish him as the head of the family, the economic provider, and the educator, the source of authority.

Perhaps the father's role is presented so clearly, more clearly than the mother's role, because it is less instinctive for a man and he needs more social guidance for this role than a woman does for her role as a mother. As we have seen, the Qur'an sets forth several examples of prophet-fathers, as well as the sage Luqman, guiding their sons and carrying out their paternal functions with justice, wisdom, and righteousness.

This role can be contrasted with the one defined by current American society. As the male's place of work has moved out of the home/farm/home-based shop or business to the distant office or factory, the importance of the role of the father in the American home has slowly diminished. The workplace does not generally recognize the role of family man, but only that of the loyal employee (employers in many Muslim countries, by way of contrast, accept lower employee output to avoid sacrificing family time to overtime, and readily recognize that their employees will be out at times for family reasons).

Books continue to emerge from the hands of psychologists to discuss fatherhood and try to figure out what it really is, even as statistics reveal how devastating the lack of a positive father image can be for children. A recently-published study reported that as many as forty percent of all the children in the United States born between 1970 and 1984 will spend most of their childhood without a father, due to the divorce or non-marriage of the parents (*Time* Magazine, June 28, 1993). This is coupled with an attitude of disrespect and casualness toward the father which suggests that he isn't really a necessary element in family life. He must either fit in with the children, like an older child to be ordered around by the mother, or the mother can do without him. Whereas a woman is never said to "babysit" her own children, a father may use this term to express the time he spends taking care of his children, revealing the role he is playing—that of a substitute mom, not of a real dad.

In this society, it is often difficult for a man to provide well for his family and also find enough time to spend with his children. Among Muslims, however, we have a support system for fathers as well as for mothers. When a man's wife and the Muslim community reflect the Islamic ideal of a father, the children can respect him as a loving father who works hard on their behalf. For Allah made children want to idealize and admire their parents, and they have an instinct to see only the good in them. A big, strong-looking man once asked a little boy, who was stronger, the man himself or the boy's small, thin father? The child puffed out his chest and forcefully proclaimed, "Daddy!"

Mommy is a key to this duty of respecting Daddy. She may be the one who always shops for the children's clothes and shoes, but she can remind them that Daddy paid for them: "Go show Daddy your new sports shoes and thank him for them!" She can consult with him in front of the children before signing them up for baseball, and otherwise demonstrate her need and desire for his advice. She can cover his faults and her disagreements with him from the eyes of the children so that their respect for him remains untouched. Naturally, the father should give similar respect and support to the mother. There should not be competition for the love of the children, but only the desire for their greatest good.

Since we live in a non-Islamic environment, however, the parents have to work harder to convey this positive, respected image of the father as a counter to the negative stereotypes portrayed in cartoons and comedies of "Dad, the bungling idiot," which is in glaring contrast to the often-portrayed image of the "supermom" or "superwoman". There's a lot more than sex and violence on TV that can corrupt our children's understanding of how life ought to be lived!

FINANCIAL RESPONSIBILITY

If a parent—more especially the father—has concerns about his ability to support his children, Allah gently reassures him, saying:

> And do not kill your children out of fear of poverty;
> We provide, sustenance for them and for you. Truly,
> killing them is a great sin. (Qur'an 17:31; 6:151)

These verses forbid both abortion and the killing of children due to difficult circumstances, for Allah is the Provider and He can send provision how and as He wills.

Two verses of the Qur'an explicitly refer to a man's obligation to support his wife and children:

> The men are *qawwamun*[2] over the women in that
> Allah has made the one of them to excel the other
> and in that they spend of their property (for the support of their families). (Qur'an 4:34)

---

[2] The Arabic term "qawwam" means one who stands firm in his own or another's business or affairs, looking after their best interest. In this sense the husband is responsible for the maintenance, protection and overall leadership of the family *(qiwamah)* within the framework of consultation and kindness.

And the mothers shall breast-feed their children for two full years, for those desiring to complete the (limit of the term of) breast-feeding, and the feeding and clothing of them rests upon the father, in a suitable manner. No soul is burdened beyond its means: a mother shall not be injured because of her child nor the father because of his child, and on the (father's) heir rests the like of that (which was an obligation for the father). Then, if they desire to wean the child by mutual consent and consultation, there is no sin upon them; and if you desire to give your children to a wet nurse, there is no sin upon you, provided that you pay (the wetnurse) what is due from you in a suitable manner. And be mindful of Allah, and know that Allah is Seer of whatever you do. (Qur'an 2:233)

The first of these two verses makes it clear that the husband is responsible, by virtue of his being a man, for maintaining his wife. And the second of the two verses makes clear his absolute, unequivocal responsibility to provide for his children. This allocation of functions, which corresponds to the biological and emotional fitrah of the male and female, ensures that the roles and functions of men and women are complementary, not competitive and not necessarily overlapping. The burdens of life —looking after the husband's needs, and bearing and rearing the children/looking after the wife's needs, and earning and providing for her and the children—are thereby equitably distributed among the males and females, without overloading one or the other.

Many ahadith encourage spending on one's family. The Prophet (S) said,

Of the dinar you spend in Allah's path or to set free a slave or as a charity given to a needy person or to support your family, the one yielding the greatest reward is that which you spend on your family. (Muslim, 2181)

The upper hand (the giver's) is better than the lower hand (the recipient's). One should start giving first to his dependants, and the best charity is what is given by a person from what is left after his expenses. And the one who refrains from asking others for help, Allah will give him and save him from asking others, and the one who is satisfied with what Allah has given him, Allah will make him self-sufficient. (Bukhari, 2.508)

O son of Adam, it is better for you if you spend your surplus, and if you withhold it, it is evil for you. There is no blame on you concerning (what you keep back for) a living. And begin (charity) with your dependents; and the upper hand is better than the lower hand. (Muslim, 2256)

When Allah grants wealth to one of you, he should spend it first on himself and his family. (Muslim, 4483)

Sa'd bin Abi Waqqas reported: In the year of the last Hajj of the Prophet (S), I became seriously ill and the Prophet (S) visited me, inquiring about my health. I told him, "I am reduced to this state because of illness. I am wealthy and have no inheritors except a daughter. Should I give two-thirds of my property in charity?" He said, "No." I asked, "Half?" He said, "No." Then he added, "One-third, and even one-third is too much. It is better for you to leave your inheritors wealthy rather than leaving

them poor, begging from others. You will be rewarded for whatever you spend for the sake of Allah,
even for what you put into your wife's mouth."
(Bukhari, 2.383A; Muwatta, 37.3.4)

Once, when the Prophet (S) ordered the Muslims to
give charity, a man said, "O Messenger of Allah, I
have a dinar." He said, "Spend it on yourself." He
again said, "I have another." He said, "Spend it on
your children." He again said, "I have another." He
said, "Spend it on your wife." He again said, "I have
another." He said, "Spend it on your servant." He
finally said, "I have another." He replied, "You know
best (what to do with it)." (Abu Dawud, 1687)

The Prophet (S) used to spend from his property on
his family, and give the residue as sadaqah . (Abu
Dawud, 2969)

Mu'adh ibn Jabal reported: The Messenger of Allah
(S) instructed me to do ten things, (and among them
was): ". . .Spend on your children according to your
means. . . " (Mishkat al-Masabih, transmitted by
Ahmad)

Hind bint Utbah said, "O Messenger of Allah, Abu
Sufyan (her husband) is a miser and he does not give
me what is sufficient for me and my children. Can I
take from his property without his knowledge?" The
Prophet (S) said, "Take what is sufficient for you and
your children, and the amount should be just and
reasonable." (Bukhari, 7.277 and 8.636)

THE WORKING WIFE

We are living in a society and in a time in which a man's responsibility for maintaining his family has become a disputed matter. As the lines between the complementary functions of male and female have become obscured and blurred by confusion and competitiveness, women have assumed the role of men and men of women. But the final guidance from the Lord of the universe, Islam, makes it clear without any doubt that providing for the family is solely the duty of the husband.

According to the Islamic teachings, if the wife is earning, her earnings are her own, to spend or save as she pleases. She has no obligation whatsoever to spend them on her own maintenance or that of her children, much less on her husband's. However, if the two decide by mutual agreement that she will be responsible for some part of the family's expenses, there is no objection, especially if she works at a job which is beneficial to herself or to others. What is objectionable is the case in which a husband withdraws from earning for the family, leaving it upon the shoulders of his wife, or in which he obliges a woman who otherwise prefers to be at home to go out and earn in his place.

To this it will be objected, "But life is expensive and one person's earnings don't go far enough to enable a family to survive." Again, if the wife agrees to work in order to help her husband make ends meet, this should be a voluntary act of kindness on her part, not something she is forced to do by her husband's pressure or unwillingness to be the provider. In such a case, he should understand that she is taking over part of his Islamic responsibility, show apprecation for her efforts, and share in the responsibility of home and children as much as possible, not taking her help for granted.

A mother may not be legally responsible for the finances of her home, but she is rewarded for anything she decides to contribute:

> A woman asked the Prophet (S), "O Messenger of
> Allah, shall I be rewarded if I spend to provide for
> Abu Salama's sons (presumably after Abu Salama's
> death), when they are my sons as well?" The Prophet
> (S) replied, "Spend on them, and you will get a
> reward for what you spend on them." *(Bukhari)*

Zaynab, the wife of Abdullah ibn Mas'ud, used to provide
for Abdullah and those orphans who were under her protection.
She enquired from the Prophet (S) whether it was permissible
for her to spend from her zakah for them. The Prophet (S) said,

> "Yes, and she will receive a double reward: one for
> helping relatives and the other for giving zakah."
> *(Bukhari, 2.545)*

POSSESSIONS

Within the Muslim family, property and possessions are
often regarded differently from the notions current in this society. For example, no practicing Muslim would buy a box of
chocolates and hide it in his room to eat all by himself. Food is
shared with whomever is present; it is not "my" food, but "our"
food. Generosity to guests, even at the expense of family
members, is the rule.

Today it is common for parents to give to their children in
excess. If my daughter has a pair of shoes for school, a pair for
play, perhaps some "good" shoes for special occasions, and a
pair of boots for winter weather, I must be thankful to Allah
that I can provide for her. But if I provide a different pair of
shoes to color-coordinate each outfit, and she has some thirty
outfits, obviously I am exceeding the limits, both of what is
correct Islamically and what is in the child's own best interest.
Concerning this, Allah says,

O you who believe, do not prohibit the good, pure
things which Allah has made permissible for you,
and do not go beyond the limit. Truly, Allah does not
like the transgressors. (Qur'an 5:90 [5: 87 in some
translations])

Say (O Muhammad): "Who has forbidden the beautiful (gifts) of Allah which He has produced for His
servants, and the good among what is provided?"
(Qur'an 7:32)

Along these lines, having a piece of candy as a special treat
now and then is a pleasant experience for a child. But if he is
given as much candy as he wants every day, he will quickly
lose his enjoyment of it; candy will become just another routine
food, maybe even one that he comes to dislike. Likewise, a few
well-chosen toys, suitable to the level and interest of the child,
can be a source of education and entertainment. However, the
usual scenario is a room full of half-broken, unused toys, and a
child who whines for more and fights with others over posses-
sion of the unused piles. And today, the overuse of television
and video games for entertainment often falls into the category
of "excess."

RESPONSIBILITY FOR PARENTS AND OTHER RELATIVES

In Islam, a male child also has financial responsibility
toward his parents when he is old enough to earn, as well as
other obligations. It is considered a bad thing for a son to
"sponge" off his father (or mother), lazily relaxing while the
other supports him; but mutual aid, depending on need and
financial ability, which is another matter entirely, is definitely
encouraged.

Muslim families have always had this kind of mutual inter-dependence. If one is in need, the other steps in to help; according to the Islamic teachings, it is both their mutual right to receive it and their obligation to give it. And needless to say, if the parents are needy and unable to take care of themselves, the children are responsible for their maintenance, particularly when the parents are old and in need of support. The following ahadith make this clear.

> The children of a man proceed from what he earns; rather they are his pleasantest earning, so enjoy from their property. *(Abu Dawud, 3522)*

> A man came to the Prophet (S) and said: "O Messenger of Allah, I have property and children, and my father finishes my property." He said, "You and your property (both) belong to your father; your children come from the pleasantest of what you earn, so enjoy from the earnings of your children." *(Abu Dawud, 3523)*.

And supplementing these are the many ahadith cited earlier, relating to service, kindness and dutifulness to parents, which includes taking care of their material needs. The basic rule in Islam is that the family should be a caring, supportive unit, whose members seek to help each other wherever there is need, financial or otherwise. This earns the pleasure of Allah and His abundant reward. Firstly, in this world we are rewarded with the warm, loving environment created in the home. At the same time, we can also hope to be recompensed for what we have done on the Day of Judgment. Whether we undertake a responsibility as a duty to Allah, because we feel it is the right thing to do, or out of love of our next-of-kin, Allah is generous in rewarding us for our efforts for His sake. He says,

It is not righteousness that you turn your faces
toward the East or the West, but rather the righteous
is that one who believes in Allah and the Last Day
and the angels and the Book and the Messengers,
and gives his wealth, out love of Him, for relatives
and orphans. . . (Qur'an 2:177)

Sometimes we may feel uncomfortable about giving "charity" to our family. Perhaps they have caused us pain, or we feel
they are lazy and that others are more deserving of our help, or
that to give to them will deprive our own family. However, if
there is genuine need, it is best to help them, as Allah created this
tie of relationship with us. Concerning this, the Prophet (S) said,

O community of Muhammad, by Him Who has sent
me with truth, Allah cannot accept the charity of
those whose relatives are in want of his kindness and
help, while he is distributing it among others, leaving them out. By Him in Whose power is my life, on
the Day of Judgment Allah will not look at such a
man." *(Tabarani)*

There is a beautiful example in the story of Abu Talha (R).
Among the Ansar (Helpers) in Madinah, he had more property
in the form of date palms than anyone else, and among his
properties, the grove called Bayruha was the dearest of them to
him. Then, when the verse, "You will not attain righteousness
unless you spend (in charity) from what you love" (3:92) was
revealed, Abu Talha (R) went to the Prophet (S), citing this
verse and saying, "Bayruha is certainly the dearest to me
among my property, therefore it is (now given as) sadaqah for
Allah, and I hope for the reward of it from Allah. O Messenger
of Allah, spend it as Allah makes you see fit." At that the
Messenger of Allah (S) commended him and said that in his
opinion, he should give it to his relatives. Abu Talha (R) said,

"I will do it, O Messenger of Allah," and he then divided it among his near relatives and his cousins. (Bukhari, 2.540)

There is also the fine example of Abu Bakr (R), who used to give help to a poor relative. Although this relative lived on this charity, he was one of the malicious gossips who spread evil rumors concerning the virtue of Abu Bakr's daughter A'isha (R), the wife of the Prophet (S). Pained by his relative's behavior, Abu Bakr (R) vowed never to give him help again. Then, soon afterwards, the verse 24:22 was revealed concerning this incident: "And let not those who have been given favors and plenty among you take an oath not to help their relatives and the poor and the emigrants in the cause of Allah, and let them forgive and overlook. Would you not like that Allah should forgive you? And Allah is Most Forgiving, Most Merciful." At that, Abu Bakr (R) started helping his relative again, saying, "I would like Allah to forgive me" (Bukhari, 5.462).

These, the noblest and highest examples from among the companions of the Prophet (S), may well serve as our guides in doing what is best and most suitable for our next-of-kin, thereby earning Allah's pleasure and generous reward.

THE EDUCATION OF CHILDREN

Within the two-parent Muslim family, there are, by definition, two educators for the child: the father and the mother. Contrary to current thinking, a father's role is not limited to paying the bills and engaging in a little consultation now and then. The Muslim father is also responsible for his child's training and education.

Concerning this, the Prophet (S) said,

> A father gives his child nothing better than a good education. *(Mishkat, 4977, transmitted by Tirmidhi and Baihaqi)*

Mu'adh ibn Jabal (R) reported that the Prophet (S) instructed him to do ten things. Among them, the ninth was, "Do not refrain from using pressure for training them," and the tenth was, "Instill in them the fear of Allah." (Mishkat, 0061, transmitted by *Ahmad)*

And in a time when baby girls were buried alive, he placed special emphasis on the reward for rearing and educating girls, saying:

"The one who brings up two girls properly until they grow up, he and I would come (close together like this) on the Day of Resurrection," and he interlaced his fingers. *(Muslim, 6364)*

The one who cares for three daughters, disciplines them, marries them off, and does good to them, for him is Paradise. *(Abu Dawud, 5128)*

These few ahadith have been included here because they specifically address parents, but there is a wealth of material in the Qur'an and hadith encouraging learning and acquiring knowledge in general. Since acquiring knowledge generally involves expense, it is natural that fathers should be informed of the obligation to educate their children. However, although mothers are not addressed specifically, they are often the major force in carrying out this obligation.

In the first Muslim community, both men and women learned their religion directly from the Prophet (S). In cases in which men were addressed, they were responsible for conveying the information to their wives and children. Women were almost exclusively in charge of early-childhood education, as well as usually being responsible for the education of girls. Men were, however, responsible for seeing that their children learned their religion and its way of life and behaved according to its teachings. They also took over the training of boys when they were old enough to start working, as most education for earning a livelihood was on-the-job training. Others, who specialized in Islamic knowledge, learned at the feet of Muslims of piety and knowledge.

KINDNESS AND AFFECTION

In their striving to Follow the example of Prophet Muhammad (S), Muslim parents should be kind and affectionate to their children as is naturally expected. As we have seen, the Prophet (S) used to kiss his grandchildren and openly display his great affection for them. There are numerous ahadith to this effect. When he greeted his daughter Fatima (R), he would kiss her, and when he went to her house, she would stand up to welcome him and would kiss him. (Abu Dawud, 5198).

We have already mentioned that once the Messenger of Allah (S) kissed his grandson al-Hasan (R) while a companion named al-Aqra (R) was sitting beside him. At that, al-Aqra (R) said, "I have ten children and I have never kissed any of them." The Messenger of Allah (S) glanced at him and said, "The one who is not merciful will not be shown mercy." (Bukhari, 8.26).

Some ornaments were sent to the Prophet (S) by Negus (the king of Abyssinia). Among them was a gold ring with an Abyssinian stone. The Prophet (S) then called Umamah (R), his granddaughter from his daughter Zaynab (R), and said to her, "Wear it, my dear daughter" (Abu Dawud, 4223).

Abdullah ibn J'afar (R), the Prophet's cousin, reported that when the Messenger of Allah (S) came back from a journey, the children of his family would welcome him. Once, when he came riding into Madinah from a journey, the young Abdullah (R) was the first to go to him, and the Prophet (S) mounted the boy in front of him. Then came one of the two sons of Fatimah (R), and

the Prophet (S) mounted him behind him, and that was how the
three entered Madinah, riding on a mount (Muslim, 5962).

Once, when the Messenger of Allah (S) was carrying his
grandson al-Hasan ibn Ali (R) on his shoulder, a man said, "You
are mounted on a fine steed, boy!" The Prophet (S) said, "And
he is a fine rider!" (*Mishkat*, 6163, transmitted by *Tirmidhi*).

The servant of the Prophet (S), Anas bin Malik (R) said,

> I have never seen anyone more kind to his family
> than the Messenger of Allah (S). (His infant son)
> Ibrahim was sent to the suburb of Madinah for nurs-
> ing. He (the Prophet, S) used to go there and we
> would accompany him. He entered the house (of the
> wet nurse), and it was filled with smoke, since the
> foster-father was a blacksmith. He took him
> (Ibrahim) and kissed him, and then came back.
> *(Muslim, 5734)*

Anas (R) further described the death of Ibrahim (R) at the
age of eighteen months:

> We went with the Messenger of Allah (S) to the
> blacksmith, Abu Sayf, who was the husband of
> Ibrahim's wet nurse. The Messenger of Allah (S)
> took Ibrahim and kissed him and sniffed him. Then
> after that we came in to him, and at that time Ibrahim
> was breathing his last, and the eyes of the Messenger
> of Allah (S) began to shed tears. At that, Abdur
> Rahman ibn Awf said, "Even you, O Messenger of
> Allah?" He said, "O Ibn Awf, this is mercy." Then he
> wept more and said, "Surely the eyes shed tears and
> the heart is grieved, but we do not say except what is
> pleasing to our Lord, and we are grieved by your
> parting, O Ibrahim ." *(Bukhari, 2.390)*

The wife of the Holy Prophet (S), A'isha bint Abu Bakr (R), reported the following incidents about her life with the Prophet (S) when she was still a young girl:

> I used to play with dolls in front of the Prophet (S), and my friends used to play with me. When the Messenger of Allah (S) came in, they would hide themselves from him. Then the Prophet (S) would call them to join me and play with me. (*Bukhari*, 8.151)

> When the Messenger of Allah (S) arrived after the expedition to Tabuk or Khaybar, the wind reard an end of a curtain which was hung in front of her storeroom, revealing some dolls of hers. He said, "What is this?" She said, "My dolls." Among them he saw a horse with wings made of rags, and he said, "What is this I see among them?" She said, "A horse." He said, "What is this it has on it?" She said, "Two wings." He said, "A horse with two wings?" She said, "Have you not heard that Solomon had horses with wings?" Concerning this, she (A'isha) said, "At that, the Messenger of Allah (S) laughed so heartily that I could see his molars." *(Abu Dawud, 4914)*

> The Messenger of Allah (S) came in to me while two slave girls were with me singing the songs of Bu'ath (a story about the war between the two tribes of the Ansar, the Khazraj and the Aws, before Islam). He (the Prophet, S) lay down upon his mattress and turned his face to the other side. Then Abu Bakr (A'isha's father) came, whereupon he rebuked me and said, "Musical instruments of Shaytan near the Prophet (S)?" The Messenger of Allah (S) turned toward him and said, "Leave them (the singers)."

Then, when Abu Bakr was not paying attention, I
made a sign to the two of them to go out and they
left. And it was the day of Eid, and the black people
were playing with shields and spears. Then either I
asked the Prophet (S) or he said, "Would you like to
see the show?" I said, "Yes." Then he made me stand
behind him, my cheek upon his cheek, and he said,
"Carry on, O Banu Arfidah," until, when I became
tired, he said, "Enough for you?" I said, "Yes."   He
said, "Then go." *(Bukhari, 2.70)*

This is the Prophet (S)—tender, tolerant, endlessly loving to
the young of his family and to all humanity. This is the holy
Messenger of Allah (S), whom we love and revere above any
other human being and whom we are honored to take as our
example. How many of us have ever even heard of this kind,
gentle, loving side of him? And why isn't this better known,
talked about, used as an example? *This* is how a Muslim father
(or grandfather), husband, and kinsman is supposed to be. May
Allah help us to be faithful followers of his blessed example,
manifesting love like this in our own lives.

PATERNITY AND ADOPTION

With all the respect Islam shows for the bonds of family
relationships, it is not surprising that any act which casts doubt
on the paternity of the child is forbidden. Accordingly, adoption as it is practiced in the West today is prohibited. And it is
important to understand why this should be so, since Islam
stresses kindness and helpfulness among the human community so strongly.

Some people view Islam's prohibition of adoption as a
reflection of male pride in controlling women and assuring
themselves that their sons are *really* their sons. However, this

is looking at the subject from a narrow point of view and describing a natural need among men in a derogatory way.

It is a fact that men are naturally vulnerable to this fear. A man wants to be certain beyond all doubt that some small act of *his* nine months earlier actually produced this baby now asleep in its mother's arms. With all the emphasis on women's needs and rights today, little effort has been made to study the male and respect his emotional ties to his children. As an example, maternal care and maternity leave are important issues in the modern world, but paternity leave has not gotten far. Abortion is considered a woman's choice; the father is not important.

It is natural and to be expected that Allah the Creator, in His Infinite Wisdom, would put all relationships in the family into the most perfect balance. Hiding the identity of the natural parents of a child is an act of the highest disrespect to the whole family, not just to the parents and to the child, but to all the relatives on both sides of the family who are related to this child, considering the immense potential of love and affection that can come through these ties, and the emotional and material support to be poured out as relatives help each other. But even more important, perhaps, is respect for the inheritance rights of relatives and mahrem relationships and obligations.

> Call them (adopted children) by their fathers' names; that is more just in the sight of Allah. And if you do not know their fathers' names, then they are your brothers-in-faith or your friends (but not your children). (Qur'an 33:5)

> No man calls himself after someone other than his father, and he knows it, without having disbelieved in Allah, and the one who calls himself after a people with whom he has no relationship, let him take his place in the Fire. (Bukhari, 4.711)

> Truly, among the worst of lies is for a man to falsely
> call himself after someone other than his father, or to
> claim to have had a dream one has not had, or to
> attribute to the Messenger of Allah what he has not
> said. (Bukhari, 4.712)

> The one who calls himself after someone other than
> his father, and he knows it, Paradise is forbidden for
> him. (Bukhari, 5.616)

At the same time that Islam protects the natural family by prohibiting adoption, it also protects the adopting family from delusions. Adoptive parents can get so attached to a child whom they love that they create a fiction around him and deny the reality of his not being their own child. They may hide the fact of adoption and create an environment in which they and the child can feel like normally related family members: "He has my eyes, his father's nose, laughs like his uncle with the same sense of humor, gets his spelling ability from my side of the family," and so on. When the fact of adoption is concealed, if the parents do not do this themselves, other people around them may, and the children also do it as they grow up and want to be part of this family. This is normal in a natural family, but it can cause great pain in an adoptive family once the lie is unmasked. Many stories attest to the long, difficult searches made by people to find their true, natural parents.

Concealing the fact of adoption can result in other kinds of harm, even worse than this. Consider the case of a boy whose adoption is concealed, living in a family with girls of his own age. As they grow up, they interact with all the intimacy of blood brothers and sisters, even though in fact the boy is a non-mahrem to them. Then he comes to know about his adoption. The boy and his adoptive "sisters" now know that he is not their brother, although through the years he has lived within the closeness of the family circle as if he were. He knows intimate

details about them that they would not have let him know otherwise. They also know him in an inappropriate way.

At the same time, Islam accepts and even encourages foster
parenting when needed, but with the clear understanding by all
members of the family that the fostered child is the child of
someone other than the parents of the family. He is called by
his father's name and inherits from him but not, unless by written bequest, from the foster parents. However, it is very awkward for a family with girls to help a boy of their daughter's
age by long term fosterage, and vice-versa, because of the
need to respect the privacy of all as the children grow up.
Logically, foster parenting, except in the short term, should be
done with children of the same sex as one's own, unless there
are large age differences between the children.

Often a child is given to foster parents because of financial
problems in his own family. However, a father or mother without resources has the right to claim help from both their relatives and the Muslim community to enable them take care of
their children. We see the example of this from the life of the
Prophet (S) himself in his adoption of the boy Ali (R).

When the Prophet's uncle Abu Talib was in financial difficulties, Muhammad (S) and his uncle Abbas each took responsibility for one of Abu Talib's younger sons, and Ali (R) joined
the Prophet's household, not as Ali bin Muhammad but as Ali
bin Abu Talib (R). We note that the Prophet also married several widows and provided for their children, and encouraged
his companions to do likewise.

When children are left orphaned, Muslims first make a
search among near relatives to find a guardian for them. When
no family member is available, other members of the community are considered. We are reminded that Prophet Muhammad
(S) himself was an orphan and he had a special tenderness for
orphaned children. The Qur'anic verses 2:220, 4:2-10, 127,
and 7:34 legislate just treatment of orphans and equity concerning their property, as do the following verse and ahadith,

And what will explain to you (Muhammad) the steep path? (It is) freeing the slave or the giving of food, on a day of want, to an orphan who is of kin. (Qur'an 90:12-15)

Did He not find you (Muhammad) an orphan and sheltered you? And He found you lost and guided you, and He found you in need and enriched you. Therefore, do not be harsh to the orphan nor repulse the one who asks, but proclaim the favors of your Lord. (93:6-9)

"I and the one who looks after an orphan (in Muslim's version, it is: whether he is his relative or not; in Muwatta, it is: whether for himself or for someone else) will be like this in Paradise," and he gestured with his middle and index fingers with a slight gap between the two. *(Bukhari, 7.224; Muslim, 7108)*

The one who strokes the head of an orphan, doing so only for the sake of Allah, will have blessings for every hair over which his hand passes; and if anyone treats well an orphaned girl or boy under his care, he and I will be like these two in Paradise," and he put two of his fingers together. (*Mishkat*, 4974, transmitted by *Ahmad and Tirmidhi*).

THE DEATH OF A CHILD

Several ahadith testify to the great reward awaiting the parent who loses a minor child while accepting it uncomplainingly as a test from Allah. The Prophet (S) said,

Allah, the Blessed and Exalted, has said, "O Son of

Adam, if you show endurance and seek your reward
from me in the first affliction, I shall be pleased with
no less reward than Paradise for you." *(Mishkat,
1758, transmitted by Ibn Majah)*

He also said,

"No woman among you will lose her three children
without there being a screen for her from the Fire."
Then a woman among them said, "O Messenger of
Allah, what if two?" She repeated her question
twice, and then he said, "And even two, even two,
even two!" *(Bukhari, 9.413 and 2.341; Muwatta,
16.13.38 and 16.13.39)*

"The one among my ummah whose two children die
before him, Allah will admit him to Paradise on their
account." A'isha asked, "Is this for one among your
ummah whose *one* child dies before him?" He
replied, "It is, O you who have been helped by Allah
to ask this... *"(Mishkat, 1735, transmitted by
Tirmidhi)*

A Muslim whose three children die before the age of
puberty will be granted Paradise by Allah due to his
mercy for them. *(Bukhari, 2.340)*

"No Muslim couple will lose three (of their children)
by death without Allah's bringing them into Paradise
by His mercy." He was asked if that applied if they
lost two, and he said it did. He was also asked if it
applied if they lost one, and he said it did. Then he
said, "By Him in Whose hand my soul is, the miscar-
ried fetus draws his mother to Paradise by his umbil-
ical cord when she seeks her reward for (the loss of)

him from Allah." *(Mishkat, 1754,* transmitted by
Ahmad and *Ibn Majah)*

Abu Hassan (R) said to Abu Hurayrah (R), "My two
children have died. Would you narrate to me anything from the Messenger of Allah, (such as) a
hadith which would soothe our hearts in our bereave-
ment? He said: "Yes. Small children are the fowls of
Paradise. If one of them meets his father" (or he said,
"His parents"), "he will take hold of his cloth," or he
said, "with his hand, as I take hold of the hem of
your cloth (with my hand). And he (the child) will
not take (his hand) off it until Allah admits his father
to Paradise." *(Muslim, 6370)*

Someone asked the Prophet (S),

"Who are in Paradise?" He replied: "Prophets are in
Paradise, martyrs are in Paradise, infants are in
Paradise, and children buried alive are in Paradise."
(Abu Dawud, 2515)

The Prophet (S) asked a man who used to come to
him together with his son, whether he loved his son,
and the man replied, "O Messenger of Allah, may
Allah love you as I love him." (Later) the Prophet
(S) missed him, and when he asked what had happened, he was told that he had died. At that, he said,
"Would you not like to find him waiting for you no
matter to which gate of Paradise you came?" A man
asked whether that applied particularly to him, or to
all of them, and he told him that it applied to them
all. *(Mishkat, 1756,* transmitted by *Ahmad)*

In a long hadith, the Prophet (S) spoke about a dream in which two heavenly guides showed him Hell and Paradise and their inhabitants. When he asked them about the meaning of the figures he had seen in both places, they replied in detail. Among their explanations was the following,

> ". . . the tall man whom you saw in the Garden is Abraham, and as for the children who were around him, every child dies on fitr (the true religion)." At that, some Muslims said, "O Messenger of Allah, and the children of the idolaters?" The Messenger of Allah (S) said, "And the children of the idolaters (as well). . ." *(Bukhari, 9.171)*

From all this, we can understand that, difficult though the death of a child is for the parents, in the long term it is a source of blessing and mercy for them, a divine favor disguised, at the time it is bestowed, as a terrible affliction. As the Prophet (S) said,

> The believing man or woman continues to have affliction in person, property and children so that they may finally meet Allah, free from sin. *(Mishkat, 1567,* transmitted by *Tirmidhi)*

Chapter Four

ATTITUDES AND METHODS FOR REARING CHILDREN

DEFINING THE PROBLEM

Each day, some people take s*hahadah* and accept Islam as their new way of life. They thereby place themselves and their families in the situation of trying to adapt the various aspects of their lives to their new faith. All their inclinations as parents, passed down to them from their own parents and social groups, are called into question. What is Islamic and what isn't? How do we go about implementing what is Islamic in our lives and getting rid of the rest?

At the same time, the Muslim world is in a state of tremendous upheaval. People born into Muslim families all over the world are also asking the same sorts of questions. Many are from countries recuperating from colonial domination, in which some elements, at least, are returning to their roots and their religion. For them there is additionally the question of what is cultural habit and what is actually Islam, and how it all relates to rearing children. Obviously there is a great deal of sorting out to be done.

Whether here or in Muslim countries, mothers often sit together over tea or coffee and discuss their children, offering each other advice about their various problems. In a homogeneous culture there are standard problems and a small range of fairly standard solutions. Because of this culturally imposed standardization, most people never imagine that their *definition* of the problem or situation they are experiencing with their child might be part of the difficulty in finding a solution.

A classic case of the perception factor is illustrated by the little joke, "A sweater is something you put on when your mother feels cold." On any given day, one child may come to school dressed to face a blizzard while the neighbor's child arrives in a light wind-breaker. The first child's mother is worried about her child getting sick. Perhaps the child *does* get sick frequently, or perhaps the mother grew up in a warmer climate and still gets chilled by a light breeze. The mother of the second child may have grown up in a cooler climate or be such an active person that she never notices the cold. One mother feels that as the care-giver, she must supervise how much clothing the child needs, since the child doesn't know, while the other mother feels that "babying" a child with protection from climate encourages him or her to be weak and to get sick more easily. And both mothers are loving, caring women, trying their best to rear their children in the best way possible.

This simple example illustrates the fact that there is more than one way to rear a child. This may sound too obvious to mention, but indeed, how a parent perceives a situation depends on his or her background, education, and individual outlook. While in a medical situation, for example, there may be one specific right answer, many times the "right" decision is one among several possibilities, its "rightness" simply depending on what course of action the parent finds most comfortable.

Some parents enjoy delving into the psychological motivations of their child's actions. Their son gave his brother a dime, and they interpret this as an act inspired by guilt because of a fight the brothers had yesterday. Some label their children and define actions in terms of labels: if *their* son gave his brother a dime they would just say that he's generous and not search any further for motives. Fortunately, Allah knows both the child and the parent, and He gave each enough flexibility to adapt to the other.

This adaptation is particularly obvious with young babies. The baby cries. His new mother has a choice of responses. Is he hungry? Or maybe he's too hot or too cold. No, he has colic from gas or drinking too fast. He's thirsty; he needs to sleep; he's bored and needs attention; he's spoiled; he's teething; he has an immature nervous system. The list can go on, and each parent goes down his personal list of remedies until the baby calms down. The precise problem may remain unknown but still some action (or at times no action) seems called for.

Perhaps Mommy has decided her baby has colic. She gives him a little chamomile tea and gently rocks and soothes him until he goes to sleep. In fact, this remedy would work for any other of the above problems. Even for hunger, a little honey or sugar in the chamomile tea would probably calm the baby for a short while. Then, after some time, the baby comes to expect a particular response from his mother to his cries. He cries, expecting that herbal tea and rocking with her. If another person tries to give him juice instead, he may push it away in rage.

In short, a strong personal element is present in any parent's approach to dealing with his or her child. This needs to be respected if the parent is to feel comfortable. At the same time, he or she doesn't always have effective ways of dealing with the problems posed by the child. If the parent comes from a different background, the approaches and solutions that were valid in the parent society probably don't work here, for new problems pose new challenges and require new solutions.

Over the past hundred years, scientists have delved deeply into the study of human behavior and have developed many techniques for dealing with problems. Much of this has simply verified the knowledge that humanity has collectively acquired during the course of its history, organizing and labeling this information so that it can be communicated effectively. At the

same time, much new information of special interest to parents
has also become available, particularly about the normal development of the child, both physically and mentally.

As Muslims, we are advised by our Prophet (S) to seek
knowledge "even if it be in China"—that is, to search for it
wherever it is to be found. Making use of scientific knowledge
or practical tips published in non-Muslim sources can be very
helpful, but a note of caution needs to be sounded. Often the
point of view, values, or specific approach in such literature can
go against Islamic understanding. Put plainly, studies which
observe children and describe their growth and development
may be very good in their descriptions, but the interpretations
of data may be colored by the ideological bias of the observer.

As an example, it is an observable fact that small children
may be shocked and worried when they first see the genitals of
a child of the opposite sex. However, to evolve from this a
sweeping theory about women's sense of inferiority in relation
to the male, as has been done, devoting pages to descriptions of
naked children playing with themselves and the possible long-
term psychological effects in their future relationships with the
opposite sex, is both nonsensical and harmful from an Islamic
point of view.

The fact of children's reaction to seeing the genitals of children of the opposite sex exists, yes, but the theory is at the
same time unproved and unprovable, as well as contrary to
Islamic teachings. Such a theory may fit into the world view of
a society which basically assumes the inferiority of the female,
and in this case the girl will sense this and will probably envy
males, even if she doesn't see her baby brother's diaper
changed. But in a society that rests its understanding of sexual
roles on the premise that the all-knowing, infinitely wise
Creator gave each male and female their respective natures, and
that He created the two sexes to complement each other, such a
theory has no place. Hence it is assumed among Muslims—
and borne out in fact—that even though children may well be

surprised and worried at first by their differences, they will quickly relax and accept these differences as natural, just as they learn to accept so many other differences among people.

Freudian psychology is particularly hostile to Islam, while behavioral psychology can usually be adapted quite well for use by Muslims. In general, however, we need to be careful of theories and interpretations. A good grounding in Islamic knowledge is important for interpreting material from non-Islamic sources. Study groups work well for Muslims in these efforts at learning, since the collective understanding of a group is usually better than the understanding of one person working alone.

ATMOSPHERE

To be confident as a parent is an act of faith. Daily we ask for Allah's help and guidance with our task, and we confidently expect to get it. Consequently, as we think, study, and plunge into coping with the child-rearing problems of everyday life, we know that Allah will never send us a test harder than we can bear.

Two common negative attitudes often characterize parents who lack such faith. One is the tendency to be overprotective of the child, fearful of what dangers might befall him. The other is the tendency to suspicion, overly worrying that the child will do something wrong or bad.

Overprotection

Is there a parent who does not worry about his or her child? Probably not. And the concerns that we face are certainly numerous enough. Did he eat enough? Is he properly dressed—not too hot or too cold? Are his friends good companions for him? Is he getting sick, and if so, how do I cope?

Will he do well in life and be happy? Will he follow the path to Paradise or get lost along the way? What can I do to influence him in the right way?

Some people surround their child with walls of "No! Don't do this, don't do that." A certain amount of direction is necessary, of course, but too much closes the child in and prevents him from growing up. In any problem situation, each parent has to weigh the danger versus the child's abilities and decide where to draw the line. Asking friends and neighbors may help, but when all is said and done, you know your child best and you alone can judge—that is, if you are not afraid to be objective—how realistic your fears for him are. You are responsible for the amount of risk you take with your child or allow him to take, and at the same time you are responsible for not allowing him to learn and grow when the benefits outweigh the risks.

While there has been no "golden age" in which rearing children was easy, it would probably be safe to say that the process is now more complex and difficult than ever before in history. There are more choices, more temptations, more of everything—excepting faith and sound values and their reinforcement in the society around us. And of course, it is here that the Muslim parent finds such tremendous comfort and reassurance in the teachings of Islam. Nothing comes to us except from Allah. We are responsible for arranging our children's lives according to our best understanding, but we cannot bear their tests for them. Through exposure to various experiences when they are young, they must mature into adults who can take responsibility and are answerable for their actions.

For each important decision, we should inform ourselves as fully as possible and talk with our child to get his input. If he is too young to give an opinion, we make our decision on the basis of our observations of him, his character, his health, his relationships with others, and a host of other factors. For example, if we are selecting a babysitter for our three-year-old, we can introduce the two and see how the child and the sitter respond to each other. It is also important to pray *istikhara*, Islam's special prayer for guidance, or simply make our own du'as throughout the decision-making period. Then when we reach a decision, seeking Allah's guidance, we go ahead with confidence, putting our trust in our Most Merciful Lord.

> And your Lord says, "Call on Me; I will answer you." (Qur'an 40:60)

> When My servants ask you (Muhammad) concerning Me, I am indeed near. I respond to the prayer of every suppliant when he calls on Me. (Qur'an 2:186)

> Three supplications are answered without doubt: that of a father, that of a traveller, and that of one who has been wronged. *(Abu Dawud, 1531)*

> The Prophet (S) said: "Any Muslim who makes a supplication containing nothing which is sinful or which involves breaking ties of relationship will be given one of three things for it by Allah: He will give him a swift answer, or store it up for him in the next world, or turn away from him an equivalent amount of evil." Those who heard it said they would then make supplication much, and he replied that Allah was more ready to answer than they were to ask. *(Mishkat, 2257, transmitted by Ahmad, Tirmidhi and Hakim)*

But perhaps after all your careful concern and prayers, something bad happens anyway. You let your thirteen-year-old son go fishing with his friend. The boys capsize the boat, losing all their fishing equipment and nearly losing themselves. You may feel a sense of having been let down by Allah. After all, you prayed a lot that He would keep the boys safe. But such a way of viewing the situation is inspired by Satan, who always wants you to look at the negative side of things. More correctly, in such situations, it is essential to realize that you are continually tested in this life in one way or another. When you have deep faith in Allah, you will often see how easy He has actually made the test for you. The boys were scared but not really hurt. They both got colds from staying too long in wet clothes and the lost equipment cost money, but there is no worse damage. Maybe there was permanent positive wisdom learned here by the boys. This accident may have helped to teach them the responsibility that would prevent them from far more serious mistakes later in life. You should be thinking: let us be deeply thankful that nothing of real consequence happened to the boys and that they learned a valuable lesson. We could also give something in charity in gratitude.

Suspicion and Trust

It is almost impossible to rear a child without being suspicious at times. Parents have so much responsibility and they worry about carrying it out well. Rearing a child is a continual effort to keep on top of the situation. Frequently with a small child, silence from the other room means he is into something and that someone needs to investigate. You may have a daughter who is doing poorly in school and you suspect she is not handing in her homework. You see your son hanging around the park with some boys you don't recognize and you suspect that they're up to no good. What makes such situations so trying for parents is that we are responsible for making the right decision.

Here the Islamic guidelines concerning suspicion come to our rescue:

> O you who believe, avoid much suspicion, for some
> suspicion is a sin, and do not spy upon one another.
> (Qur'an 49:12)

Beware of suspicion, for truly suspicion is the falsest of speech, and do not spy upon one another and do not eavesdrop and do not have enmity. (The *Muwatta* version adds: Do not compete with each other and do not envy each another and do not hate each other and do not shun each other), but be (Muwatta: slaves of Allah,) brothers. . . *(Bukhari, 7.74; Muwatta)*

The Messenger of Allah (S) mounted the pulpit and called in a loud voice, "You who have accepted Islam with your tongues but whose hearts have not been reached by faith, do not annoy the Muslims or revile them or seek out their faults; for he who seeks out the faults of his brother Muslim will have his faults sought out by Allah, and he whose faults are sought out by Allah will be exposed by Him, even though he should be in the interior of his house." *(Mishkat, 5044,* transmitted by *Tirmidhi)*

We are not supposed to ignore our concerns, but it is better to avoid showing suspicion, especially as in many cases it turns out to be unfounded. Assume the best, but be prepared for the worst. When checking up on a child, the approach should never be: "What trouble are you into this time?" "I know you're up to *something,*" "What mess am I going to have to clean up now?" This just tells the child that his mother expects bad or annoying behavior from him—in other words, that *he is bad.* In short, he has been accused of something that he may or may not have done, which leads to shame, which leads to guilt, which leads to endless anxious and uncomfortable feelings. If such scenarios as these are repeated frequently, the uncomfortable feelings tend to go far beyond the immediate issue and call into question not only the child himself but his mother and his relationship with her. A far more positive, loving, productive approach is: "Hi, honey, have you found something interesting to do?" "Are you there, pumpkin? Do you need anything?" "Anything you want help with in there?"

How many parents treat a child's problems with homework by asking, in an accusing manner, "Well, have you done your homework, or do you still have an hour left to go?" "Are you *sure* your homework's all finished? When did you do it? I didn't see you sit down to anything." This can destroy the home atmosphere for a child evening after evening, and teach him that he isn't trusted, or, just as bad, that his parents don't really value him for himself but only care about his not shaming them by making poor grades.

Among the many non-suspicious approaches available to a parent are the following: (1) Sit down with the child and casually discuss school, asking the child's opinion about school work, teachers, social relationships, and the school environment, discreetly searching for the reason why homework is not being done and for other school problems. (2) Provide a quiet area for study and remind the child once, maximum twice, to do his work, no TV on anywhere, no headset on his ears. Then trust the child to complete it. If he doesn't, let him experience the consequences of his own negligence, for many children are able to learn only by having to deal with the consequences of their actions. (3) Calmly and without reproach take charge of the child's assignment notebook and check off each task as it is done. With a small child, small rewards such as stars or smiley faces may add motivation. (4) Set an example by doing your own studying, reading, or other "assignments," and showing off a bit what you've earned from it. (5) Reward good grades and cut off privileges for bad ones.

The rule of thumb here is to expect and hope for the best, but at the same time to be aware of what is happening with the child, his school, his friends, and his entire world. Accusations should never be made, but questions should be tactfully asked to elicit the truth. Small faults should be passed over in silence, saving "ammunition" for big issues. Searching out small faults in a child, who will always be far from perfect, can amount to harrassment in severe cases. As Allah is Most Generous and Most Forbearing in overlooking our faults, so too should we be with our children and others around us. The Prophet (S) said,

> If you search for the faults of the people, you will corrupt them, or will nearly corrupt them. *(Abu Dawood, 4870)*

> Allah, the Exalted, has said: "O son of Adam, I shall surely continue to pardon you as long as you call on Me and hope (for My forgiveness); whatever your faults and sins may be, I do not care. O son of Adam, even if your sins mount up as high as the sky and you ask for My forgiveness, I will forgive you. O son of Adam, if you come to Me with an earthful of defaults and meet Me, not associating anything with Me, I will come to you with an earthful of forgiveness." *(Mishkat, 0442, transmitted by Tirmidhi)*

Concerning our child's choice of friends, we have a delicate problem. We cannot oblige our child to like or dislike someone. We may introduce them to someone we like but they may or may not "click," or we may not want him to associate with someone we feel is not good for him, but he may stick to him like glue.

Up to a certain age we can prevent our child from seeing children we disapprove of simply by denying visiting privileges. However, we cannot control who they meet at school and who they see when they are older (this realization should impel us to realize the importance of giving them a good understanding when they are young so they will have a strong inner ability to steer away from dangerous "friends"). What a parent *can* be adamant about is not letting a child go to visit in a home when the parents have never met the family, and can insist on being informed about the circumstances in the home, the address and telephone number. Another alternative is to have the other child come to visit in your home, or to take him or her on various outings with your own child and thereby get a feel for what kind of a child this is. This will enable you to discuss elements of the relationship with your child on the basis of your observations rather than on the basis of suspicion or "hunches," which may or may not be correct. Suspicion involves mistrust, predicting the future based on unfounded assumptions, on past acts, and on judging a person as "bad," which is very different from informed knowledge.

Allah is Forgiving and Merciful. He allows us so many chances to wipe clean our past mistakes and start afresh. Our children are basically good, but they need loving, positive, firm guidance. It is particularly important that they not associate Islam and its guidelines with a series of "No's," negating and denying everything they want to do and value—and this is all-too-common a problem among us. Islam is so balanced a way of life; let us not unbalance it by emphasizing the negative. The negative is there, but there is so much positive, mercy and compassion, and just plain common sense for the pure in nature. Presented in perspective, it is not hard to secure the child's cooperation and support in keeping things running within its framework.

MANAGEMENT TECHNIQUES

Our training of children rests on two bases: the theoretical relationship between parent and child, and the practical, everyday experience of putting ideals into practice. A variety of management techniques that suit different occasions and situations, and different children and parents, is suggested for Muslims. These may be summarized briefly as follows:

Rewarding Positive Behavior—through praise, attention, and special treats.

Teaching Desired Behavior—by talking together in a constructive manner.

Modeling—positive learning by example.

Decreasing Inappropriate Behavior—by ignoring it, substituting other action, modifying the environment, allowing natural consequences to occur, using "time-outs," and, rarely, physical punishment.

Rewarding Positive Behavior

This is a very basic concept in Islam. While the Muslim society acknowledges good behavior by giving positions of respect and trust to those who deserve it, Allah appreciates and most generously rewards the smallest good we do:

> Whoever comes with a goodness, for him there will be ten (goodnesses) like it, and whoever comes with an evil, he will not be recompensed except with the like of it. (Qur'an 6:160)

More than this, our Lord's generosity is so great that He rewards even the *intention* to do good, as the following ahadith attest:

> Indeed, Allah the Almighty and Glorious wrote down the good deeds and the bad ones, and then made that clear. Then for the one who intends a good deed but does not do it, Allah writes it for him with Himself as one whole good deed. And if he intends it and does it, Allah writes it for him with Himself as from ten good deeds up to seven hundred times up to many times over. And whoever intends a bad deed but does not do it, Allah writes it for him with Himself as a good deed, and if he intends it and

does it, Allah writes it for him as a single bad deed. *(Bukhari, 8.498* and *9.592; Muslim, 0233)*

O people, deeds are only (judged) by intentions, and every person will have only (the reward of) what he intended. *(Bukhari, 9.85)*

Of special interest to those of us who are converts is the following:

If a slave (of Allah) accepts Islam and then makes his Islam excellent, Allah covers all his past sins, and after that starts the settlement of accounts. The recompense of his good deeds will be ten times to seven hundred times for each good deed, and an evil deed will be recorded as it is unless Allah forgives it. *(Bukhari, 1.39A)*

The entire basis of the message of the prophets is that we are presented in this life with a choice between good deeds and bad, between submission to Allah and going astray. For this we are recompensed either with reward or punishment. However, the reward/punishment ratio is not balanced. Under all circumstances, the punishment is equal only to the bad deed itself, while the reward is at least ten times and possibly infinitely many times greater than the good deed done.

This point needs to be emphasized and repeated: that parents build the world-view and understanding of reality into the mind of a child. When a mother and father create an environment of accountability to Allah in their home, even without speaking about it, they prepare their children for a clear and correct relationship with Allah. Even a quite young child who has been taught about accountability to Allah can be motivated by the desire to please Him and hope for His reward, and not to displease Him. Allah knows best our true nature, and He guides us with this simple, clear view of Reality, which is our model in guiding our children.

Avoiding Excesses

Measuring the appropriate level of rewards is difficult for many parents. With the emphasis on material possessions today, too many of us feel that rewards can only be in the form of *things*. But the fact is that in affluent societies like ours, children are quickly satiated with toys, clothes, and other possessions, so that such rewards become meaningless. A piece of candy used to be a great gift, but now children have their own money and are able to buy whole boxes of candy. We are reminded of Allah's saying:

> O you who believe, do not prohibit the good, pure things which Allah has made permissible for you, but do not go beyond the limit. Truly, Allah does not like the transgressors. (Qur'an 5: 87)

In the context of rewards, a child and his room can only absorb so many *things*, but the child can never get enough special attention from his parents. A wise parent rewards good behavior with a smile, a comment, a hug or kiss, a small treat, or a present. We recall that the Prophet (S) did not shower his wives or children with gifts. In fact, when his daughter Fatimah (R) came to him and asked for a servant, telling him about the hardship of her household work, he said:

> "May I inform you of something better than that? Say 'Subhanallah' when you go to bed thirty-three times, and 'Alhamdulillah' thirty-three times, and 'Allahu Akbar' thirty four-times." *(Bukhari, 7.275; Muslim, 6580)*

Having his parent's approval can make the sun shine for a child on a cloudy day; it can mean more than the most expensive toy. However, we have used the word "wise" in describing this sort of attention, and this is important because exaggerated praise is a form of lying. This is a dangerous practice, because it does not give a child a correct, objective standard against which to measure himself. Whatever he does, it earns acclamations from his parents just because *he* did it. In such an atmosphere, with time a child may come to believe the exaggerated praise and imagine himself to be "the greatest." This is the spoiled brat who becomes an arrogant adult.

This happens in families. Sami draws a picture. Mommy praises it. Then Daddy and Grandma praise it. In some families, Sami might grow up believing that he is a fantastic artist, while actually his skill is only average. Most children, however, are quick to sense it when an adult exaggerates. Even if they don't want to admit that they are not geniuses, they can always compare their work with other children's. The adult who exaggerates usually loses credibility and respect in the eyes of the child. It is very important, when giving rewards, not to exceed the limits of both what is truthful and what is appropriate.

And shun the false word. (22:30)

Two ahadith are mentioned in Bukhari in which the Prophet (S) strongly discouraged exaggerated praise of anyone. On one occasion, a man praised another in front of him and the Prophet (S) said to him:

"Woe to you, you have cut off your companion's neck! You have cut off your companion's neck!" He repeated it several times and then he said, "If anyone among you must praise his brother, he should say, `I think him to be such-and-such, but Allah knows the exact truth. And I do not attest to the truth of any-

one in front of Allah, but I think him to be such-and-such,' If he (actually) knows that about him."
(Bukhari, 3.830)

On another occasion, the Prophet (S) heard a man praise another in an exaggerated manner, and he said:

"You have destroyed or cut the back of the man."
(Bukhari, 8.86)

And on another occasion he ordered his companions (figuratively) to throw dust upon the faces of those who indulged in exaggerated praise (Muslim, 7142).

Adults who exaggerate in praising or rewarding children are often those who most desire to be in favor with the child. Their praise or rewards are an attempt to get something from the child, and in response, the child will often try to manipulate them into giving more and more.

Encouraging Goodness

As we reward our children for good deeds, we can mention that there will also be that other reward, far greater than any we can give. Little by little the child's comprehension expands to look forward to the heavenly rewards promised by Allah on the Day of Judgment. In what better way can we show our love for our children than by encouraging them to do what is pleasing to Allah, hoping for His acceptance and reward?

Apart from the forbidden and discouraged acts, of which there are few, there are literally millions of acceptable, constructive, useful, enjoyable ways to use time, both for ourselves and our children. We, the parents, must set the example to our children of constructive uses of time. But to use our time in doing deeds that are useful and beneficial for others, particularly in light of the endless encouragements which Islam offers, is best of all.

And for all are degrees (or ranks) according to what they did. (Qur'an 6:132).

Sadaqah (charity) is due on every joint of the people for each day on which the sun rises. To judge justly between two persons is sadaqah; and to assist a man with his riding animal by helping him to mount it or by lifting his load onto it is sadaqah; and the good word is sadaqah; and every step taken toward salah is sadaqah; and removing something harmful from the road is sadaqah. *(Bukhari, 4.232)*

It is part of the excellence of a believer's Islam that he should leave off whatever is of no benefit to him in this world and the Hereafter. *(Mishkat, transmitted by Tirmidhi).*

A servant of Allah will remain standing on the Day of Judgment until he is questioned about his life and how he spent it, and about his knowledge and how he utilized it, and about his wealth, from where he acquired it and in what he spent it, and about his body, how he used it. (In the Tirmidhi version, the fourth is added: "What he made his youth pass in doing.") *(Mishkat,* transmitted by *Tirmidhi).*

All sorts of small acts can count as good deeds for the child. As we know from the words of the Prophet (S), even a smile earns reward from Allah when it is done with the pure intention of pleasing Him. It is important to teach a child to try to please Allah, Who has brought him into this world and given him everything he has. How? By pleasing, helping, and making others happy, particularly his parents. There is no end to the list of kind, considerate, helpful things a child can do, even a young child.

The Prophet (S) said,

> "Allah will give shade to seven (kinds of people) on the Day when there will be no shade but His." The second of these which he mentioned is, "A youth who has been brought up in the worship of His Lord." (Bukhari, 1.629)

> Behave appropriately and draw close (Bukhari, 8.474 has: "And give good tidings"), and know that your deeds will not make you enter Paradise, and that the deed most dear to Allah is the most regular and constant one even though it is little. (Bukhari, 8.47, 8.474, 1.34)

The Prophet (S) was asked,

> "What deeds are most dear to Allah?" He said, "The most regular, constant ones, even if few." And he said, "Do not force upon yourselves deeds which are not compatible (with your abilities)." (Bukhari, 8.472)

> There are six good manners which one believer should display to another: he should visit him when he is ill, be present when he dies, accept his invitation when he gives one, greet him when he meets him, say 'Yarhamak Allah" (in response to his saying "Alhamdulillah") when he sneezes, and act sincerely toward him, whether he is absent or present. (Mishkat, 4630, transmitted by al-Nasa'i)

In teaching our children to act for the sake of pleasing Allah, we are teaching them to be useful, giving, caring people. Too many parents today fail to convey this message to their children and consequently end up with children who only know how to take and expect to be served—often by their parents. In its extreme form, this may manifest as demanding one's "rights" by protesting or suing others for any minor inconvenience in life.

Such attitudes do not suit Muslims, for Islam encourages self-sufficiency and discourages asking from others. It emphasizes serving and not being served, giving and not being given to—in short, doing one's end of things without expecting or waiting for others to do theirs. It is an active, not a passive mode, a giving, not a taking way of life.

> By Him in Whose hand my soul is, one of you taking his rope and gathering firewood on his back is better for him than to come to a man, asking him (for something), and he may give to him or may refuse him. (Bukhari, 2.549 and 2.550)

> The upper hand is better than the lower hand (that is, to give is better than to take), and start with whomever is related; and the best charity is to protect one's honor. And the one who refrains from asking, Allah will protect his honor, and the one who shows independence, Allah will enrich him. (Bukhari, 2.508)

> The upper hand is better than the lower hand, for the upper hand is the giver and the lower is the beggar. (Bukhari, 2.509, and Muwatta)

> A man came to the Prophet (S) and asked his permission to go for jihad. The Prophet (S) asked him, "Are your parents living?" He said, "Yes." Then the Prophet (S) said, "Then strive for (the welfare of) the two of them." (Bukhari, 4.248)

A child will fill his time, his mind, and his heart with *something*. Left to himself, he can drift in various directions, both good and bad. Too much guidance can rob a child of a sense of initiative, restrict his desire to explore the world, and stifle his budding independence. A middle-of-the-road, moderate, regular course is needed, following the Prophet's deeply wise advice:

> The Prophet (S) was asked, "What deeds are most dear to Allah?" He said, "The most regular, constant ones, even if few." And he said, "Do not force upon yourselves deeds which are not compatible (with your abilities)." (Bukhari, 8.472)

> Do (good) deeds which are within your capacity, for Allah does not get tired but you get tired, and the best (good) deed in the sight of Allah is that which is done regularly. (Bukhari, 1.41)

Teaching Desired Behaviors

After providing for the child's basic physical and emotional needs, training, teaching, and guiding him or her is a basic duty of parents. By studying the Prophet's actions and words, we can see that he was above all a teacher. His every act, word, gesture, and even his silence, were the means of teaching his companions, and ourselves as well, the religion. And he said,

> Learn the obligatory acts and the Qur'an, and teach them to the people, for I am a mortal (who will die). (Mishkat, 0244, transmitted by Tirmidhi)

> The Messenger of Allah (S) was asked which of two people among the Children of Israel was superior. One of them was a learned man, keeping the salah and then sitting and teaching the people goodness, and the second fasted during the day and prayed

during the night. At that, the Messenger of Allah (S) said, "The superiority of a learned man who observes the salah and then sits down to teach people goodness, over the worshipper who fasts during the day and worships during the night, is like my superiority over the lowest in rank among you. (Mishkat, 0250, transmitted by Darimi)

Mention was made to the Messenger of Allah (S) of two persons, and the one was a devotee and the other was a learned man. At that, the Messenger of Allah (S) said, "The superiority of the learned man over the devotee is like my superiority over the lowest in rank among you." Then the Messenger of Allah (S) said, "Truly, Allah and His angels, and the inhabitants of the heavens and the earth, and even an ant in its hole and the fish (in the sea), invoke blessings upon one who teaches people goodness." (Mishkat, 0213, transmitted by Tirmidhi; Mishkat, 0250; Mishkat, 1932[R])

The Prophet's nephew, the great Islamic scholar Abdullah ibn Abbas (R), spoke about his illustrious uncle's manner of teaching directly:

Once I was riding behind the Prophet (S), when he said, 'O boy, I want to teach you something. Be careful to follow Allah's orders steadfastly, and Allah will protect you; safeguard His rights, and you will always find Him with you; if you are in need of anything, ask from Allah; and when you need help, ask Allah alone for that. Know that if all the people joined together to grant you some benefit, they would not be able to, excepting in what Allah has decreed for you, and know that if all of them joined

together to do you harm, they would not be able to,
excepting in what Allah has decreed for you. The
pens have been lifted and the ink (of the book of
divine decrees) has dried. (Mishkat, 0062, transmitted by Tirmidhi)

But in spite of the fact that he possessed more knowledge
of Allah, of true Reality *(Haqq)*, and every kind of religious
knowledge, the Messenger of Allah (S) was careful not to over-
burden people with too much teaching or rules. It is reported
in Bukhari that

Whenever the Messenger of Allah (S) ordered (anything for the Muslims), he would order them to do
deeds which were within their capability. . .
(Bukhari, 1.19)

And he said,

Truly, the religion (Islam) is easy, and no one makes
the religion harsh without being overcome. Therefore,
behave appropriately and draw close, and receive
good tidings, and seek help in the mornings and after-
noons and some part of the night (Bukhari, 1.38)

If it were not burdensome for my ummah, I would
have ordered them to use the miswak (tooth stick) at
each salah and to delay the night prayer until the first
third of the night is over. (Mishkat, 0390, transmitted
by Tirmidhi and Abu Dawud, and Mishkat, 0611,
transmitted by Ahmad, Tirmidhi and Ibn Majah)

It is essential to feed the slave, clothe him, and not
burden him with work which is beyond his power.
(Muslim, 4095)

A Bedouin stood up and urinated in the mosque. The
people confronted him, but the Prophet (S) ordered
them to leave him alone and to pour a bucket of
water or a cupful of water over his urine, "for truly,
you have been only been sent to make things easy
and not to make them difficult." (Bukhari, 1.219)

Abdullah ibn Abbas (R), whom we mentioned above,
learned this lesson well from his beloved master (S), for he
instructed the Muslim preachers:

"Preach to the people once a week, and if not that,
then preach to them twice, and if you want to preach
more, then let it be (not more than) three times. And
do not make the people bored with this Qur'an. If
you approach people who are holding a conversation, do not interrupt their conversation by preaching, lest you should cause them to be bored. Rather
be silent, and then if they ask you, preach to them
while they are eager for it." *(Bukhari, 8.349)*

The Prophet (S) often taught by means of his silence; what
he did not say was as meaningful as what he said. This is clearly evident from the reports of his servant, Anas bin Malik:

When the Messenger of Allah (S) came to Madinah,
he did not have a servant. Abu Talha (R) (Anas's
step-father) took me to the Messenger of Allah (S)
and said, "O Messenger of Allah, Anas is a clever
boy, so let him serve you." Then I served him on
journeys and at home. He never said to me about
anything I did, "Why did you do this?" nor about
anything I did not do, "Why did you not do this?"
(Bukhari, 4.29; Abu Dawud, 4756)

Anas (R) also said,

> The Messenger of Allah (S) had the best disposition among people. One day he sent me on an errand and I said, "By Allah, I will not go," but it was in my mind that I would do as the Messenger of Allah (S) had ordered me. I went until I came upon children playing in the street. Then the Messenger of Allah (S) arrived and he caught me by the back of my neck from behind. As I looked at him, I found him smiling, and he said, "Unays (Anas's nickname), did you go where I ordered you to go?" I said, "O Messenger of Allah, yes, I am going." Anas said further, "I served him for nine years, but I do not know that he ever said to me about anything I did, why I did that, or about anything I had neglected, why I had not done that." *(Muslim, 5724)*

But look at our methods of teaching, in contrast to our Prophet's (S). How many of us parents constantly scold and nag at our children? "Wipe your feet before coming in! Hang up your jacket! Brush your teeth. Go do your homework." *This is teaching?* The child listens to such orders over and over until he doesn't hear them any more. Is it not therefore far, far better to follow the example of the Prophet (S), overlooking the child's frequent mistakes, and saving ourselves stress and breath, while reminding our children occasionally of their responsibilities? In short, if you want to be listened to seriously, keep the heavy stuff for serious occasions.

Other techniques which replace nagging are far more effective. A little reward of praise or appreciation reinforces a child when he does something right without being asked. For example, "Oh, you've brushed your teeth already? My, aren't you getting big, to remember that all by yourself!" "You remembered to take out the garbage last night, son. I'm really proud of you!" "You've already prayed? That's great! You're getting to be such a grown-up girl."

Problem Solving

With children, adults often need to break down an idea into parts and introduce them slowly. "Please clean your room" can be a very complex statement to a young child. A child needs to know what constitutes "cleaning" to his mother. Perhaps in his mind it simply means clearing a path from the door to the bed, but Mommy may see it differently. He also needs some guidance about where to begin his task, and probably a lot of help and encouragement as he learns. The whats and how-to's of "Clean your room" may need not only explanation, but the parent needs to do it with the child. If this is done, after a few times the child will be able to do at least part of it on his own.

Adults often don't see the child's view of a situation. Neatly arranging stacks of toys on a shelf might be easy to Mommy, but it actually involves a complex evaluation of the size and weight of objects, and experience in knowing what will stay on top of what. Children learn these skills slowly. In the early stages, they may do best with a toy box into which they can toss their things, as they slowly develop the coordination and understanding of more advanced organization.

Problem-solving can be clearly separated into parts.

1. What is the focal point of the problem?
2. What information needs to be given to enable the child to do the task? (Here it is important to screen out which information is unnecessary to solve the problem. Problem-solving is often hindered by too much extra information that confuses a clear view of the important things.)
3. What do we do to get the desired results—i.e., what skills are necessary?
4. What do we expect to achieve in the end?

For the messy-room situation, the child probably needs to

know what it looks like when it is orderly and clean. He needs to understand that we arrange things so that they are easier to find later, so that they are protected from breaking, so that we have space to use for other projects, as well as for the pleasure of seeing a clean, pretty, orderly room.

To achieve this goal we need a vacuum cleaner, broom, or dust mop, a dust cloth, and places to put things, such as shelves, drawers, closet, boxes, etc., and we need to know how to use the dust cloth, vacuum, and so on. We also need a plan about what items can best go where. Unnecessary information might include that this doll is from Auntie Hala and what sort of sounds are made when different toys are dropped from the top of the bunk beds into the toy box.

This analytical approach can be applied to all sorts of projects with children, including homework. Take the symbols 3 + 2 = ?, for example. Does the child understand the concrete meaning of the symbols, that there are three things here and two things there (apples, oranges, whatever), and that we want to do something with them? Is it clear that the number of objects is important, not their color or the container they are in? Is it also clear that the required manipulation is to put them together? Can the child actually count to 5? Since this problem is so simple for an adult, this may sound like making too much out of too little, but by breaking it down in this manner with a child who is having a problem, we can find out exactly *what* he doesn't understand. This is clearly a better method than injuring the child's self esteem by scolding or yelling at him that he's stupid or isn't trying.

A less obvious and more complex problem-solving situation would be an analysis of what to do when Tahera lied about eating her brother's cookie. We can approach the problem this way:

1. There are two problems here, hardly separable from each other: one, Tahera lied, and two, she took something that wasn't hers. So is her mother's objective to teach her not to lie,

not to take things from others, how to respect her brother, how to restrain herself from eating between meals—or all of these?

Tahera needs to learn all these lessons, but a child can only absorb so much at one time. Which goal should be emphasized this time? What action or words of Tahera's will show that she understands?

2. If Mommy wants to teach Tahera through this incident not to lie, are the specifics of this little episode important? Looking at the broader picture, does the child know what a lie is, or the difference between an imaginary situation and a fact? At what age are children clearly able to separate fact from fiction? Is Tahera afraid of some enormous punishment for stealing? Why did she lie?

3. Mommy must weigh the gravity of Tahera's fault and how upset the child is about it. Suppose she ate her brother's cookie because she found it on the table after she finished hers. Mommy then needs to show Tahera how lying gets found out and discourages people from trusting her word in the future. She also needs to stress that Allah loves truthfulness and hates lying, and that a Muslim is supposed to be truthful (of course, in order for Tahera to make sense out of that, Mommy must be truthful herself).

4. Mommy can observe the effectiveness of her approach and see if more work needs to be done on the subject of lying, for this is a complex problem which can be handled in a variety of ways. When we analyze it, we can appreciate how important it is to have guidance from Allah, for as we reflect on the best thing to do and try to make the wisest decision, at the same time, we ask for His guidance and help. Then we act, with the best of intentions, trusting that He accepts this good intention, has guided our action, and will forgive our mistakes.

It works well to have an idea of priorities in deciding what to teach. Which concepts are the most important to learn just now? Just like adults, children cannot learn everything at once. As an example, we often see young adults with excellent manners and behavior, taught them by their parents, but who do not know how to pray. The parents did an excellent job with one aspect of training but totally neglected another, even more important one; in short, their sense of priorities was, for a Muslim, not a correct one.

It may be noted that when we teach our religion, we are automatically teaching manners, too. But some parents can and do teach manners to their children without any tie-in with religion, morals, or understanding of accountability; to them, manners are totally outside the sphere of religion. In such a case, they remain merely manners, while in the case of a conscious Muslim, they are *aadaab al-Islamiyah*, the good behaviors and usages peculiar to Islam—in other words, the correct, acceptable way in which Muslims are expected to act in various situations.

Rapport

Instruction is given in a vacuum if a parent does not listen to a child: his or her feelings, fears, hopes, and all the rest. Many parents and teachers lecture on and on without pausing to notice if the child is listening and understands. If he or she isn't or doesn't, they decide that it is the child's fault for not accepting their valuable efforts to teach. Ali bin Abu Talib (R) put the matter so well, saying:

> The hearts of the people have desires and aptitudes; sometimes they are ready to listen and at other times they are not. Enter into people's hearts through their aptitudes. Talk to them when they are ready to listen, for the condition of the heart is such that if you force it to do something, it becomes blind. *(Al-Kitab al-Kharaaj* by Abu Yusuf)*

This relates to rapport, and rapport is necessary for teaching. The Prophet (S) did not merely give lectures. Rather, he interacted very intimately with his people, and when he spoke, he spoke to people's hearts, not just to their minds. And because the sight and sound of him, and the teachings he brought, filled their hearts, they were ready to obey him, even to sacrifice everything for him and his divine cause. Throughout the history of mankind, it is probable that no human being was ever as deeply loved and revered as he was. The collections of hadith contain a vivid record of his loving, intimate manner and the impact he had on the lives of his Companions, children as well as adults.

Zayd bin Haritha (R), for example, was a young slave in Khadijah's house. He was so happy in Muhammad's service that he chose to remain with him as a slave rather than return- ing to his father and to freedom. Muhammad then freed him and adopted him as a son. Zayd (R) was later to become one of the earliest converts to Islam.

A certain companion reported that during his childhood he used to throw stones at the palm trees of the Ansar in Madinah. For this he was once brought before the Prophet (S), who asked him:

> "O boy, why do you throw stones at the palm trees?"
> He said, "To eat (dates)." The Prophet (S) said, "Do not throw stones at the palm trees but eat what falls beneath them." He then wiped (his hands over the boy's) head and said, "O Allah, fill his stomach." (Abu Dawud, 2616)

The Prophet (S) said to another companion,

> "Come near, my son. Mention Allah's name, eat with your right hand, and eat from what is next to you." *(Abu Dawud, 3768)*

A companion named Ikrash (R) reported,

> We were brought a platter with a large amount of *tharid* and slices of boneless meat, and I plunged in my hand in all directions while the Messenger of Allah (S) ate what was in front of him. He caught hold of my right hand with his left and said, "Eat from one place, Ikrash, for it is all one kind of food." Afterwards we were brought a plate containing various kinds of dates and I began to eat what was in front of me, while the hand of the Messenger of Allah (S) went around on the plate. Then he said, "Eat where you wish, Ikrash, for it is not all one kind. . ." *(Mishkat,* transmitted by *Tirmidhi)*

Similarly, the companion Umar ibn Abu Salamah (R) reported,

> I was a boy under the guardianship of the Messenger of Allah (S), and my hand used to wander around the dish (while I was eating). Then the Messenger of Allah (S) said to me, "O boy, mention (the name of) Allah and eat with your right hand, and eat from what is closest to you." Thereafter I did not lapse from this way of eating of mine. *(Bukhari, 7.288)*

Rapport cannot exist where there is putting-down, degrading language. Perhaps the most frequent exhibition of bad manners among parents consists of rebuking, reproaching, shaming, and name-calling: "Dummy, how many times do I have to tell you?" "When will you ever learn?" "Bad boy!" "You little devil!" "Stupid idiot!" "Think about how much I sacrifice for you!" Some use much worse epithets— "Moron!"—as well as others not even fit to print. It's amazing how often otherwise polite, well-mannered people turn on their children and hurl abusive language.

Three common reasons for this behavior are,

1. Many adults regard it as proper to use good manners only with other adults. Children are considered lesser, uncivilized beings who are not entitled to respect. They (a) must be kept down so they won't get out of hand, or (b) don't merit the trouble of being treated politely.

2. Within the intimacy of the family circle, when no one else is around to notice, manners don't count. Mommy can say whatever she feels like in this relaxed atmosphere. In public, however, she will be polite.

3. When a parent is frustrated with life, tense and stressed out, or upset with another adult, patience can desert him (or her) in dealing with the multitude of childish demands that require patience. He lets loose all his frustrations and tensions—and who else is there to let them out on except the children, who cannot defend themselves? Result: instead of yelling at the neighbors for the loud party they had last night, Daddy yells at little Tariq for spilling the milk at breakfast. "You clumsy brat! When are you going to learn to pour without spilling!"

This might seem like a very minor matter to us, but Allah tells us otherwise:

> And do not defame one another, nor call one other by (offensive) nicknames. Evil is the name denoting wickedness after faith. And those who do not repent, they are wrong-doers. (Qur'an 49:11)

> Call to the way of your Lord with wisdom and goodly admonition, and argue with them by that which is best. (Qur'an 16:125)

And what about the Prophet (S)? Didn't he ever get angry and use bad language or curse? Yes, he got angry, but his anger was for the sake of Allah. But he never used bad language, cursed, or insulted people. His behavior is a matter of historical record. The Prophet's wife A'isha (R) reported:

> The Messenger of Allah (S) was not improper or obscene in his language, nor was he loud-mouthed in the streets, nor did he return evil for evil, but he would forgive and pardon. *(Mishkat, 5820,* transmitted by *Tirmidhi)*

Anas bin Malik (R) said,

> The Prophet (S) did not use insults or bad language or curse. . . *(Bukhari, 8:58)*

Abdullah bin Amr (R) said,

> The Messenger of Allah (S) neither talked in an insulting manner nor did he ever speak evil intentionally. He used to say, "The dearest to me among you is the one who has the best character." *(Bukhari, 5.104)*

And the Prophet (S) himself said,

> The most perfect believer in respect of faith is the one who is best of them in manners. *(Abu Dawud, 4685)*

> Four (characteristics are such that) whoever has them within himself will be a total hypocrite, and whoever has one of these characteristics within himself, there will be one of the characteristics of hypocrisy within him until he gives it up: When he is trusted, he betrays, and when he speaks, he lies, and when he makes a covenant, he acts treacherously, and when he quarrels, he reviles out. *(Bukhari, 1.33)*

> Abusing a Muslim is fusuq (wickedness) and killing him is kufr (unbelief). *(Bukhari, 1.46)*

> A believer is not given to accusing others or cursing them, nor is he immoral or shameless. *(Mishkat, 4847, transmitted by Tirmidhi and Baihaqi)*

> A believer does not taunt, curse, abuse, or talk indecently. *(Mishkat, 1740, transmitted by Tirmidhi)*

Nowhere in the Qur'an or hadith is it stated that we should speak nicely to adults but can say anything we like to children, as so many adults do. In fact, it is wrong to abuse or curse even inanimate objects.

Once, in the time of the Prophet (S), the wind snatched away a man's cloak and he cursed the wind. The Prophet (S) said,

> Do not curse it, for it is under (Allah's) command, and if anyone curses a thing undeservedly, the curse returns upon him. *(Abu Dawud, 4890)*

Children are much like that cloak, blowing in the wind. They track in mud on a clean floor because it just happened that way. They spill, drop, and break things because their muscles just can't manage any better. Generally they don't make mistakes, messes, or problems because they're mean or like to cause trouble. They're just young and thoughtless and have a lot of learning and growing to do. They are *children*.

Rebuking and reproaching, scolding, shaming and belittling, using sarcastic and vulgar language—all of this is the result of an attitude that says, "I'm better than you. I'm a big, important adult and you're just a stupid kid." Children quickly carry over such behavior in their language and attitude toward each other. Young and old, people are resourceful in finding ways of saying "I'm better than you are." This is self-righteousness and arrogance, the very opposite of the humbleness and absence of pride which Allah wants from His sincere ones.

Recall again that children's bad deeds are not recorded, while ours are. They are innocent, while we have had so many more years to commit sins than they have. If they die now, they will be in Paradise, but can we be so sure of our own fate? Then how can we possibly justify putting them down? Negativity on our part begets negativity on theirs, and all negativity is inspired by Shaytan.

Chapter Five

PRACTICES, MANNERS, AND VALUES

MODELING

When a child is reard by practicing Muslim parents and his ties with practicing Muslims in the community are fostered, he has multiple examples to copy and support him in growing up as a sound Muslim.

As a general rule, the single most important factor in the growth and development of a child is the example of his parents. Quite naturally, the child tries to copy them. Books on psychology and education term this a teaching technique and label it "modeling." Children observe, try to copy, make mistakes, forget, temporarily try alternative ideas, and, for better or worse, generally pattern themselves on the parental model.

Since the time of the first parents on earth, Adam and Eve (S), parents all over the world have relied upon modeling as the first method of training their children. Muslims traditionally have used not only their own examples but also the examples of the prophets, and especially those of Prophet Muhammad (S) and his Companions, and of other great Islamic personalities, as models for themselves and their children.

In the Muslim home, morals, manners, and religious practices may best be taught by modeling. However, it should be obvious that modeling is counterproductive if we, the parents, do not provide sound models. We are expected to practice our religion before trying to tell our children to practice it. The example of the parents' actions is far more powerful than all of the words they preach.

> Do you enjoin righteousness on the people but forget (to practice it) yourselves, while you read the Scripture? Then will you not understand? (Qur'an 2:44)

> O you who believe, why do you say that which you do not do? It is odious in the sight of Allah that you say that which you do not do. (Qur'an 61:2-3)

> There are two qualities which can never coexist in a hypocrite: good conduct and understanding of religion. *(Mishkat,* transmitted by *Tirmidhi)*

> A man will be brought on the Day of Resurrection and thrown into the Fire, and his intestines will come out in the Fire and he will go around as a donkey goes around its millstone. Then the inhabitants of the Fire will gather around him and say, "O such-and-such, what is wrong with you? Did you not enjoin on us what was good and forbid what was bad?" He will say, "I used to enjoin on you what was good but did not do it myself, and I forbade you what was bad but did it myself." *(Bukhari, 4.489)*

Let us now look at various approaches to training Muslim children in the basic elements of their faith.

TAHARAH (CLEANLINESS)

The first principle of Islam that a child will probably learn is cleanliness. Just as *wudu* (ablution) precedes *salat* (prayer), so *taharah* is the first requisite of this religion. The Prophet (S) said,

> Cleanliness is half of faith. . . . *(Muslim, 0432)*

> The key to Paradise is prayer and the key to prayer is cleanliness *(wudu)*. *(Mishkat,* transmitted by *Ahmad)*

The Prophet (S) gave very complete instructions about matters of cleanliness and hygiene. Since urine is a pollutant and cannot be on our bodies, our clothes, or anywhere near us when we pray, so we are very careful about toilet habits and work to keep our children and our homes as clean as possible. The first element of this concerns cleaning the urine of an infant if it falls on the clothing or body. He said,

> The urine of a female (child) should be washed and the urine of a male (child) should be sprinkled over until the age of eating. *(Abu Dawud)*

The distinction between a male and female toddler is not stated in the hadith, but is usually understood as a difference between sprayed urine and puddles. It has nothing to do with discrimination against girls. We clean any clothes or surfaces as best we can.

A Muslim mother cleans her baby with water at every diaper change. As the child grows older, she, or another member of the family, assists the child in washing at the toilet, so the child is always clean. In Muslim countries, most toilets may not have toilet paper but they all have water for washing. A boy can be trained from the beginning to urinate sitting, according to the instructions of the Prophet (S) to Umar ibn al-Khattab (R), who said:

> The Messenger of Allah (S) saw me urinating while standing. At that, he said, "Umar, do not urinate while standing." *(Mishkat,* transmitted by *Tirmidhi* and *Ibn Majah)*

The reason for this is not stated but probably it relates to the possibility of the splashing of urine on the body or clothing. The Prophet (S) indicated that being polluted with urine is a cause of torment to a person in his grave (Bukhari, 1.215).

By the time the child is a few years old, he or she will be able to make wudufor salah. Children vary greatly in their ability to wash properly and regularly. In this regard as in all others in dealing with young children, it is better to be indulgent, not harsh. Allah will not hold the child responsible for such mistakes, so why should *we* be severe?

> The one who puts people into difficulties, Allah will put him into difficulties on the Day of Resurrection. *(Bukhari, 9.266)*

Friday *(Jumu'ah)* is the day of community prayer for Muslims, the most important day out of the seven, and it should be treated as a special day. Children can be trained from an early age to take a shower *(ghusl)* on Friday, especially boys. This act is commendable, not fard, and it might not have as much meaning today in families with the means and the habit to shower every day, but it is in the sunnah of the Prophet (S),

> O company of Muslims, this is a day which Allah has appointed as a festival, so shower, and if anyone has perfume, it does him no harm to apply some of it; and you should use the tooth-stick. *(miswak).* (Muwatta)

Ghusl (showering) on the day of Jumu'ah is incumbent on every male who has reached puberty. *(Riyadh-us-Saleheen 1152)*

As the child grows older, approaching puberty, he will learn the rules of *tahara,* what voids *wudu,* what is commendable of the practices, what is fard, obligatory, etc. The book *At-Taharah —Purity and State of Undefilement,* by Jamal Badawi, is a good book for young people on this topic. This is usally part of the program in Islamic schools, and can be included with sex education programming, but certainly may also be taught at home.

RESPECT FOR RELIGION

Respectful behavior is an extremely important value in Islam—respect for parents, grandparents and other relatives, elders, teachers, Muslims, and human beings in general. However, we are living in an environment in which lack of respect—for others and for themselves—seems to be a hallmark of the young generation.

Unfortunately, this prevailing attitude of disrespect often carries over even into religion. It is not uncommon to hear youngsters referring to the prophets and to Prophet Muhammad (S), the very best and noblest of mankind, as "those guys," may Allah forgive us. Maybe no disrespect is intended; perhaps this is merely the only way children today know how to express themselves. In addition to this, some children speak of Allah Ta'ala without the proper respect, treat the Holy Qur'an with disrespect, sit with feet toward it or on a table upon which it is placed; put it on the floor; put other things on top of it; recite it while playing about—even, may Allah forgive us, in the bathroom—or without the proper *adab* in general). Generally acting flippant toward religion is not acceptable behavior. A parent does not need to be harsh or mean about this, but merely be firm and consistent in not allowing disrespectful behavior.

SALAH (PRAYER)

For a child born into a practicing Muslim family, salah is a constant factor in his or her life from the time of birth, a never-changing, regular, fixed feature of the days and nights. It is something he or she gets used to, like getting up in the morning or eating meals, part of his acculturation process.

When a child is small, there is often a period when he wants his mother's attention during salah and cannot understand why she does not respond. All young children go through this, and we solve the problem according to the example of our Prophet (S). It is reported that the Prophet (S) was seen praying while holding his granddaughter Umamah (R). When he prostrated, he put her down and when he stood up again, he picked her up (Bukhari, 1.495; Muwatta; Abu Dawud, 0918). A mother may sometimes need to do this too.

This certainly does not mean that parents should habituate their children to being held during salah, or that children—of any age—should be allowed to cavort around and disrupt salah as a regular habit. But it does mean that we are tolerant of the behavior of babies and little children who are too young to understand or control their behavior.

This changes once the child can follow simple directions and has some degree of self-control, for the salah of an adult is an obligation and it should be carried out in as respectful and dignified an atmosphere as possible. The child should be trained in appropriate salah-time behavior as soon as he or she is able to understand, together with other manners related to prayers, such as removing the shoes and not walking in front of a praying person. But children are not always easily controllable. It is here that adults must exercise consideration and good judgment. In time, the child will start to join others in salah. At first this takes the form of his standing momentarily beside Mommy or Daddy, hands placed one over the other, moving his lips in silent imitation of his parents. Often he may try to imitate prostration and end up standing on his head, in practice for the real thing. Later, when he has a more serious understanding of the matter, he stands in the row with the adults (at this point, it's best to put him at the end, not in the middle, of the row, so that if he drops out there won't be a gap). Even though a child's attention span is short and he is likely to wander off, nonetheless he will feel that prayer is a part of his life and enjoy the warmth of being a part of a group of praying Muslims.

Since children ordinarily like to be with their parents and do what they do, the best way to get children to pray, and to want to pray, is to have them pray with us. Obviously it is both useless and dishonest for parents to order a child to pray when they don't pray themselves. When prayer is an established routine in the household, participating in it comes naturally to a child. Then, when the time comes that his parents ask him to pray seriously, he will be ready for it.

Many parents assume that a youngster is supposed to start praying at the age of puberty. However, this is incorrect. The Islamic guidelines concerning this are made clear by the following ahadith of the Prophet (S):

> Order your children to observe salat when they reach the age of seven and spank them for not observing it when they reach the age of ten, and arrange their beds (for sleeping) separately. *(Abu Dawud)*

> When a boy distinguishes right hand from the left hand, then command him to pray. *(Abu Dawud)*

A simple, workable method for initiating _salat_ with a young child is the following. On his fifth birthday, ask him to begin regular prayer with the family once a day. This should be treated as a special event, a significant landmark on his road to growing up. The most suitable prayer to begin with is generally _maghrib_, when the whole family is at home and can pray together. Then, when the child reaches five and a half, initiate the second salah, any one out of the five you choose. On the sixth birthday, the third salah is added; at six and a half, the fourth; and by the seventh birthday, he has all five prayers regularized.

It is suggested that the child pray only the *fardrak'ats*at this stage. He can keep adding the *sunnah rak'ats*from the time he has all the *fards* completed—that is, from his seventh birthday—so that by age ten he has the entire *salat, fards* and *sunnahs,* complete. This suggestion is made for a child who lives in a stable Islamic environment, but in some situations it may be too much—or too little. *How much* depends upon the individual child and his or her individual situation.

Another workable method is to casually mention in the child's presence, as the occasion arises, how some older child prays all his or her prayers regularly. Little discussions can take place, in the car on the way to the grocery store, or while washing dishes, where parents and others can express their expectations of the child. "Before I was eight I could do all my prayers regularly, without my mommy reminding me," Grandma might be able to say. Or Daddy could mention the hadith above and tell his child that he knows his child will be big at 7. Then the family can simply call the child to participate at any and every prayer possible, while reminding him often of the reward for prayer.

Naturally, even after age seven, and sometimes after age ten, the parent will have to remind the child again and again that it's time to pray, and gently but firmly see that he or she does so. Making salaha habit does not come overnight. However, if the mother or father have the child pray with them, it makes the whole task of learning to regularize it so much easier. When a child forgets, is late, or misses a prayer, it should not be a cause for blame or shame, but simply a tiny, insignificant incident on his road to learning to be responsible for himself. The recording angels start recording bad deeds for missed prayers at puberty, as discribed in chapter 1, but the intentions and efforts toward prayer are recorded as good deeds for the child as early as Allah knows best.

As we have seen from a number of ahadith, wiithin the community of the Prophet (S), children were tolerated with gentleness. They were not cut off as being too little or a nuisance, nor shut into a child's world away from the adult world. And this was the case inside the mosque as well as outside it.

In contrast to many of our present-day *imams,* the Prophet (S) was acutely conscious of the situation of the Muslims praying behind him and concerned about their feelings. It is reported that during the salah, when the Mesenger of Allah (S) would hear the crying of a child who was with its mother, he would deliberately recite a short surah, saying:

> When I stand up to pray, I want to be long in it, but then I hear the crying of a child and at that I refrain (from this) in my salah, hating to give trouble to its mother *(Bukhari, 1.675; Muslim, 0951). (*In *Bukhari 1.677*and *1.678,* it is: "Then I refrain due to what I know of the stress its mother feels because of its crying . ")

And Anas ibn Malik (R) reported,

> I never prayed behind any imam a lighter or more complete salat than the Prophet's (S). If he heard the crying of a child, he would make it shorter out of fear of being a trial for its mother. (Bukhari , 1.676)

An imam whose congregation includes children will hopefully show this same sort of consideration for the feelings of the mothers (and fathers), and for the children themselves. At the same time, parents need to show good judgment in the matter of taking a child to the mosque.

The Islamic center or mosque is not a playground or a place in which to pass empty time but rather a house of Allah in which one behaves with the utmost respect. We go there for prayer and other specific purposes, not simply to "hang out." Parents need to be on top of the situation and keep their children under strict control in the *masjid* setting. The occasional crying of a little child is one thing, but disruptive, rude, aggressive behavior is something else, and a child who exhibits this sort of behavior should, for the sake of decency, be kept at home.

As a rule, the child will be at home with his or her mother. However, a considerate husband will make opportunities for his wife to go to the mosque when she wants to go, while he stays home with the child or children. After all, they are *his* children too, and it is a piece of blatant injustice to require a woman to be in constant, unbroken attendance upon them while their father never is.

There is nothing in the Islamic teachings which suggests that the care, training, or education of the children are the sole responsibility of the wife, while the husband is free to be away from the family as much as he likes; the verses we cited earlier concerning the husband's responsibility make this absolutely clear. Consequently, while *praying* in the mosque is an emphasized duty for Muslim men, spending long hours at the local Islamic center in socializing, sports, and other activities is neither required nor recommended by Islam. Once the primary duty of *salah* has been fulfilled, the family's needs have priority.

For the future of his children's Islam, it is very recommended that a father teach them religion and other matters, make *salah* with them frequently, and interact closely with them so that they will identify with him and his values. Otherwise, there is a strong possibility that they may see him as the always missing parent, and possibly in time come to reject him and his values because he is not a present force in their lives.

SIYAM (FASTING)

Because meals are usually eaten in company, a small child, even a six-month-old baby, may temporarily refuse to eat alone when his parents fast, especially if he is used to eating with the family. It can take two or three days for young children to return to normal eating habits as they adjust to the fact that parents and older brothers and sisters are not eating with them.

Perhaps the first thing a Muslim child notices about Ramadan is the time of the maghrib prayer. He joins the family in awaiting the arrival of sunset, whether by standing on the balcony listening for a cannon shot, as in some Muslim countries, or waiting for the call to prayer on television, or maybe just running to check a clock he can't read and asking everyone whether it's time yet. He catches the special atmosphere of the family and the joy of the evening meal that breaks the fast.

Although it sometimes seems strange to non-Muslims, children in the families of practicing Muslims often beg to be allowed to fast with the rest of the family. When they are small, from four to six, they can "practice" fasting, say from breakfast to lunch or from lunch to supper, as the equivalent of a half-day's fast. Just as playing with dolls or cars or soldiers prepares them for adult life, being able to pretend to fast and talking about it also prepares them for their later obligation.

At around five or six, many children are able to fast from breakfast time when they wake up in the morning up to the evening meal. If they manage to do this, they should earn praise for it, but there is no need to be rigid about it. Whatever the child can do is good; however, he is still quite young and fasting is not obligatory until puberty, although it is desirable that a child have some experience of it before it becomes an obligation.

Various families have various strategies for the learning years. Some children fast on Mondays and Thursdays in Ramadan. Others fast a few days at the first of the month and a few at the end, or on weekends. And some plunge in from the beginning of the month and fast the whole month from the age of seven on.

Islamic fasting differs from the fasting of other religious communities in some notable aspects: (1) It is total fasting; (2) the period of fasting is from dawn to sunset; and (3) two meals are prescribed. The special hallmark of Islamic fasting is *suhoor*, the pre-dawn meal. The Prophet (S) said,

> Have suhoor, because truly there is blessing in suhoor. *(Bukhari, 3.146)*

Today many Muslims are fasting without suhoor; they argue—especially those who must go to work early in the morning—that they need sleep more than food. However, going without suhoor deprives the fasting one of the blessing of keeping the Prophet's *sunnah* and recommendation concerning the pre-dawn meal. If children fast, it is particularly essential that they have suhoor in order to maintain strength during the day. Without this, fasting may come to be seen as an unbearable hardship, one which a child apprehends with dread instead of anticipation of his own growing ability to master his desires.

It is recorded in Bukhari and Muslim that the early Muslims made simple toys and arranged distractions for their children who were learning to fast. When a person, whether a child or an adult, is occupied with something interesting, time seems to fly. Active games keep the adrenalin flowing and the blood sugar up, so a person pays less attention to hunger and thirst. And while fasting children may have long since given up their nap time, a nap helps time to pass and makes up for the sleep lost in the early morning hours when they are up for suhoor and *fajr* prayer.

The fasting of a child is sometimes harder on the mother than it is on the child. We mothers like to see our children eating well, and naturally we are concerned about their health. One mother insisted that her children pass a doctor's visit and blood test before she would allow them to fast. However, in the case of healthy, normal children, this constitutes gross overprotection. Allah has not asked anything of us which is beyond our abilities. Instead of parents imposing objections and restrictions that are a product of their own minds, let the child decide what he is capable of handling. Test him gently — let him test himself.

Whenever there is any sign that a child is becoming over-tired or ill from fasting, or, in a summer fast, dehydrated, a parent may order his child to break fast. This can be a sensitive issue, requiring a great deal of tact. The child may resist breaking fast and need comforting. It is hard for Abdullah to see his best friend Haroon fasting with ease, out playing tennis in the sun, while he himself is dizzy and tired. But children grow at different rates and fasting presents different levels of difficulty. And just because Abdullah wasn't able to complete his fast today doesn't mean that he won't be able to a week from now, when conditions may be a bit different.

Two children of the same age may have very different levels of self-control, too, aside from their physical stamina. One may refuse a plate of cookies offered by a well-meaning neighbor without effort, while another may try to fast but end up trying to sneak a snack in the kitchen when no one is looking. As parents, we provide the model by our own fasting, as well as positive support to the child in his learning. We share in his pride at his accomplishments, great or small, and celebrate the Eid together.

An important reinforcement to the child's fasting is to invite other fasting Muslims for *iftar*. This assists in the child's socialization and teaches him that Ramadan is a time for sharing and being together. The fasting child also becomes aware of being part of a vast company of people fasting besides his own family. If his parents stress his tie with Muslims throughout the world who are fasting for the pleasure of Allah, the child will feel special pride in his being part of this great group.

When the child is of an age to think and reflect, we can share more details about why we fast. It could be mentioned that fasting has been a practice prescribed by God in every divinely-revealed religion:

> O you who believe, fasting is prescribed for you, as
> it was prescribed for those before you, in order that
> you may be mindful of Allah. (Qur'an 2:183)

It is important that the child understand that Allah does not ask him to give up the food and drink he normally takes for granted during the daylight hours because He enjoys seeing people hungry and thirsty. Rather, he is imposing upon himself, not permanent deprivations, but temporary controls so that he may come closer to Allah. Compassion for the hungry and poor is of course another aspect. He will learn to see Ramadan not as a time of deprivation but of growth for his soul—not merely as a month of denial of bodily appetites, but a month with a full program of spiritual work, including giving charity, reading the Qur'an, and attending tarawihprayers.

Before the prayer of Eid al-Fitr, the *zakah al-fitr* (the sadaqah of the feast) is due, according to the instructions of the Prophet (S):

> The sadaqah of the breaking of the fast is obligatory
> on every Muslim, male or female, freeman or slave,
> young or old, consisting of two mudds (measures) of
> wheat or its like, or a sa' (measure) of grain.
> *(Mishkat,* transmitted by *Tirmidhi)*

> Abdullah ibn Abbas (R) reported that the Messenger
> of Allah (S) prescribed the sadaqah related to the
> breaking of the fast as a purification of the fasting
> from empty and obscene talk, and as food for the
> poor. For the one who pays it before the (Eid)

prayer, it will be accepted as zakah (al-fitr), but for the one who pays it after the prayer, it will be a sadaqah like other sadaqahs. *(Abu Dawud)*

When the child is old enough to be aware, it is good to tell him about this obligation and that it has been met. However, to respect the dignity of those who receive sadaqah in the community, we can hide their identity.

ZAKAH AND SADAQAH (OBLIGATORY AND VOLUNTARY CHARITY)

The calculation and payment of *zakah* (obligatory charity) is the responsibility of the parents. Children cannot participate with them in this, but, at an appropriate age when they know about this obligation, they can be informed that it has been paid for the year. This will give them the understanding that this is an obligation, to be met by them, if they have sufficient means to do so, when they become adults, and they will feel satisfaction in the fact that their parent has taken care of this obligation.

Beyond the obligatory zakah, voluntary charity *(sadaqah)* is mentioned again and again in the Qur'an and in ahadith. Charity, whether obligatory or voluntary, is a religious obligation second only to salah.

The Prophet (S) said, "Sadaqah is (obligatory) on every Muslim." Then they asked, "O Prophet of Allah, what about one who cannot find (anything to give)?" He said, "He should work with his hands and benefit himself and give charity (from what he earns)." They asked, "But if he cannot find (even that much)?" He replied, "He should help the anxious, needy one." They asked, "But if he cannot find (the means for that)?" He said, "Then he should do good deeds and keep away from evil ones, and surely that will be sadaqah for him." *(Bukhari, 2.524)*

The one who gives sadaqah from good earning—and Allah only accepts the good—it is as if he placed it in the palm of the Most Merciful to rear it, as one of you rears his foal or young camel, until it is like the mountain (in magnitude). *(Muwatta)*

Sadaqah appeases the Lord's anger and averts an evil death. *(Mishkat,* transmitted by *Tirmidhi)*

The believer's shade on the Day of Resurrection will be his sadaqah. *(Mishkat,* 1925, transmitted by *Ahmad)*

Abu Dharr (R) asked Allah's Prophet (S) to tell him what the reward for sadaqah would be, and he received the reply, "Many times as much, and more still with Allah." *(Mishkat, 1928,* transmitted by *Ahmad)*

A child of any age can participate in giving *sadaqah*. For example, every mosque has collection boxes for the poor and for other causes. The family may also keep a box in which a certain amount is put on a regular basis—for example, the family members' change or a fixed amount daily. Children intrinsically love doing good things for other people, and they will enjoy the responsibility of doing this or reminding the parents of this obligation.

Beyond this, the child should be taught that sadaqah is not only money or material things given in charity, but any sort of help, goodness, or useful action with which Allah is pleased. For example, parents can ask them to take food to a neighbor in need, help pack blankets and food to be sent to refugees, or give some of the clothing they don't need to help someone who can use them. The list is virtually unlimited. And every sadaqah is rewarded. The Prophet (S) said,

> Every act of goodness is sadaqah. *(Muslim, 2197)*

> Sadaqah is due on every joint of the people for each day on which the sun rises. To judge justly between two persons is sadaqah; and to assist a man with his riding animal by helping him to mount it or by lifting his load onto it is sadaqah; and the good word is sadaqah; and every step taken toward salah is sadaqah; and removing something harmful from the road is sadaqah. (Bukhari, 4.232)

> When you smile in your brother's face, or enjoin what is good or forbid what is wrong, or guide someone who has lost his way, or help a man who has bad eyesight, or remove stones, thorns and bones from the road, or pour water from your bucket into your brother's, it counts for you as sadaqah. *(Mishkat 1911,* transmitted by *Tirmidhi)*

HAJJ (PILGRIMAGE) AND UMRAH

Children have participated in hajj and *umrah* (the "lesser pilgrimage") since the time of the Prophet (S). Although this participation does not fulfill their obligation of performing hajj unless it is done after they reach puberty, they are rewarded for it, as is the parent.

> The Messenger of Allah (S) met some riders at ar-Rawha and asked who they were. They replied that they were Muslims. They said, "Who are you?" He

> said, "The Messenger of Allah." A woman lifted up a
> boy to him and said,"Will this child be credited with
> having performed the hajj?" At that, he said,"Yes,
> and you will have a reward." *(Muslim, 3091)*

Today, due to the very crowded conditions, hajj has become
so physically difficult that parents need to look closely at their
circumstances before taking their children along. However, it
is good to talk about *hajj,* its significance and rites, with children and make them familiar with it, especially in the context
of the life-story of the prophet Abraham (S) and the feast of
Eid al-Adha. Umrah can be done in less crowded conditions
and is a very rewarding experience for children when possible.

ADAB (MANNERS)

To many people, the word "manners" conjures up the list
of do's and don'ts of polite society—in short, social etiquettes.
The Islamic definition of *adab* (plural, *aadaab*), good manners,
however, is far wider and deeper than this. Good manners, the
correct way of conducting oneself, equals good behavior, and,
conversely, good behavior equals good manners. Good adab is
closely tied to good *akhlaq*—that is, good character and morals.
Hence, all the Islamic guidelines for sound interaction among
human beings rest on this dual foundation of good akhlaq and
good adab. Numerous ahadith clarify this point.

> Abdullah ibn Amr reported: Truly, the Messenger of
> Allah (S) was not foul-tongued nor did he participate
> in foul speech. He used to say, "The dearest to me
> among you is the one who has the best character and
> manners." *(Bukhari, 5.104, 8.56)*

The Prophet (S) used to pray, "O Allah, I seek Your

protection against undesirable manners, deeds, and desires." (*Mishkat*, transmitted by *Tirmidhi)*

The most perfect of Muslims in faith is one who has the most excellent behavior, and the best among you are those who behave best to their wives. *(Mishkat, transmitted by Tirmidhi; Abu Dawud)*

Equanimity, gentleness and good behavior are one twenty-fifth of prophethood. *(Muwatta)*

Nothing is weightier in the scales of a believer on the Day of Judgment than his good behavior. Allah treats with displeasure a person who is given to loose and vulgar talk. *(Mishkat,* transmitted by *Tirmidhi)*

However, as Muslims we are not to judge others, for Allah alone has that right. And one of the most important functions of good manners is to protect ourselves and others from acting on our private perceptions and internal judgments of others.

Everyone forms opinions about those around him; this is a part of our nature. Fortunately, Allah does not hold us accountable for our thoughts or feelings as long as they are not translated into actions. Initially we may not like a person: his accent is "funny," he looks strange, or his clothes are not pleasing. But in the Islamic framework, such feelings are not a reason to treat a person disrespectfully. To this end, among others, Allah has prescribed a code of manners or adab, some general, such as being good to parents, and some specific, such as forbidding children to enter their parents' bedroom without permission. These Islamic manners form a basic framework on which positive relationships can be built.

Supposing, after some acquaintance, we still don't like a person. Nevertheless, he is a member of the human family and may also be a fellow Muslim. In either case, he has a right to decent and just treatment. If his actions are bad, we may need to protect ourselves from him and from the evil he does, but Islamic manners prevent us from being unjust and exceeding the limits prescribed by Allah.

Take, for example, the Qur'anic command,

> And when you are greeted with a (courteous) greeting, greet with better than it or (at least) return it. (Qur'an 4:86)

The obligation of greeting itself is supported by the following ahadith:

> A Muslim has the right to five things from (another) Muslim: to return the salam (Islamic greeting), and to visit the sick, and to follow the funeral processions, and to accept the invitations (of other Muslims), and to respond to the one who sneezes (by saying *"Yarhamak Allah"*) *(Bukhari, 2.332).* (A sixth and seventh duty, "To help the oppressed and to fulfill oaths," are mentioned in *Bukhari, 2.331)*

Following this basic order, *whom* to greet and *how* to greet is made clear by other ahadith such as the following:

> A man asked the Prophet (S), "Which (expression of) Islam is good?" He said, "Feeding (the hungry), and greeting those whom you know and those whom you do not know." *(Bukhari, 1.11)*

> The young should greet the old, and the passer-by (should greet) the one who is seated, and the small group (should greet) the large group *(Bukhari, 8.250; Muwatta).* (In addition to these,"The rider should greet the walker," is found in *Bukhari, 8.251)*

And the Prophet (S) said to Anas bin Malik (R),

> Son, when you enter your home, greet your people
> with the salam. It will be a source of blessing for you
> and for the members of your family. *(Mishkat,*
> transmitted by *Tirmidhi)*

Abdullah ibn Salam (R), who prior to his acceptance of
Islam was a prominent Jewish scholar, tells about how he recognized Muhammad (S) as being a true prophet, saying,

> When the Prophet (S) came to Madinah and I
> went and examined his face, I recognized that it
> was not the face of a liar. The first thing he said
> was, "If you (Muslims) greet all whom you
> meet, feed (the hungry), take care of your rela-
> tives, and pray at night when people are asleep,
> you will enter Paradise in peace." *(Mishkat,*
> transmitted by *Tirmidhi, Ibn Majah, and Darimi)*

Greeting is so much of an obligation that it is due even to a
person with whom we are at odds, and the one who greets the
other first is the better of the two, according to the Prophet's
saying:

> It is not permissible for a Muslim to shun his brother
> for more than three nights—that is, they meet, and
> this one turns away and that one turns away. The
> better of the two is the one who gives the salam first.
> *(Muwatta)*

Following this, we understand that the Islamic adab of
greeting is not just a piece of polite etiquette, but a means of
building respect, harmony, good relations, and reconciliation
among human beings. One of the benefits of this injunction is

that it opens the door for the creation of relationships when none existed before and the repairing of relationships which are strained. Because of it, strangers, as well as those close to us, feel respected and welcomed.

How greatly Allah Ta'ala honored and respected human beings is clear from His having ordered the angels to prostrate to Adam (S), the prototype of humankind (see 2:34; 7:11; 17:61; 18:50; 20:11). And He says,

> And We surely honored the Sons of Adam. (Qur'an 17:70)

How then can *we* take it upon ourselves to disrespect those to whom the Lord Almighty gave so much honor? Thus, the adab of Islam establishes the minimum basic respect due to another person just because he is a fellow human being created by Allah. It has nothing to do with whether we like or "approve of" someone or not. It relates to doing what is commanded and what is right, just because it *is* right.

As we have seen, the respect and kindness due to parents is irrespective of whether or not they are good parents; it is due just because they are parents. The help due to the poor and needy, the care required for an orphan, the duties ordered for neighbors—all of these are also irrespective of our personal feelings of liking or disliking, or our judgment of a person as deserving or undeserving. He is deserving because Allah said so, not because we, with our limited understanding. decided that he is.

A hadith makes this point clear. A man asked the Prophet's (S) permission to visit him. When the Prophet (S) saw him, he said confidentially to his wife A'isha (R), "What an evil brother of his tribe and what an evil son of his tribe!" But when the man sat down, the Prophet (S) behaved toward him in a correct and polite manner, and was completely at ease with him. When the man had left, A'isha said to the Prophet (S), "O Messenger of Allah, when you saw the man, you said this and that about him, but then you behaved in a correct and polite manner toward him, and you enjoyed his company." The Prophet (S) then said,

> O A'isha, when have you seen me behaving in a shameful manner? Truly, the people who will have the worst station in front of Allah on the Day of Resurrection will be those whom the people leave to avoid their evil. *(Bukhari)*

Now, back to the children. The easiest, most natural way to teach children manners is by providing them with good examples and lots of opportunities to practice what they have learned in an easy, non-threatening atmosphere.

For example, we are required to visit the sick. Mommy can select an occasion or two for taking little Layla with her, preferably to visit people Layla knows and who will enjoy seeing her (visits with contagious people can be carried out over the telephone). With advance preparation, Mommy can see to it that Layla's need for food, drink, and something to keep her occupied are satisfied before arriving at their destination, particularly when it is a hospital visit. As they get ready to go, Mommy can tell Layla where they are going, why, and what is expected of her.

A visit to a sick person is usually short in any case, and particularly when children are present. Layla may grow fidgety and bored if the visit extends too long, and Mommy wants her to enjoy visiting, not to regard it as a boring obligation. The sick person also will not benefit from the presence of a misbehaving child, and the main goal of the visit is to please the invalid, not to teach the child or please it.

Layla will learn how to greet an ill person by listening to Mommy and then trying out her own efforts at a greeting. She will learn what to say and what not to say for such occasions, and when a gift is appropriate. With time, Mommy can take her more often, and she will feel at ease in this now familiar situation.

Sharing

Sharing is a subject that occupies whole chapters in Western "how to rear kids" books. Such works detail the developmental stages that precede the child's ability to accept sharing.

As Muslims, we value sharing highly because we recognize that everything we have is a trust from Allah; it is not ours but His. However we also respect private and personal property and the right of people to exercise control over what has been entrusted to them. Allowing young people to have a special box or place for a few special treasures that are only for themselves may be appropriate in teaching respect for property and giving them more security to share other things. It isn't necessary to expose or oblige a child to share *all* his playthings with visiting children, especially if the young visitors are known not to have respect for others' things or to be destructive.

With thought, parents can find many special things (including experiences, sights, sounds, and feelings) to share with their children, and older children's things can be shared with the younger ones without fear of damage. One mother, for example, had a "mother box" full of tiny shells, interesting little rocks, and other small treasures that she brought out on occasion to share with a sick or miserable child as a special privilege.

Now and then items of clothing can be shared, particularly for special occasions. Parents can also demonstrate this concept by showing the child how they share with each other, or with relatives or friends. For example, Daddy puts his jacket around Mommy's shoulders when she forgot to bring her jacket and is cold; Mommy shares sweaters or jewelry with her sister, and later with her daughter as she grows up. As the child observes examples of his parents' sharing and giving, he will learn that giving and sharing do not diminish his own share, and that it feels good and right.

Food is one of the best things to share, and it can be done so many ways, dividing a candy bar among children, cutting apples into slices and passing them around, or letting everyone dig into the popcorn bowl together. Extra or special food can be shared with neighbors, Muslim and non-Muslim, as a gesture of neighborly warmth. This sharing is taught to a child through the hospitality which his or her parents show to guests, an Islamic obligation.

Hospitality

Honoring and showing hospitality to guests is so important as to be considered a religious obligation in Islam. Part of "honoring" is to greet a visitor with respect and affection, and to part with him or her in the same way. Even if someone arrives at a *bad* time, such behavior is the standard; a guest should always be made to feel welcome, never a burden.

Hospitality means to take care of the guests' needs, to make them feel comfortable and at home in one's house, to serve them food and drink appropriate to the occasion, and, if they are staying, to make them comfortable for the night. Numerous ahadithattest to the importance of this obligation. The Prophet (S) said,

> The one who believes in Allah and the Last Day should be generous to his neighbor (in another version it is: "Should not injure his neighbor"), and the one who believes in Allah and the Last Day, should be generous to his guest to his satisfaction." It was said: "And what is 'his satisfaction,' O Messenger of Allah?" He said: "A day and a night (of generous hospitality); and guesthood is for three days, and whatever is (given) beyond that is a sadaqah for

him." (Another version has, "And it is not permissible for one to stay with him [his host] until he is put
into difficulty" *[Bukhari, 8.156]*. And the one who
believes in Allah and the Last Day should (either)
speak what is good or be silent." *(Bukhari, 8.48,
8.158)*

A Companion said, "Messenger of Allah, tell me—
if I come to a man who does not give me any entertainment or hospitality, and he afterwards comes to
me, shall I entertain him, or treat him as he treated
me?" He replied, "No, entertain him." *(Mishkat,*
transmitted by *Tirmidhi)*

It is a part of the sunnah that a man should accompa-
ny his guest to the door of the house. *(Mishkat,*
transmitted by *Ibn Majah* and *Baihaqi)*

The force of this obligation is so strong that, according the
Prophet's words, if a guest comes and hospitality is not shown
to him, he has the right to take what is due to him as a guest
without the host's permission.

The one who is a guest of people who do not give
him hospitality, he is entitled to take from them the
equivalent of the hospitality due to him. *(Abu
Dawud, 3795)*

Uqbah bin Amir (R) reported, "We said, 'O
Messenger of Allah, you send us out and (at times)
we come upon people who do not ask us to stay with
them. Then what do you think about this?" The
Messenger of Allah (S) said: "If you come upon
(such) people and instruct them concerning what is
appropriate for a guest, accept it. But if they do not

> do it, then take from them the right of the guest, whatever is appropriate for them (to give)."
> *(Bukhari 8.159; Mishkat, 4040)*

The child will not fail to learn the proper treatment of guests from his parents' behavior, whatever it may be. A child who grows up in a home where there are no visitors, or where visitors are not welcomed or treated with respect and generosity, may have a hard time learning to share food and other possessions, perhaps regarding them as being all for himself. But in a home in which guests are welcomed and honored, a child learns that this is the behavior which is appropriate for himself as well as his parents. As he grows older, he can help in serving visitors, cleaning house, and setting tables in anticipation of the arrival of visitors, greeting and saying goodbye to them at the door, and the like.

These are just a few examples of Islamic manners, a subject about which great numbers of books have been written. The best way for parents to teach such manners is to learn them themselves, practice them, and let the child join in to the extent that he or she is able.

Tactfulness

Many Muslims are concerned about the distinction between honest manners and hypocrisy. No one likes insincere remarks or acts done only to show off or gain some advantage. But the question is, does being polite and nice to others when one doesn't feel like it constitute a lie, or possibly a piece of manipulative behavior?

In this regard, parents need to be alert to the motivations underlying their children's behavior. For example, Fatima has learned that if she smiles and talks sweetly to Daddy, she can get him to agree to whatever she wants, even when Mommy has already said "No." Here Fatima is not practicing nice manners, she is manipulating Daddy.

Identifying this problem will depend a lot on the perceptive ability of Fatima's parents in evaluating her intentions. Clues are usually obvious with children. Fatima may boast to Mommy, "If *you* don't let me, Daddy will." There may be some arrogance in her behavior that reveals that she thinks she has a system for managing things her way. Other children in the family may be overheard discussing this with her; in fact, they may deputize her to ask for collective favors.

It's good that Fatima has learned to search for the reward that comes from good manners rather than using more aggressive tactics. Her father has taught her that. But even though a child has asked in a nice way, a parent needs to use common sense in granting requests. Once the habit of asking politely has been learned, it is wise to lower the reward level.

But is being nice when you don't feel like it lying? It all depends upon one's intention—and, as the Prophet (S) informed us, actions are judged by the intentions underlying them.

> O people, truly, actions are only (judged) according to intentions, and truly, a man will have only what he intended. Therefore, the one who emigrated for Allah and His Messenger, his emigration was for Allah and His Messenger, and the one who emigrated for what this world gives him or in order to marry a woman, his emigration was for whatever he emigrated for. *(Bukhari, 9.85)*

We could define a lie as something said for the purpose of falsifying the truth for a wrong purpose, as in the following ahadith:

> A woman asked the Prophet (S), "If one of us women said that she had no desire for a certain thing even though she had that desire, would it be considered a lie?" The Prophet (S) said, "Falsehood is writ-

ten as falsehood, and a small falsehood is written as
a small falsehood." *(Muslim)*

A woman said, "O Messenger of Allah, I have a co-
wife. Then, is it a sin for me if I make known concerning my husband (that he gave me) what he has
not given me?" Thereupon the Messenger of Allah
(S) said, "The one who expresses gratification with
what he has not been given is like one who wears a
double garment of falsehood." *(Bukhari, 7.146;
Muslim, 5311)*

People are guilty of small lies every day. The phone rings
and Mom says to her daughter, "See who it is, and if it's
Martha, tell her I'm not home. I don't have time to talk to her
right now." Why not just tell Martha that Mom is busy now
and will return the call later? Sufyan comes to school wearing a
very strange shirt. Ali says, "Oh, what a cool shirt!" when he
actually thinks it's awful. To avoid small lies like this, silence is
best, and if we are pressed for an opinion, we can try to be honest and tactful at the same time: "It's different, but I like your
blue shirt better."

Even in joking with children we need to be very careful.
Children often don't understand the intended humor, and sarcasm and innuendo, which are prohibited in any case, go over
their heads.

A believer cannot have complete faith unless he
gives up falsehood in his jokes and debates, even
though in all other matters he speaks the truth.
(Ahmed)

A woman called her little son to herself in the presence of the Prophet (S). She told him to come so
that she could give him something. The Prophet (S)

asked what she wanted to give her child and she replied that she had a date for him. The Prophet (S) said, "If you had not given him this date, then the committing of a falsehood would have been entered into your record of deeds." *(Abu Dawud)*

If one calls a child, saying that he will give him a certain thing and he does not give it, it is a lie. *(Ahmad)*

I guarantee a house in the surroundings of Paradise for a man who avoids quarrelling even if he is in the right, a house in the middle of Paradise for a man who avoids lying even if he is joking, and a house in the upper part of Paradise for a man who makes his character good. *(Abu Dawud, 4782)*

It is important to be clear about our intentions in joking. Are we teasing someone with our superior knowledge or ability, so that they will feel or look stupid? This is a form of arrogance, and the arrogant one will not enter Paradise. Are we secretly putting down someone, either because of his race, cultural background, handicap, because we don't like him, or for any other reason? This is likewise arrogance. Even laughing at ourselves is not good if the tone is condemning. Intention is of first importance, then the tone of the joke as it is perceived by others. It may not have been intended to insult. Nevertheless, someone got hurt, so it was a mistake.

This doesn't mean Muslims can't tease or joke, or that they can't indulge in fantasy. The Prophet (S) himself had a subtle, gentle sense of humor. As we have seen, on one occasion he was amused by a toy belonging to his wife A'isha (R), a horse with wings. He saw the humor in it and didn't forbid it on the grounds that horses don't have wings. He nicknamed one of his Companions "Father of the Cat," and Muslims to this day call Abu Hurairah (R), the prolific transmitter of great numbers of ahadith, by that affectionate title. An old woman came to him and asked if she would go to Paradise. Gently teasing her, he told her that no old women would be allowed to go there, and then he gave her the good news that she would be there in her best form, freed from her old, sickly body.

In teaching children not to lie or deceive, there are those who believe it is not right to insist on manners that are not felt by the heart. Why insist that a child say he is sorry if he obviously isn't? Why take him to visit Grandpa in the hospital when he doesn't like it?

Such a question may seem confusing, but the answer to it is really quite simple. A Muslim is not responsible for his feelings, only his actions, and we want to do the right thing in the sight of Allah even if we don't feel like it. Visiting Grandpa in the hospital, saying "Sorry" to a friend when we aren't really sorry, acting as if everything is all right when one has been hurt—all these are forms of doing the right thing despite our feelings, for the rule is that, regardless of how we *feel* about something or someone, we must do what we know to be right. And, in this society where what one feels is considered all-important, we must teach this understanding to our children. *This* is submission to Allah and is central to the whole meaning of Islam.

Mataz, age four, catches Sabrina playing with his car. He grabs it from her furiously, rudely pushing her to the floor. He is still seething mad that she violated *his* toy, and for very little he wouldn't mind hitting her again. When ordered by Mommy to say "Sorry," he does so with the worst grace.

However, by accepting to apologize, Mataz is learning that right and wrong are determined by laws which exist outside of himself, laws which he must learn to live by. Feeling sorry requires knowing right from wrong, although Mataz hasn't learned the rules well enough to understand quite *why* he was wrong. After many such experiences, he will learn to understand the system, start to internalize the standard of right and wrong, and feel really sorry for actions of his that hurt others.

Many things in life are more easily learned by doing than by listening to a lecture.

This difference between telling the hard, cold, painful truth and saying what is appropriate in a given situation often causes problems for new Muslims, since many of us come from backgrounds in which it is believed the truth must be told, straight, direct and head-on, no matter how much it may hurt. But if one thinks for a moment, he will realizes that there are many ways to tell a story of what happened, many ways of shading the account, depending on one's point of view or emphasis. Some ways are more tactful, less painful than others. It isn't necessary to explain every detail of the story. We will never know absolutely all the details, and in particular we will never know all the intentions of the people involved. Therefore, why mention or elaborate on aspects of a situation or story which, if played down, would be less hurtful and more productive in the long run? Truth is essential, without question, but not every single truth is to be told to every single person if it is going to hurt someone's heart or produce disastrous results.

Ala and Shireen are asked if they cheat in school. Both answer "No." The fact is that Ala actually did once, but he felt terribly guilty and asked Allah for forgiveness, and he has never done it again. He is not lying; he does not cheat in school. Shireen cheats whenever she can. She is lying.

Sa'ud is asked why his brother is late for school. Sa'ud tries to avoid the question by answering, "Are you sure he was late? My mother tries so hard to get us off on time." He knows his brother pretended to be sick this morning and had a big fight with his mother before getting off late. When pushed to answer the question, he says, "I think he had a little problem this morning and got off to a late start."

In general conversation we cover each other's faults. We all have them. People are known by their actions, not by any false rumors others may spread. The exception to this is when justice must be done, and then we should speak only to those responsible for securing fairness and justice and to those who must be warned for their own safety. In other words, we don't talk about bad occurrences or the bad actions of people just for the fun of it or to shock others.

> Allah does not like evil to be talked about openly
> except by the one who has been wronged, and Allah
> is All-Hearing, All-Knowing. (Qur'an 4:148)

An example: Iman saw Mai take a pen from a classmate's book bag in a suspicious manner. She talks over the situation with Mommy and asks what she should do. Mommy tells her that it wouldn't be right ("Allah wouldn't like it" or "Islam tells us not to do this") for her to go around the school telling the story to everyone and calling Mai a thief. Her alternatives: (1) She can talk to Mai privately, telling her what she saw and advising her to return the pen. Maybe there was an acceptable reason for her taking it. (2) If the girl who owns the pen asks Iman about it, Iman can direct her to Mai. (3) She can tell the teacher privately that she saw someone take something, without mentioning names. The teacher can give a little talk about the evils of stealing. 4) However, if the teacher or another responsible person privately asks Iman about a stealing problem in class, Iman must tell what she saw Mai doing. But if another child comes to her and scornfully calls Mai a thief, Iman can say, "Why, did you see her doing it? How can you be sure?" or, "Why do you want to talk like that about somebody? How would you like it if someone did that to you?" and change the subject, instead of blurting out her own suspicions. She has already done what it was right to do about the matter.

Frequently people talk when they should keep silent because the story, problem, event, or whatever, is burning a hole in them. They think they just *have* to get it out; then they will feel better. A way of combatting this tendency to talk too much is to understand, and teach our children, that whatever we have seen of the private or secret affairs of others is a trust, *amanah,* and as such it should not go beyond us. When we carry something for the sake of Allah and for His pleasure, it becomes easy. Otherwise we are likely to blurt out everything we know just to get it off our chest.

Thus it will be seen that the etiquette of conversation requires a sense of what is right and wrong, and a lot of practice. Many adults go beyond the bounds of right in this, and these daily errors accumulate into sins. The closer we come to Allah, the more correct our sense of balance, moderation, and wisdom in conversation will be.

When we start nudging our children to practice good behavior and sound manners at a young age, they learn when they are least self-conscious. Doing new things is uncomfortable for people in general. Too often feelings of awkwardness and insecurity prevent adults and older children from doing what they sense is right. Small rewards will encourage the establishment of good habits, but one of the best encouragements is for the parents to practice what they preach.

> Those who do good shall have good and even more
> (as a reward). Neither darkness nor abasement shall
> come near their faces. They are Companions of the
> Garden; in it they will remain. (Qur'an 10:26)

ALL ABOUT SEX

Gender Role Modeling

Since the beginning of man's life on earth, gender roles have been transmitted to children through modeling. As is only natural, as a rule children pattern themselves and conceive of their own sex roles after their parents' example.

A boy whose father is passive, laid-back, and uninvolved with his family is unlikely to grow up into an active, supportive, caring family man—that is, unless he patterns himself after his involved, giving, dynamic mother. A girl whose mother reflects no feminine values and is like a pseudo-male is likely to grow up with a strong masculine component to her personality. Again, what we portray is what we are most likely to see in our children. Hence, any attempt to influence our children's perception of their sex roles requires a high degree of self-examination, honesty, and the willingness to admit and try to rectify mistakes.

Children of all ages tend to act out their perception of their sex roles in play. As described by both Dr. Benjamin Spock in his book, *Rearing Children in a Difficult Time*, and F. Ilg and L. Ames in their classic work, *Child Behavior from Birth to Ten,* children from three to six, for example, are naturally curious and sensitive to their social environment. They play pretend games, imagining themselves in adult gender roles, modeling themselves after their parents. Such play is quite spontaneous—and, incidentally, is a marvellous way for parents to tell how their children think and understand things.

This age is very special because the child is absorbing his concept of his identity—by what he is defined and who he is in the eyes of others. By the age of seven or even well before, a child knows, without any formal instruction, what his sex, religion, nationality, and language are. His identity as a boy, her identity as a girl, has long since crystalized and become part of his or her personality.

When parents live in a stable, supportive community and are certain of themselves and their values, children of this age automatically absorb their understanding of the behavior appropriate to their sex from their environment and are tied in to it as they grow up. But today it is relatively hard to find such communities. People move around, lacking permanence; nothing is as it was before and nothing stays as it is. The hallmark of this time is impermanence and constant change.

In addition, the family is under attack and under pressure from all sides. Role models are confused, particularly gender role models. Women are alternately portrayed as seductive, manipulative, competitive pseudo-males in feminine form. Men are portrayed as victims of women, or as barely coming out even. There is a great deal of militancy about women's rights, and men's needs are ignored; both are increasingly portrayed as being out to exploit the other. Homosexuals' demands that their lifestyle be regarded as normal and correct are being listened to and met.

This is in complete contrast to the Islamic view of men and women as partners in society, cooperating and sharing their different strengths to provide a stable base for their children. Since a good deal of literature is available about the relationship between men and women in Islam, it need not be repeated here. Nonetheless, we need constant reflection and guidelines on how to steer our children clear of negative influences and models, so that they may grow into adults who can function effectively and usefully in the modern world.

Controlling the Environment

As much as possible, parents should try to control the environment of a young child so that he doesn't get drawn into "bad" stuff—and seeing and hearing is the first step toward being "drawn into."

Even when something is right in front of a young child, it can pass over his head if his attention isn't drawn to it. It's not necessary to tell a three-year-old that the couple across the street is living together without being married. We must still fulfil our obligations to them as neighbors, but we don't have to have more contact. The child will assume that they are married because the model he perceives is that of a married couple. Later on, when he is more world-wise, he will understand, and that will be time enough.

On the other hand, even though the dirty jokes in a television program may pass over a child's head, it is still best to protect him from them, first, because of the generally unsavory atmosphere of the program as a whole. Second, we don't know at what point the child will start to notice (and he *will* notice the response on the laugh track and the snickering of any older people watching with him, which will cue him in to noticing earlier than he otherwise might), and even if he doesn't understand at the moment, perhaps he will remember and put the pieces together later. Third, parents themselves provide a good example in turning off programs that they feel are inappropriate, either for the child or for themselves. The message is, *if* something doesn't seem good, don't opt to have it around—or, alternatively, take yourself away from it.

> Coarse talk does not enter into anything without disgracing it, and modesty does not come into anything without adorning it. *(Mishkat,* transmitted by *Tirmidhi)*

> Modesty is part of faith and faith is in Paradise, but obscenity is a part of hardness of heart and hardness of heart is in Hell. *(Mishkat, transmitted by Ahmad and Tirmidhi)*

Some guidance is necessary to help the child protect himself from harmful influences without cutting him out of the world so much that he cannot function in it. As the child grows older, we cannot simply turn off the television; after all, he can watch at the neighbor's or at home when we aren't present or paying attention. He will talk to other children at school and hear all sorts of things; even if he attends an Islamic school, there will still be less-sheltered children who will talk. And perhaps sheltering isn't the answer anyhow. We can't rear our children in a vacuum. But we *can* train them to fight against evil, whether in the outside world or in the secret desires of their own egos.

Often there is more than one approach we can follow. Again, take television watching. One course of action would be that time after time we voice our disapproval of a TV show and leave the room. Then the child will either be his own policeman and turn it off himself, or he will watch, perhaps trying to understand for himself why his parent disapproves. In the latter case, however, the harm will be done. A second approach would be to order him to turn it off, whether he likes it or not. Reasons for our stand may be given, or a parent may ask the child, "Why do you think I didn't want you to watch that?" and a discussion follows.

Another approach would be to sit with the child and discuss the show as it progresses, pointing out what we object to and why. Obviously this is by far the most constructive approach, for it builds and cements a common understanding between child and parent, building the child's value system through close communication with his primary teacher, his mother or father. It also provides the child with ammunition so that he is able to defend his parents' moral code when other children talk to him about the show. And if a parent's moral code is clearly defined to a child, he will often prefer it to anyone else's, at least until he reaches the age of thinking for himself at around puberty. When a youngster is well armed against the ridicule of his peers, he may be less likely to be swayed by them.

Part of modifying the environment for our children surely involves modifying ourselves. We Muslim parents must make a conscious effort to provide our children with the best models possible—in ourselves, our friends, our home life. This involves trying to improve our own behavior so that we will be as perfect examples as possible. If Daddy doesn't have enough self-control and fear of Allah to control his own television watching, for example, how can he possibly expect Ahmad and Naila to? If Mommy isn't in the habit of telling the truth, how can Jilan learn that lying is a serious sin? If one or both parents don't consider it important to pray regularly, how can they imagine that their children will? Even when we try to hide things from them, children pick up what we do.

Shielding young children as much as possible from bad environments and unsuitable models by limiting contact is essential. The television can be turned off, or even done without. Undesirable books and movies can be avoided. Contacts with unsuitable family members and neighbors can be limited and controlled. How to do this is discussed in chapter 8.

Modesty and Sexual Issues

Allah Ta'ala says,

> O Children of Adam! We have revealed to you garments to conceal your shameful parts and to be an adornment, but the garment of *taqwa* (mindfulness of Allah)— that is best. This is among the signs of Allah, in order that they may remember. (Qur'an 7:26)

And the Prophet (S) said,

> Every religion has a distinctive quality, and the distinctive quality of Islam is modesty. *(Muwatta)*

> Modesty is part of faith and faith is in Paradise, but obscenity is a part of hardness of heart and hardness of heart is in Hell. *(Mishkat,* transmitted by *Ahmad and Tirmidhi)*

> Indecency disfigures everything, while modesty enhances the charm of everything. *(Mishkat,* transmitted by *Tirmidhi)*

> Once the Prophet (S) saw a man washing in a public place without a lower garment. At that, he mounted the pulpit, praised and glorified Allah, and said: "Allah is characterized by modesty and concealment.

So when any of you washes (the private parts of his body), he should conceal himself." *(Abu Dawud)*

And he said,

Avoid being naked, for with you are those (angels) who never leave you except when you are relieving yourselves and when a man has intercourse with his wife; so observe modesty in front of them and honor them. *(Mishkat,* transmitted by *Tirmidhi)*

It is easy to teach modesty to children when they are small. In a home in which the adults behave with modesty, a child automatically learns to close the door when he or she is in the bathroom or getting dressed, usually by the age of four. The child is discouraged from parading around in his or her underwear. Example is now reinforced by verbal instruction. "Nadia, fix your dress. That's not polite, dear." or, "We need to cover properly in front of other people, Anwar."

Some parents do allow very small children to see them naked, while changing, or bathing, or even at the toilet. Each parent knows his or her reasons. We should, however, remember our position as role models in defining modesty. A clear injunction to respect the parent's right to privacy in the intimacy of the bedroom is contained in Surah al-Nur:

O you who believe, let those whom your right hand posesses, and those among you who have not reached puberty ask permission (to come into your presence) three times: Before *salat al-Fajr,* and when you put aside your clothing at noontime, and after *salat al-Isha*—three (times of) privacy for yourselves. There is no sin upon them or upon you (at times) other than that, attending to one another. Thus Allah makes clear the signs, and Allah is

> Knower, Wise. And when the children among you reach puberty, let them ask permission (to come into your presence), even as those before them asked permission. Thus Allah makes clear to you the signs, and Allah is Knower, Wise. (Qur'an 24:58-59)

Little girls love to dress up around the house and enjoy making themselves pretty when Daddy comes home or Grandma comes to visit. Observing their mother and her friends wearing special dresses for outside and for inside, they want to imitate them. If they are allowed to play with scarves and complimented for wearing them correctly and at the right time, they will feel comfortable with them and be better ready to cover when they reach puberty.

Modesty extends to other areas as well, and is learned early, usually before school age. For example, if the mother or sister wear *hijab*, a child learns not to let in a visitor without making sure that the women of the house are properly covered. Children also learn to protect the privacy of the home by closing the curtains before turning on the lights in the evening. Such elements of modesty taught to little ones, both girls and boys, makes the transition to normal adult modesty easy.

All this is part of the groundwork which prepares children to resist pressures against their modesty as they grow up. If this foundation is laid, the child will grow up aware of a tremendous contrast between himself and his values, and those of others.

Children in public schools will need their parents' assistance to protect this modesty we desire. Often they are required to change in front of other children for school plays, and especially for sports activities. Sports uniforms may be too skimpy for our children, and in schools with pools, swimming activities may also breach our code. Showers in the school locker rooms may lack proper privacy curtains. Older children are frequently shy to mention these facts to their parents so parents should inquire for details from the gym teacher.

General Sex Education

By puberty, a Muslim youngster will be aware that many non-Muslim children are having a difficult time because of the heavy emphasis on having relations with the opposite sex. Because of the earliness with which non-Muslim children start such relationships, and the heavily sexually-charged atmosphere of American society as a whole, we need to discuss such matters with our children early, probably before sixth grade. Parents can ask other parents with older children for advice concerning the local situation.

The Islamic ideal of marriage needs to be explained to the Muslim child and continually reinforced. Children need to know early, well before the dating age, how we expect them to find a mate in life, and how we will help them. We can point out to our children that non-Muslim youngsters engage in so much talk about sex to cover their inexperience and anxiety about what, to a Muslim, is a wholesome and beautiful matter in the correct context—marriage. Kids tell dirty jokes to relieve their stress and boast to cover their insecurities about dating and attracting members of the opposite sex. In such an environment, Muslim youngsters need support in realizing that their feelings of shyness are normal and that, although no one admits it much, they are experienced by most of their non-Muslim classmates as well.

Our children, observing their classmates at school or characters in books or movies, with all of the problems created by the current emphasis on sexual freedom, may feel a sense of relief at being Muslim and not having to worry about a date, which will offset their feeling of being left out of the "stuff" other kids are into. However, it usually requires tactful discussion on the part of parents to make these issues clear to children.

Unfortunately, many foreign-born Muslim parents shy away from talking to their children about anything involving the shameful, taboo word, "sex." This is a disastrous, head-in-the-sand policy, often reflecting the parent's sense of guilt and impotence concerning the environment in which his child is forced to spend his school hours, due to his—the parent's—decision to settle in this country. It also reflects the parent's background where this topic was considered too private for open family discussion. But this does not change the realities of the child's situation.

The fact is that the child is immersed in and bombarded with sexual stimuli and sex talk during all his hours in school. He needs tools for dealing with this, and the firm backing of adult values and support to cope with it. Where children are not aided by their families in learning skills to act as Muslims in the non-Muslim world, they will invent their own ways of dealing with school and peer preasure. Too frequently, being normal humans who want to join the group of their peers, they develop a sort of split personality, dividing themselves into two different worlds, joining the world and acting like everyone else in school, where they hide the fact that they pray and fast, and hiding the forbidden schooltime activities from parents at home. "Mom and Dad just don't understand." They can do this with every aspect of their Islamic identity, often starting with adopting a nick name at school that hides their Islamic name.

If we put ourselves into our child's place, we can readily grasp how inviting the non-Muslim scene may be. It is inevitable that some of our children will try to become part of this scene. At some point in their growing years, these young people will try cigarettes, alcohol, drugs and/or sex; some may even get pulled into homosexual behavior. These behaviors represent almost the worst- case scenario to us parents, short of involvement in gangs and violent crime.

How can we head off this possibility with our children? The answer is that possibly we may not be able to; it is only by Allah's grace that they—and we ourselves—are saved from such sins. But we can try.

It is best for a young person to be able to talk frankly to his or her parents about the situations found in school and among friends, and this should be encouraged wherever possible. However, young people are learning to be adult, to be responsible for themselves, and their desire for independence can strain parent-child relations just when they need their parents' support the most. Some parents listen and respond to kids better than others. If parents are unable to keep their cool when one of them finds a note "You're cute, signed Bill" in their 13-year-old daughter's coat pocket, they need help. In the difficult age we live in, a discrete parents' support group is a real help.

A support group among Muslim teens with a "hip" Muslim advisor would also be a big plus. Islamic communities can do a lot to aid parents by providing such support groups for older boys and older girls. These groups could be modeled as social clubs or Islamic study groups, but they can function to allow our children to discuss their problems coping with others in similar situations. The best Islamic teachers are needed for these groups to guide the children. These teachers would specialize in the delicate topics children and parents have trouble discussing .

As a word of warning to parents, the dangers of the unIslamic lifestyle should be discussed frankly and openly but without exaggeration. In one girl's home, the parents provided her with a good model of conduct, but they told her that with only one sip of alcohol she would become an alcoholic, lost forever in drunkenness; Allah would also punish her and she would surely go to Hell.

Once, when she met friends from school at a party, she was horrified to see them drinking. They offered her a drink and she refused. As a result of this incident, she began to think about her parents and what they'd taught her. She saw that her friends were not alcoholics; they drank some at the party and even became a little high, but the next day they were back to normal, her regular friends, acting as usual. She decided that her parents didn't know anything about American society, especially about alcohol, and she became a social drinker. The punishment of Allah on the Day of Judgment seemed more distant than the threat of becoming an alcoholic in this life, and she discarded that fear, too.

When a child finds that his parents have grossly exaggerated their warnings of danger, he is likely to assume that they don't know what they are talking about. "My folks are from the old country, so they don't really understand what's going on, see?" "My folks are RELIGIOUS, see. They always overreact to things." It therefore becomes easier for him to ignore their warnings. So much scientific, accurate information and statistical data about rape, AIDS and other sexually transmitted diseases, unwed motherhood, homosexuality, etcetera, is available to Muslim parents today to support our stand against dating, alcohol and drug use, the gay lifestyle and all the rest, that we have no excuses for not properly informing our children about the *real* dangers.

The foregoing story illustrates another danger. Many well-meaning parents try to inculcate in their children the evil not only of the non-Islamic lifestyle, but also of non-Muslims in general. While a child may recognize the validity of this in an abstract manner, we must remember that he spends six hours a day, and often more, with these same "evil" companions. To him, it may seem as if his friends, whose innate goodness as human beings he recognizes underneath their wrong behavior, are being attacked. So recognize that goodness too, and that potential for change in them. Don't condemn individuals, condemn general behavior. Otherwise, at some point, overgeneralizing parents may come to seem like liars or like closed-minded, prejudiced people. *They* are talking theoretically, but *he* knows his "unIslamic" friends as concrete, often basically decent individuals, even if some of them are heavily into drugs, alcohol or sex, or even homosexual practices. Then it becomes parents versus friends—and at this age, the parents often end up as the losers.

In summary, we keep communication open about all subjects with our young people, surround them as far as we are able with sound, appealing models, and provide them with safe, enjoyable outlets. Many youngsters, surrounded by endless parental restrictions, come to equate Islam with prohibitions, with negations of almost everything they like or want to do—haram this and haramthat. And this is a dangerous and often costly error. Parents may have made some trifling, temporary gains by restricting a youngster from various social activities, but have lost him to Islam as a result.

Even with our best intentions and efforts, however, our young people may make mistakes, may even commit serious sins. But it is important to recognize that one step off the track, or even more, does not condemn a human being forever. An individual's account in front of Allah is not complete until he takes his last breath, and we never give up hope of His guidance and help. If our child does something *haram*, even continuing it over a period of time, we continue to hope that he or she will realize the mistake and return to right conduct. The correct response is to remain loving and open, not condoning an errant youngster's misbehavior but trying to affect him or her by love, and not closing our hearts or our home to our child. Is it not an article of faith that Allah forgives all sins? Then how can we be less forgiving than Allah? The tremendous weapon we have, which is more powerful than any misbehavior, is prayer, for Allah surely responds to the prayer of a parent for a child.

For recent converts with adolescent children, there are no easy rules or guidelines for converting these children into model Muslims overnight. Kathy is fourteen; she has been attending dances for two years and dating occasionally. She just started going with a "really cute guy" in her history class at school. Then one day, her parents come home from a class at the mosque and say, "Here are some scarves to wear, and from now on, no more dating."

Such parental behavior reflects a real break with reality and with wisdom. Regardless of their own enthusiasm, how can they suppose that this girl, with her background and present orientation, can possibly be ready for such a step? *They* are Muslims; *she* isn't.

Kathy's parents will certainly want to encourage her strongly toward Islam, but they must, in all fairness, recognize that there is no compulsion in religion; if they don't, they are running the risk of driving her away from them. Even though she may have reached the age of accountability to Allah, she has to make her own decision about her religion. Remember that the Prophet himself (S), our example and guide, was sent to convey a message, not to force anyone to accept it. The above suggestion about an Islamic study group for girls or boys is particularly needed for this situation, if the child will accept to attend.

Negative Models

Since modeling is so important in teaching children, the impact of negative models is obvious.

We live in an environment dominated by non-Islamic values and behavior, and, like any parents who have strong religious values, we are, quite justifiably, fearful of the effects of this contamination and corruption on our vulnerable children. And of course, this contamination appears not only in the realm of ideas and values but also includes peers, who can point the way to all kinds of evil behaviors—sexual misbehavior, homosexuality, substance abuse, atheism, and all the rest. Unfortunately, it also includes adult influences as well—teachers, counselors, sports or entertainment figures. The list goes on and on.

Most unfortunate of all, it also includes Muslims. It has often been said that it is easier to rear Muslim children here than in Muslim countries because here the issues are clear-cut: there is Islam and non-Islam, Muslims and non-Muslims. However, this is far from accurate.

Perhaps the most dangerous of negative models to which our children are exposed are Muslims who either do not practice or who practice with a bias—that is, they take what they like of Islam and leave the rest. The result is a terrible imbalance, both in thinking and in behavior, which can affect our children just as it does our adults.

Perhaps the worst of such an influence is the "Islamic" model which, like some Christian evangelists, stresses the "Hellfire and damnation" approach. Allah is seen as a vengeful deity who is eager to consign His servants to Hell for the smallest mistake. There is little room in such a conception of Islam for mercy, softness, gentleness, or anything which would move the heart. Instead there is a heavy emphasis on "do's and don'ts," the haram-ness of things, and practicing by rote and not from the heart.

Another negative model is that which relegates Islam to one small corner of one's life. The approach is secular and utilitarian, and extremely superficial. One does the minimum to get by with, and for the rest operates pretty much like any non-Muslim member of this society. The Prophet (S), the most exalted of Allah's creations, is seen as an ordinary person "just like anyone else," who happened to be chosen, like some postman, to bring Allah's final revelation for mankind. Taking him as a life-example by following his sunnahis looked upon as fanatacism, or, if you will, fundamentalism. Ideas and practices alien to Islam are seen to be cropping up among people who hold this kind of thought, and it is likely that among their children almost nothing will survive of Islam.

The fact is that there is no "safe" community of "good" Muslims in which we can take refuge to protect our children from outside influences—and indeed if there were, it might be just as dangerous in the long run, as it would leave our children ignorant of the choices and errors possible in the world. As one mother said to her child, "You have to know the word 'pig' and how to spell it. You have to know also the words 'sow' and 'hog' and 'piglet,' and 'ham' and 'bacon,' and whatever else. You have to know what pork looks like and the common dishes in which it's served. This is part of your education for living in the world today."

Allah, our Most Merciful Lord, is fully aware of the tests we encounter in rearing our children in such an environment. He has promised that He will not give us a test harder than we can bear. Good parenting takes time, thought, persistence, and effort, but with Allah's help, we do the best we can. Because of the effects of negative models, we have to be more strict with ourselves in providing positive models. We also need to be more open in communication with our children, discussing with them the deeper meanings of what they see around them, why we do things, and why others do otherwise. And again, we need to make *du'a* without ceasing for the well-being of our children and their success in this life and the Hereafter.

Chapter Six

MODIFYING INAPPROPRIATE BEHAVIOR

SIX STRATEGIES FOR DEALING WITH PROBLEMS

No child or parent is perfect. There are bound be troublesome issues, conflicts, and problems in their relationships, even in the best of situations. And some approaches are better than others. We present here six methods a parent can use in dealing with problems. The choice of which one to apply depends on the situation and the child. Since all children are unique individuals, some techniques work better with a given child than others.

IGNORING FAULTS AND ERRORS

If we are realistic about ourselves, we have to admit that we would drive ourselves and our children crazy if we tried to correct their every mistake. Taking the Prophet Muhammad (S) as our example, we note that he spent the first thirteen years of his mission trying only to teach *tawheed,* the oneness of Allah. He either ignored minor faults in his companions or trained them so that they could eventually overcome their own faults.

We have already seen how leniently he treated his young servant, Anas bin Malik (R), passing over his mistakes and refraining from asking him about why he did or not do something. We have also read Abdullah bin Masud's statement that the Prophet (S) admonished his companions only occasionally, out of concern that daily admonishment would be too burdensome. The Prophet also discouraged people from telling tales about each other and encouraged them to hide one another's faults:

> The servant (whose fault) Allah conceals in this world, Allah will also conceal (his faults) on the Day of Resurrection. *(Muslim, 6266)*

> O community of people who have believed by their tongue but whose belief has not entered their hearts, do not backbite Muslims and do not search for their faults, for if anyone searches for their faults, Allah will search for his fault, and if Allah searches for the fault of anyone, He disgraces him in his house. *(Abu Dawud, 4862)*

> None of you should tell me anything harmful about my companions, for I want that, as long as I come to you, my mind should be clean in respect to each one of you. *(Abu Dawud)*

> The one who covers the failings of someone in this world will have his shortcomings covered by Allah on the Day of Judgment. *(Muslim)*

Bad behavior has its reasons. However, if it is from an error committed with good intentions—for example, making a mess in the kitchen while trying to fix a surprise breakfast for parents—the good intention is far more important than the results. Hadi threw the toast at Firas for not listening to his orders and spilling the milk; an egg was broken on the floor. But the kids were smiling with their big surprise when Daddy came in to get his coffee. In such situations, far more positive and constructive to appreciate the good effort and ignore the mistakes for the present. Parents often have to bite their tongues to keep from making negative comments and thereby hurting feelings or humiliating a sensitive child.

If Mommy sees Danah making a mean face and lifting her arm to hit her sister but stopping herself before she actually does it, Mommy should ignore Danah's aborted attack and talk to her about something else. Or she can praise her for not doing the mean thing she was about to do; even though Danah *thought* about doing something bad, she didn't do it, and that requires praise and appreciation (we recall that on the Day of Judgment, Allah will reward believers for bad intentions which for His Sake are not carried out).

Samir is doing poorly in school. All on the same long day, he forgot the books he needed for his homework, lost his eraser, broke his pencil, couldn't remember what the assignment was, spilled his juice, and called his sister a bad name. Where does Mom start? A quiet personal du'a for patience might be most appropriate, for a start! Then she could gently start unraveling what, of his homework, he is able to do, help him clean up, organize his work in a quiet corner, and get him started. When someone is drowning, we throw him a life preserver; we don't start yelling at him about why he got into the deep water.

As a rule, much of the annoying or bad behavior of children is outgrown without our ever having to do anything about it. However, ignoring bad behavior should be a deliberate course of action taken by the parent as the best technique for the given circumstances. It should never be the lazy parent's excuse.

Modifying the Environment

Confrontation does not provide easy solutions to problems; as a rule, it produces hard feelings and poor results. Therefore, to avoid it is best. One strategy for solving problems and avoiding confrontations is that of modifying an environment for the better. And this is in conformity with the words of Allah Ta'ala:

> Allah desires ease for you, and He does not desire hardship. (Qur'an 2:185)

> Whenever the Messenger of Allah (S) had a choice between two matters, he would choose the easier of them so long as it was not sinful; but if they were sinful, he would stay as far away from them as possible. *(Bukhari, 8.777)*

> You (Muslims) have been sent to make things easy and not to make them difficult. *(Bukhari, 1.219)*

> Whenever the Messenger of Allah (S) ordered (anything for the Muslims), he would order them to do deeds that were within their capability... *(Bukhari, 1.19)*

An often-overlooked strategy is for parents to change a situation in order to avoid creating behavior problems with their children. A good deal of bad behavior occurs when children's needs and limitations are not properly considered. A classic example is the situation in which parents keep expensive decorative objects within a child's reach and then spend days yelling at the child not to touch.

Children are curious and fascinated by anything that catches their fancy. This is not because they are innately "bad"—no, not at all. Rather, Allah created them this way, with lots of energy to go out, investigate, and conquer the world. When we anticipate this need and provide them with friends to play with, areas that are safe, and interesting things to do at their own level, we can relax. They will still need our attention but it can be much more constructive and positive attention, overseeing their games as the situation calls for rather than playing "mean old policeman."

An obviously inconsiderate action of parents is placing their young children in situations in which they have to sit still or go without food for longer than they can easily bear. Sometimes their need for sleep is not considered by parents who want late evening visits with friends, just as they did before having children, or they are taken out at mealtimes and left hungry while Mommy attends to her own affairs.

Children are quite flexible and adaptable. They can make some sacrifices for special occasions or when the welfare of the family requires it. However, parents usually find misbehavior occurring as a result of their children's unwarranted sacrifices, which represent a denial of their most basic needs. Thus, crankiness is common among hungry or tired children; hyperactivity is frequently seen in children fed too many sweets and little nutritious food. Likewise, children who seem glum and sullen may brighten up considerably when allowed more daily exercise and regularly scheduled meals and sleep.

Substitution

Substitution is an approach that might be regarded as part of modifying the environment, but we visualize it differently. Substitution means that we can change a child's behavior by giving him something else (desirable) in the place of what he already has (undesirable). So, if nine-month-old Ahmed is playing with Nadia's dirty shoe, distract him with a ball or something else. If the children are watching a television show that turns out to be unsuitable, send them outside to play tag or upstairs to play a board game.

Even when a situation or a behavior is not really bad, substitution can be useful, helping us to apply the advice of the Prophet (S):

> It is a part of the excellence of a believer's faith that he leaves off whatever is of no benefit to him in this world and the Hereafter. *(Tirmidhi)*

We also find many ahadith in which the Prophet (S) pref-
aced his advice to someone by saying, "May I tell you about
something that is better than this?" The general meaning of
this is that, if something is not useful or beneficial, find something else.

We have the opportunity to use our time in many different
ways. Simply put, those activities that are pleasing to Allah
bring us reward, and those that are displeasing bring punishment. Some bring benefit, some bring harm, and others bring
nothing. We will never lose if we encourage our children to
look for the activities that Allah likes.

A word may be said here concerning motivation. A young
child brought up in Islam has a natural disposition to love
Allah. He or she wants to please Him, not to displease Him.
The desire to please and not to displease Allah can be a powerful motivator, even of quite young children. Just as a child
wants to please and not displease his parents, he has the ability
to feel the same toward the Most Beneficent God Who created
him and gives him everything.

Natural Consequences

Allowing children to taste the consequences of their mistakes and misdeeds is an excellent method of changing behavior. And part of the consequence, inevitably, is the need to
apologize or make reparations.

As a parent, we may feel a strong desire to protect our
child, but we are not doing him a favor when we protect him
too much from the natural consequences of his acts. All too
soon he will be an adult, responsible and accountable for his
own deeds. By shielding our child from tasting the consequences of his own actions, we may spoil him and weaken him,
making him unfit for the tests that will surely come to him with
time, a time when we will not be present or able to help him.
Allah says,

And no bearer of burdens bears another's burden,
and if one heavily burdened calls another to bear his
load, he will not be able to carry any of it, even if he
is a relative. (Qur'an 35:18; 6:164)

O mankind, be mindful of your Lord, and fear a Day
when no parent will be of any avail to his child, nor
will a child be of any avail for his parent. (Qur'an
31:33)

Training children to accept the consequences of their
actions should begin early. In a fit of rage, Isa throws his toy
plane to the floor, breaking it. Maryam sneaks Mom's sharp
sewing scissors out of the drawer, although she isn't supposed
to touch them, and tries them out on her shirt, cutting a big hole
in the front. And there is a price for such wrong-doing. Isa's
plane is wrecked and Maryam's shirt is ruined.

This can be a good learning experience, but only if parents
allow it to be. If Daddy, feeling sorry for Isa, who after all has
cried and apologized, runs out and gets him a new plane, perhaps he will have learned nothing; if Mommy replaces
Maryam's shirt with a new one very quickly out of pity for her,
the lesson may not have sunk in.

The lesson that needs to be learned is that destructive
behavior, whether intentional or not, results in loss. It is easiest
to show children how wrong actions destroy things. As they
grow up they will better understand how wrong actions can
destroy relationships.

Islam highly recommends following a bad deed with a good
deed:

Truly, good deeds remove evil ones. (Qur'an
11:114)

Repel evil with what is better. (Qur'an 23:96)

Nor can Goodness and Evil be equal. Repel (Evil) with what is better; then will he between who and you was hatred become as it were your friend and intimate! (Qur'an 41:34)

Fear Allah wherever you are, and do good deeds after doing bad ones; the former will wipe out the latter. And behave decently toward people. *(Tirmidhi)*

The one who has wronged his brother concerning his honor or anything else should ask his forgiveness before the Day on which he will have neither dirham nor dinar (that is, neither wealth nor possessions to help him). If he has good deeds, they will be taken from him in proportion to his wrong doings. And if he has no good deeds (to his credit), the evil deeds of his companion will be taken and loaded upon him. *(Bukhari, 3.629)*

If a child spills something, he should clean it up to the best of his ability. If he breaks his brother's space ship, he should fix it or replac it, depending upon his age and ability. If he is lazy and repeatedly dawdles in the morning, missing the school bus and having to walk may do more to solve the problem than all the scolding and pushing his mother can do to get him off in time. If he doesn't bother to show up at the table at mealtimes, he may change by learning that he has to reheat his meal and serve himself, eat and clean up after himself all alone.

But a word of caution is needed here. The foregoing applies to problems that the child causes by negligence, forget-fulness, and the like. But the parent must be honest and sincere in evaluating each situation. Does the child wake up too late to catch the school bus because the parent has not imposed any rules concerning bedtimes and the child isn't getting enough sleep? Is the twelve-year-old not getting to the table on time because he doesn't know that it's expected, because he isn't being called soon enough, or because, due to some personal reasons, he'd rather eat alone than with the family? All these factors need to be taken into account and dealt with straightforwardly. Often it's the parents who are to blame for a problem that's attributed to the child.

We need to tell children clearly what we expect of them and help them arrange a program to carry out our expectations. Then, after a short breaking-in period when they get used to a new responsibility, we can impose appropriate penalties for nonperformance.

It is also important to balance the desirability of our mercy and forbearance with the child's need for responsibility and accepting the consequences of his actions. It's important to be flexible in our use of methods. For example, if Mom is in a hurry and her child spills milk, she may just cover the accident and quickly clean up the mess herself. If she has time, she may teach him to clean it up himself (i.e., with rags or a mop, carpet shampoo and the like). If he's at the verge of learning to pour things himself, he may also need instruction in how to do it and when it's best to ask for Mommy's help. He doesn't need to hear reproaches and rebukes, as if he created the accident intentionally. It's wiser, more just, and probably more accurate to assume good intentions on the part of our children whenever possible.

Even though the child's efforts to make amends may be more symbolic than useful because he can't really clean up or fix things too well, the intentions and feelings behind his effort are very important. Overlooking the lack of skill and praising his effort, no matter how inadequate it may seem, will produce long term positive results that far exceed short-term inefficiency.

Some deeds may not be easy to rectify. When four-year-old Maryam calls Grandma an "old fatso" in a fit of anger, it might take some thought and effort to make amends. However, this is

Maryam's problem and she needs to do something to fix it. In the discussion that follows, Mommy or Daddy can help Maryam realize what she has done and think of possible good deeds she can do as reparation. Maybe she can pick some flowers for Grandma, or color her a picture for an "I'm sorry" card. Maybe she can offer to run errands for her. Maybe a simple kiss and hug with a nice request for forgiveness will be enough. Ultimately, it will depend on Grandma herself.

Time Out: Dealing with Anger and Negative Emotions

This technique is described in childcare books as a system of calming a child who is out of control, by isolating him temporarily, whether in a corner or a separate room, or by having him lie down in seclusion for a period. It is a term borrowed from sports, with connotations that suit the situation. We will use it here to discuss and describe methods for both parent and child to regain control of emotions.

Now and then anyone may lose control, whether in anger or tears or laughter; emotions take over, and logic and reasoning cease to function. This fits with the Prophet 's description of emotional outbursts:

> The Sons of Adam have been created of different types. Some get angry late and return to normal soon. Some become angry soon and return to normal soon, and some become angry late and return to normal late; the return to normalcy (of such people) is according to their quickness in getting angry. But be careful! Some people get angry soon and return to normal late. Listen—the best people among these are those who get angry late and repent at once, and the worst among these are those who get angry soon but return to normal late. *(Tirmidhi)*

Often there is no way to deal *rationally* with a person in an emotionally upset state. Fortunately, it usually doesn't last long. If we wait until it has passed, we can often do much better in dealing with whatever brought on the outburst of emotion. Time out does not necessarily mean "end of problem"; it means to stop normal activity in order to calm down, so that when normal life resumes, we can go back and do something constructive.

Children are very prone to such outbursts. Little ones are so obvious in their ability to switch from tears to laughter, from anger to affection, for they have not lived long enough to learn other ways of handling their emotions. The time-out technique takes a little persistence and patience on the part of parents, but it offers long-term benefits by teaching a child the habit of giving himself time and space to regain self-control when strong emotions hit.

People who use this technique generally attach a time limit to it so that the child is reassured by knowing that it's temporary. Time lengths for small children should be short because they can generally switch in and out of emotional states very quickly, and because they have short attention spans. Parents can define a time-out in a variety of ways to adapt to the current situation and whatever works with their particular child. Time-outs should be imposed calmly and without anger. The child should know that this is not a punishment as such, but rather a means of helping him get under control.

In some cases—for example, when a young child is running around the living room screaming—he or she can simply be swept up and placed in a bedroom. "You need to be here for the next five minutes (or until you calm down)." The door is then closed firmly and in a business-like manner, without anger. The child may accept this in a reasonably peaceful manner since he knows that time-out for such behavior is the rule of the house. Recognizing the justice of the consequences of his action, he may even be asleep or quietly playing when the time is up and Mom opens the door. A variation is to put an egg timer or stop watch in the room with the child so that he can time himself and know when it's time to come out.

But children are unique individuals and what works well for one may be devastating to another. A different child might feel totally cut off with the above method and respond much better to standing quietly in a corner of the room, sitting like a quiet statue in a chair, or with his head down on a table. One mother described having her two sons lie down on the floor at opposite ends of the room with furniture in between them so they couldn't see each other. She would sit quietly in a chair between them, reading or knitting for the required time.

This method can resolve a lot of the bad behavior that starts when a group of children gets giddy and excited together, or starts one of those common fights in which everyone says, "He started it!" Usually no follow-up is needed, because the collective spell is broken by the time-out. However, if necessary, some calm group discussion of the problem may be in order afterwards.

It is not uncommon for a child to model his behavior on that of a parent who has a quick, hot temper which he feels it is his right to unleash on the members of his household, and even outside, whenever it happens to flare up. Such a household is always churning with the energy of uncontrolled emotions, either of the parent or the child. A parent of this sort may be after his child for having a short temper, but he never asks himself where the child gets the example for this. Because he is not in the habit of taking an accounting of himself, such a parent never deals with the issue of how he can expect to teach his children to control their emotions if he doesn't control his own. Conveniently forgotten or ignored are also the innumerable Islamic injunctions about controlling anger.

Be quick in the race for forgiveness from your Lord
and for a Garden whose width is that of the heavens

and the earth, prepared for those who are mindful of Allah: those who spend (freely), whether in prosperity or adversity, and who restrain anger and forgive people—and Allah loves those who do good; and those who, when they commit an indecency or wrong their souls, remember Allah and ask for forgiveness for their sins—and who forgives sins except Allah?—and do not persist in what they did while they know (that it was wrong). (Qur'an 3:133-135)

A man said to the Prophet (S), "Give me (some) advice." He said, "Do not be angry." He (the man) repeated it several times. He said , "Do not be angry." *(Bukhari, 8.137)*

A man came to the Messenger of Allah (S) and said, "O Messenger of Allah, teach me some words which I can live by. Do not make them too much for me, lest I forget." The Messenger of Allah, said, "Do not be angry." *(Muwatta)*

The strong one is not the one who throws (people) down, but the strong one is the one who controls himself in the face of anger. *(Bukhari, 8.135,* and *Muwatta)*

No one swallows anything more excellent in the sight of Allah, the Great and Glorious, than anger which he restrains, seeking to please Allah Most High. *(Mishkat, 5116,* transmitted by *Ahmad)*

These are the words of Allah Ta'ala and His noble Messenger (S). They contrast sharply with present-day attitudes concerning the expression of one's feelings. Modern psychology would have us believe that it is emotionally unhealthy to repress anger, as well as being useless, because the anger will express itself later in a different way. But the theories of any discipline reflect the overall orientation of the society in which they originate. This theory may appeal to the understanding of non-Muslims, but it is completely at odds with the Islamic teachings.

Anger is an emotional expression. All emotions are natural feelings. We are responsible for our acts, but not for our feelings. Therefore someone may feel angry, but he is not guilty of anything until he allows his anger to push him into saying something nasty, or hitting, or doing some other negative act. Because a Muslim knows of the perfect justice of Allah, anger does not need to be expressed by drawing violent pictures, screaming, or kicking the garbage can. When he controls himself and the violence of the emotion passes, he can work on remembering the justice and rewards he will have for doing the right thing. If some justice can be obtained here on earth, from whatever made him angry, he can now seek that in an appropriate way. This doesn't mean that he won't still feel anger, but it will be an emotion under control. Maybe he will see the situation differently when he has time to reflect. Maybe he will feel sorry because *he* was wrong. If not, he knows Allah will never let him be the loser if he acts according to Islam, and no one will ever get away with wrong doing forever.

> Deal not unjustly and ye shall not be dealt with unjustly. (Qur'an 2:279)

> And fear the Day when ye shall be brought back to Allah. Then shall every soul be paid what it earned and none shall be dealt with unjustly. (Qur'an 2:281)

And the Prophet (S) left some clear directives about how to deal with anger.

Two men insulted each other in the presence of the Prophet (S), and one of the two became angry, and his anger increased until his face became swollen and changed. Then the Prophet (S) said, "I know a word such that, if he says it, whatever is with him will go away." Then the man was told of the saying of the Prophet (S), and he said, "Seek refuge in Allah from Satan the Rejected. . ." (*Bukhari, 8.74; Abu Dawud, 4762)*

When one of you becomes angry while standing, he should sit down. If the anger leaves him, it is well; otherwise he should lie down. *(Abu Dawud, 4764; Mishkat, 5114)*

Some are swift to anger and swift to cool down, the one (characteristic) making up for the other; some are slow to anger and slow to cool down, the one making up for the other; but the best of you are those who are slow to anger and swift to cool down, and the worst of you are those who are swift to anger and slow to cool down. Beware of anger, for it is a live coal on the heart of the Son of Adam. Do you not notice the swelling of the veins of his neck and the redness of his eyes? So when one experiences such a thing, he should lie down and cling to the earth. *(Mishkat, 5145,* transmitted by *Tirmidhi)*

Anger comes from Satan. Satan was created of fire and fire is extinguished by water; so when one of you becomes angry, he should make wudu. *(Abu Dawud, 4766)*

Now let's return to the concrete realities of dealing with anger in two examples. In our first example, it's been a long hard day. Mom is busy cooking supper. The children have started running around in the next room, screaming wildly. Suddenly they dash through the kitchen while she's carrying the salad to the table. As Majid darts around her, Abdul-Kareem bumps into her. Suddenly, there is salad all over his head and on the floor. First one and then the other doubles up with laughter at the funny sight, as Mom looks at the salad oil stains appearing on Abdul-Kareem's shirt. Mom sees that she now has a major clean-up of the kitchen to do and will have to give Abdul-Kareem a bath before supper besides—and meanwhile Daddy is sitting in the living room, relaxing with a magazine and calling for his dinner.

Mom's patience snaps. She starts yelling and tries to swat the salad-covered child on the seat. He dodges and runs out of the room, spreading the salad mess onto the carpet. The other boy runs for cover. By the time Mom has everything back in order, supper is late, she is frantically upset and exhausted, and the kids are resting up for the "before bed" uproar.

Actually, Mom is a diligent, devoted, thoughtful parent. She tries hard to keep a neat, well-run home, feeding her family good nutritious meals. But at times she does allow her children to play noisily in the family room and run around the house, particularly when the weather is bad outside. She accepts this as normal but realizes that sometimes it gets out of hand.

For another example see Daddy, a hard-working man, and his work is all for his family. Every evening he comes home tired from the noise and pressure of his job. His vision of home is a haven of peace and quiet where he can relax. Unfortunately, his three children frequently start acting up shortly after he sits down to relax. Sometimes they are just noisy, wrestling on the floor or running around. Often, though, they erupt into fights.

Ignoring them at first in the hope that they'll stop by themselves, Daddy slowly propels himself to take charge and yells at his children to stop the noise. Calm ensues for a few minutes. Then things are "back to normal," as the children, knowing their father, resume their usual interaction.

Daddy yells again. In response, Sara comes crying to him that Umar took her doll and won't give it back. Daddy explodes, pulling himself out of his chair, ordering the children to their rooms, screaming and threatening. Fifteen minutes later, dinner is served to the tired, ill-tempered family. An hour later, the kids are off to get ready for bed. All they've seen of their father tonight is a hot-tempered grouch.

In fact, Daddy is right to expect a pleasant, peaceful home to return to at the end of the day. Why shouldn't he have sweet, loving children who greet him and make him feel relaxed instead of this uproar? He is a good man with high ideals for his family, and he usually manages well with them on weekends and vacations. The question is, how could he manage a situation like this better?

Controlling anger and other negative emotions may sound all very well in theory, but putting it into practice frequently seems impossible. In an old example of how difficult it is to change, a young man fresh out of an agricultural college once tried to tell an old farmer about new farming ideas. The old farmer stopped the young man short, saying, "Sorry, son, don't bother me with all that new stuff. I already know more about what I should be doing than I can do right now."

How many of us are like that farmer? We know the Islamic teachings, are aware of our faults and wish we could do better, but somehow seem unable to change. Preoccupied with other affairs, we squeeze in managing our children by yelling at them to "stop that fighting" or "clean up that room." Setting a good table and having a proper meal on time is often a higher priority for mothers than controlling the kids, which is often seen as a nuisance, an unwanted intrusion into her well-planned schedule. Fathers often feel no responsibility for child behavior and react badly when called upon to "do something" about misbehavior. It's either not their job or they always—stress *always*—have "more important" things to do.

The first step toward change is making the decision that a change should be made, and giving this change priority. Knowing both what Islam teaches about yelling, scolding and losing control, and how unproductive it is, parents have to commit themselves to change. The second step is to actually control anger. Before any other changes can be made, a person must be in control of himself. And giving us this self-control is among the purposes of praying and fasting.

The following are more Islamic guidelines for the control of anger. We can use them ourselves and can teach them to our children when they are old enough.

> And if an evil suggestion from Satan incites you, seek refuge in Allah. Truly, He is All-Hearing, All-Knowing. (Qur'an 7:200)

> If the Prophet was angry and he was standing, he would sit down. If he was seated, he would lie down, and the anger would go away. *(Abu Dawud* and *Ibn Abi Dunya)*

> If you are angry, keep silent. *(Ahmad)*

> Practice silence. This is a way of causing Satan to run away. It is a support to you in the matter of your religion. *(Ahmad)*

> The one who keeps silent will be safe. *(Mishkat, 4836,* transmitted by *Ahmad, Tirmidhi, Darimi* and *Baihaqi)*

> A judge should not judge between two persons while he is angry. *(Bukhari, 9.272)*

Do not invoke Allah's curse, Allah's anger, or Hell.
(Abu Dawud, 4888)

Al-Ghazali, the noted twelfth century Islamic scholar, offered a list of useful aids in controlling anger:
1. Recognize that you are angry.
2. Remember the reward for not being angry.
3. Remember the consequences and punishment that may come from it.
4. Remember how ugly you look when angry.
5. Reflect on why you think punishment of the culprits would be better than forgiveness.
6. Accept Allah's Will when circumstances are beyond your control.

One stage in learning to control anger is seen when a person trying to control his anger utters a prayer for help and forgiveness, but does so with the expression and tone of an angry person who is cursing. The words and the expression clash, and may seem humorous and perhaps hypocritical. But in fact, this is a very positive sign. The person has learned the first step toward control, control of the tongue, and gradually this will extend to the controlling of the rest of him, until his heart and emotions come under his control.

But once parents are in control of themselves, that is not "the end of these problems." Controlling emotion is but one step toward getting the mind free and clear to solve problems in a positive, rational way. We should not just suffer or blunder passively through life's tests. Rather, we are expected to actively think and investigate the multiple possibilities available for solving our problems. Allah Ta'ala gives us some guidelines in this direction:

The good and the evil deed are not alike. Repel (evil) with what is better. (Qur'an 41:34)

Then it was by mercy from Allah that you were gentle
to them. And if you had been severe and hard-hearted, they would have broken away from you; so pardon them and ask for (Allah's) forgiveness for them,
and consult them in (deciding) affairs. (Qur'an 3:159)

For our first example, once Mom avoids screaming abuses at
her children, or, alternatively, aboids laments and complaints about
how much she suffers, or running after them, trying to catch one to
vent her anger with a swat (a common parental approach), she may
find a multitude of better ways to manage her situation. An older
child might be asked to help finish the meal preparation or get the
salad-covered child into the shower. Daddy might be called in to
help. Another child might be asked to pick the salad off the floor,
set the table, or help in making more salad. Mom might also
require the children to apologize to her for being so careless.

Additionally, she might consider how they could spend their
time at the end of the day more constructively. They, too, are
tired and hungry. A mid-afternoon snack of apples and milk or
yogurt might keep them in better control until the evening meal.
Fighting with them, however, is sure to make any positive outcome very difficult. In short, positive problem-solving approaches will yield constructive results. Anger, arguing, blaming, shaming, scolding, and complaining are all negative and cannot be
expected to yield any useful short- or long-term results.

For our second example, Daddy has an important role to
play. He has the right to respect from his children and family.
If he wants a quiet, relaxing period when he returns home from
work, they should respect his wishes and try to cooperate.
Multiple possibilities toward that end exist, depending on the
family and their perception of the problem.

Perhaps changing Daddy's idea of homecoming a bit can
smooth the atmosphere. Instead of coming in and plopping
himself down in front of the television or hiding behind a news-
paper, he could plan ten to fifteen minutes of relaxing on the

couch with his children. "Come and see Daddy! I've missed you all day." Children get bored with Mommy by the end of the day, just as she gets tired of being alone with them and her housework for hours on end. A few minutes of positive attention from Daddy, reinforced by a hug, can often give a child the boost that keeps him from teasing his sibling. Remember, misbehavior and fighting between siblings are frequently used by children as a way of attracting the parents' attention.

Physical Punishment

We now come to a controversial and somewhat difficult subject, that of physical punishment. In this society, burdened as it is with horrendous forms of child abuse, corporal punishment has become almost a bad word. Even young children know that to secure intervention from the authorities, all they have to do is call 911 and claim that their parents hit or otherwise abused them. In some states, any form of corporal punishment other than hitting a child on the bottom with the flat of the hand legally constitutes abuse. Where then does this leave parents in enforcing discipline with their children?

Let us begin by examining the Islamic guidelines. It is mentioned in hadith that the Prophet (S) never struck anyone with his hand, neither a woman nor a servant (Muslim, 5756). However, he also gave the instruction to,

> Order your children to pray when they become seven years old, and spank them for it when they become ten years old . . . *(Abu Dawud, 0495, 0494)*

In addition, Mu'adh bin Jabal (R) reported that the Messenger of Allah (S) instructed him to do ten things. The ninth and tenth among them were,

> Do not refrain from using pressure (on your children) with a view to training them. Inculcate in them

the fear of Allah. *(Mishkat, 0061,* transmitted by *Ahmad)*

Physical punishment is therefore not prohibited in Islam. Rather, the necessity of it under certain conditions is recognized and upheld. The Prophet (S) himself was patient for years under the oppression of the pagans of Makkah, but when the order came from Allah to resort to force, he was ready for that. And Allah, the All-Knowing, was best aware that all other options had been tried.

By utilizing the techniques outlined above, we can usually manage most situations with our children without resorting to force. However, there are times when taking that extra step is warranted and desirable. Allah is Compassionate and Merciful, but He is also infinitely Just, and Hell does, after all, exist.

Let's suppose that in a given situation all other methods have failed and Mom or Dad feels a spanking is in order. The main purpose of a spanking is to demonstrate to the child the seriousness of his mistake and his parent's displeasure. It is not intended to hurt severely but rather to embarrass the child with the knowledge that his parent had to resort to this most severe step. When it is used only on rare occasions by a parent who is normally kind and in control, it will have a very strong impact without requiring a hard-handed approach.

There are no specific ahadith defining physical punishment for children, with the exception of those dealing with praying which we have already cited. However, the Islamic guidelines, derived by scholars from hadith, are the following:
1. Do not hit the face, head, or tender parts of the body.
2. Do not hit hard enough to leave a mark on the skin.
3. Do not spank when you feel you might lose control.

Let us now look at a case in which physical punishment might be appropriate. A mother noticed that her two boys, ages five and seven, were fascinated by matches. She had strictly forbidden the boys to touch them, but while checking up on them one day, she found them hiding in the garage trying to light matches. Recalling an incident in which a neighbor's three-year-old set fire to the house by lighting matches in her closet, she thanked Allah that she had found them in time. She immediately confiscated the matches and sent the boys to sit quietly in the house for a five-minute time-out.

Several days later, the mother saw a scorched mark on the garage wall and several burnt matches on the ground that had not been there previously. She summoned the boys, who hung their heads and evaded her eyes as she questioned them. The crime was serious: they had disobeyed her, had done something she had warned them was dangerous, and had deliberately hidden their act from her.

Although she had never hit her sons before, the mother was very disturbed about their having repeated this dangerous act. Trembling in her concern, she took each boy in turn by the arm and gave him two firm swats on his seat with her hand. Then she walked away and avoided speaking to them until they pleaded for forgiveness fifteen minutes later.

Such punishment teaches a lesson that no amount of talking can, especially to small children who are not used to being spanked. But what of a child who is so disobedient, rebellious, or difficult that hitting is the only way to get through to him? He is repeatedly spanked by his mother, beaten by his father, but nothing changes. And such children are not uncommon.

Behavior of this kind—both on the part of the child and on the part of the parent who has to keep resorting to force— points to some underlying problem with one or both. It is the basic problem which must be addressed; the repeated beatings are only a symptom of some deeper disturbance operating on the child or his parent, or on the interaction between them.

The child's problem could be of various kinds: he has an extreemly strong need to be in control, he was spoiled when little to the point at which he rebels at all authority and discipline, he has found the best way to get attention from his parents is through disruptive behavior, he has an undetected physical problem or biochemical imbalance, he has a learning disability, or any number of other possible problems. The parent's (or parents') problem might be the following: consistently chosing to exhibit angry, uncontrolled behavior instead of reasoning and offering gentle but firm guidance; a conflict of approach between one soft, gentle parent and a stern, harsh parent, with the child caught in between; lack of parenting skills; and, in the worst case, a pathological desire to hurt and humiliate the child. It is also possible that the parent may be too exhausted by the various demands upon him or her to cope more effectively, or that he or she may have some undiagnosed physical or emotional problem.

For all of these there is help. The first help is through patience and prayer, seeking guidance from Allah. And the second, help from human sources, deserves a section all to itself.

GETTING HELP

Sometimes a situation gets so out of hand that the parents feel they need outside help. At other times, the parents feel they don't need and don't wish to seek outside help, although it is called for and needed.

Wise, older close relatives are usually preferred for advice in settling disputes. An Islamic scholar, *imam,* or simply an understanding, mature individual in the community, man or woman, can be consulted. When a Muslim is available to consult with, it is preferable to consulting a non-Muslim, since a Muslim will obviously understand the Islamic point of view and orientation more easily than someone else would.

> And if two groups among the believers fight, make
> peace between them. But if one of them has trans-
> gressed against the other, fight against the one which

has transgressed until it returns to Allah's orders. Then if it returns, make peace between them with justice and fairness. Truly, Allah loves those who are fair. The believers are but brothers, so make peace between your two (contending) brothers and be mindful of Allah in order that you may be shown mercy. (Qur'an 49:9-10)

The Prophet (S) used to fast on Mondays and Thursdays, and when someone remarked on this to him he said, "On Monday and Thursday Allah forgives every Muslim, excepting two who are at variance, for He says they must be left until they make peace with one other." *(Mishkat, 2073,* transmitted by *Ahmad and Ibn Majah)*

The gates of Paradise are not opened except on two days, Monday and Thursday, and then every servant (of Allah) is granted pardon who does not associate anything with Allah, excepting the person in whose (heart) there is enmity against his brother. And it will be said, "Look at both of them until there is reconciliation, look at both of them until there is reconciliation, look at both of them until there is reconciliation." *(Muslim, 6222; Muwatta)*

An example: Timmor and his twelve-year-old son Yunus are bitterly at odds. Timmor has been strict about sending Yunus to the weekend Islamic school but the boy rebels, refuses to study, and creates a discipline problem at the school as well as at home. This father and his wife have exhausted all their efforts to talk to the boy, encouraging him to study through rewards for good grades, punishing him by withholding privileges, grounding him, and forbidding him allowance money or TV time.

Living far away from their families, they have no relatives to turn to for help. The public school and Yunus' non-Muslim friends seem to encourage the boy to rebel. In despair, they go to speak with a mature woman in the community, knowledgeable about the Islamic faith and with the experience of having reard boys older than Yunus, who are recognized in the Muslim community as well-adjusted.

This woman talks to the parents and listens to their story. Then she talks to Yunus alone and finds that his sole desire is to be "normal" like his friends at school, one of their crowd. This desire is stronger in him just now than his desire to please his parents, much less Allah. In addition, he sees many people and occurrences at the Islamic school that he finds unacceptable, Islamically and otherwise, and which compare unfavorably with his public school. Attendance at the school also cuts off his Saturdays from participating in sports and other activities with his friends.

There are many ways of handling this problem, each option determined by the particular circumstances of the family and their personalities. The boy might profit from a summer, or perhaps a whole year, of staying with Muslim relatives and enjoying the companionship of his cousins and their friends. Islamic summer camp is a good option where available, one that might encourage strong relationships between Yunus and other boys his age from similar backgrounds. Yunus's distance from his parents during the time away might help him to discover that he *can* have fun with Muslim friends, without his parents' constant reminders that they want him to.

Perhaps travel is too expensive. The advisor knows two other families who have boys of similar age and whose parents probably would easily mix socially with Yunus' family. They could invite them over for a barbecue. Go to visit them. Make friends within the Muslim community to strengthen the support system necessary for the whole family. The parents could start a boys' club, organized sports, camping trips, outings to bowling alleys, science museums, or whatever, encouraging the boys toward clean, healthy fun together. After rapport is established, hopefully Yunus will enjoy being part of a circle of Muslim boys his age. In later years, this may be a motivation for him to work to acquire the knowledge that will help him become a leader or at least an important member of the Muslim community.

At the same time, the parents need to listen to Yunus' objections concerning the local Islamic school, investigate them for themselves, and, if his claims are well-founded, they need to let Yunus know that they share his concerns. Perhaps there is constant misbehavior among the children at the school, or harsh attitudes on the part of the teachers. Perhaps the building is so shoddy and poorly maintained that it stands in sharp contrast to Yunus' other school, or it may be that the organization of the school, the curriculum, and so on, are not workable. If parents see that their child's objections to the school are not entirely without basis, they will have more sympathy for his feelings on the matter. And this should impel them to take some action to improve the school for their son's sake, volunteering in whatever capacity they can fill best.

Being a good neighbor and on friendly terms with non-Muslims is important and necessary. Nevertheless, our faith community is the Muslim community, and it is there we can expect to receive, and also to give, the greatest support. We need to encourage social relations among Muslim children so that they are not obliged to choose exclusively non-Muslim friends. If the Muslims around us are not so admirable, this may be simply a reflection of the difficult conditions that the Muslim ummah, and indeed the entire community of human beings, is passing through at this point in time. Our challenge and responsibility is to try to improve the condition of the Muslim community around us, and to find other like-minded people who share the same values, in the process of which we will reach out into the non-Muslim community as well.

No solution to problems between parents and children can be expected to work overnight. It is normal for such relationships to change as a child becomes an adult, and Yunus is entering that stage of transition. Are his parents still treating him like Mommy's little baby? Gradually parents and children need to adjust to allow the emerging young adult more responsibility and more say.

When does a parent decide that he or she needs more help than is available within the Muslim community—in other words, when it's time to talk over the problem with a non-Muslim counselor, therapist, or psychiatrist, if no such Muslim professionals are available? There is no easy answer to this, but when the parents reach the point of being so worried and upset by the situation that they feel something must be done about it, it is clearly time.

If the problem relates to a handicap or a disability of some kind, of course any sensitive qualified specialist is probably good, but when the problem is psychological, the moral character of the advisor should be of the highest priority. Psychological problems can be viewed as illness or as troubling of the soul. Certainly there are a variety of possible treatments, and medication may be necessary in extreme cases. While comming closer to Allah (SWT) is perhaps only part of the cure, it is essential for a Muslim and we need understanding from any advisor on this point.

Many Muslims will feel a sense of humiliation or uneasiness about consulting a non-Muslim professional. In some ways this is justified. No one wants to open his or her deep personal problems to a stranger, and a non-Muslim stranger at that. This naturally gives rise to the fear that this non-Muslim will not understand our point of view as Muslims, that he or she will try to impose non-Islamic values or solutions on us. There might also be the uneasy sense that we have in some sense violated Islam by opening the problems of Muslims to the eyes of an outsider.

But there are therapists and therapists, doctors and doctors. No one is committed to continuing with a professional—of any kind—whose services do not satisfy or who does not do what one senses needs to be done. If help is needed, it is best to choose a therapist who is known and recommended by someone whose judgment we trust. If this is not possible and one is forced to pick a name at random out of the telephone book in making the initial appointment, specific questions should be asked of or concerning the therapist.

What is his or her method of approach? Is he or she religious, and if so what is the orientation? If the answers to these questions are satisfactory, an initial appointment may be made. Then, if the therapist seems to be a person who is respectful of the Islamic viewpoint, and a good therapist will honor the belief system and values of his or her clients, we may continue with him or her. If not, we simply do not go back and we find one who is more suitable, even if this involves several trials. Continuing therapy when the "chemistry" or understanding between oneself and a therapist is not a good one may do more harm than good. It must be repeated that a therapist who is committed to respect for his or her clients will not attempt to impose solutions which originate in the therapist's own worldview, but will try to work out solutions that fit with the understanding of the client.

PARENTAL RESOLVE

> O you who believe, save yourselves and your families from a fire whose fuel is men and stones. (Qur'an 66:6)

> And know that your possessions and your children are only a test, and that with Allah is a tremendous reward. (Qur'an 8:28 and 64:15)

Be moderate and stand firm in trouble that falls to
the lot of a Muslim, as that is an expiation for him,
even stumbling on the path or the pricking of a
thorn. *(Muslim, 6243)*

The Prophet (S) used to pray: "O Allah, I beg of
You steadfastness in (my) affairs and determination
in (doing) righteousness." *(Mishkat, 0955,* transmitted by al-Nasa'i*)*

These verses and ahadith remind us of the necessity of
standing firm with our children on important issues. When a
parent is loving and caring, it is sometimes very hard for him to
say "No" to his or her child. However, children are born to test
the limits of their parents' resolve. Some children are more
strong-willed than others and can even prove to be more strong-
willed than their parents. "Be easy on him, he's little," may
sound loving and kind, and it probably is intended to be, but the
fact is that we are *not* kind to our children when we allow them
to develop bad habits, manipulate us into obeying them, get
away with rude or obnoxious behavior, or act irresponsibly.

There is room for indulgence, because children are children
and cannot be expected to learn mature behavior overnight.
But by continually working with them and encouraging them
toward better ways of behaving, we may gently guide them
toward good habits, manners, sharing, helping and cooperating
with others, remembering Allah and striving to please Him, and
all the other good characteristics that we hope to instill in our
children.

There are no hard-and-fast rules on handling an obstinate
child who refuses to put his coat on before leaving the house on
a cold day, or refuses to wash his dirty hands, or starts screaming in a store because Mommy refuses to buy him some toy.
Allah, in His Wisdom, has trusted parents to be sensitive to
their children and to use their common sense.

An example: It's freezing cold outside but Huda refuses to put on her coat before going out with Daddy. If it's not really necessary to take her, Daddy can simply leave her there. In situations like this, instead of engaging in a screaming match or argument with a stubborn child, just walking away and letting the child taste the consequence of stubbornness serves as an excellent shaper-upper.

However, if Huda *must* go, Daddy may be obliged to put the coat on her as she screams and kicks, and then cart her off to the car as matter-of-factly as possible. Alternatively, he might decide to take her and her coat separately, and wait until she asks for it once she is outside. Again, another member of the family might intervene to break the deadlock. A time-out might work here. The important thing is that the parents remain in charge. Daddy and Mommy decide the rules, not their child, by whatever means of manipulation he or she may choose to use at the moment. Some rules are flexible and others are unchangeable. And one unchangeable, fixed rule is to respect the parents and their word.

All children want and need limits and guidelines. If none are set, they often become more and more naughty, and at the same time more anxious, for they sense that they are out of control and need to be stopped. In such a situation, a child will test his parents and push them until they set limits for him, either by stopping him or by punishment. Many parents suppose that a child out of control is merely being naughty, while in reality he is demanding that controls—which he is unable to impose upon himself due to his immaturity—be established.

A young child's misbehavior should be stopped either by words or simple physical restraint or redirection. "Ahmed, now we're going to go to the other room to play with the new puzzle instead"; "Time to eat now, Sajidah. You don't want to? Well, let's get you into your high chair anyhow"; "Rami, let's get you headed to bed now. You can listen to this tape tomorrow." However, many parents make the mistake of entering into discussions with young children, or asking them what they would like to do: "Do you want to go now or later?" "Would you like peanut butter or cream cheese on your sandwich?" "What do you want to wear—your red sweater or your white one?"

But while this is appropriate in dealing with an older child, it certainly is not with a young one. Mothers or fathers are supposed to make such decisions for young children; then life proceeds smoothly and without questions or challenges. Otherwise, if everything becomes a matter for discussion or opinions, we have a long series of "No," "But," arguments and challenges from the child that can go on and on until some firm action is imposed by the parents.

Early childhood is not a time for entering into discussions or asking a child's opinions. It is a time when children learn routines and what is expected of them in the normal course of life. A case in point is bedtimes.

No young child ever wants to go to bed or goes voluntarily; there are too many exciting things to do while awake. But if there are rules about bedtimes, no discussion or argument should be allowed concerning it. On the special occasions when the child is allowed to stay up late, this should be because the parents feel it is suitable, not because the child badgers or bullies them into saying yes. As a general rule of thumb, parents should never give in to such tactics but should make sure that the child knows that he cannot manipulate them in such a way.

Many parents have difficulty distinguishing between firmness of purpose and stern force. Either they are overly permissive, allowing their children to rule them, or they are overly strict, yelling and slapping their children into obedience. Such parents are unable to enjoy their children because they have not worked out a system of getting good behavior out of them. Other parents are models of inconsistency; their "no" means "maybe" and "maybe" means "yes." If the child pouts, wheedles, teases, or behaves nastily enough, they will give in, per-

haps without a struggle. But something is seriously wrong
with such approaches.

Firmness of purpose is a quality necessary for sane parenting, in keeping with Allah's command to the Prophet (S):

> Then, when you have determined (on a course of
> action), put your trust in Allah. Truly, Allah loves
> those who put their trust in Him. (Qur'an 3:159)

It involves deciding what is right in a given situation and
acting on it with determination. Especially when the commands
of Allah are involved, we need to take decisive action and stand
firm—for example, in the case of lying, bullying other children, treating adults disrespectfully, or refusing to pray, naturally taking the child's age and level of development into account.
We can emphasize to our children that these are the rules which
Allah made, and we submit to them ourselves and expect them
to do likewise.

As regards rules coming from human sources, we can be
much more flexible. A pediatrician may advise an eight p.m.
bedtime, for example, but it happens that a particular child isn't
sleepy that early and seems to do fine with an eight-thirty or
nine o'clock bedtime. A neighbor's daughter of the same age
may fall asleep on the sofa at 7:00 every night if her mother
doesn't get her into bed first. No need to make an issue over
this; on any given night, fifteen or twenty minutes more or less
will never be noticed.   But caring for our child's health is part
of our responsibility to Allah. We need to allow for adequate
sleep and to be firm about it, even in our flexibility.

At the same time, it is important to avoid standing firm "for
the sake of Islam." Make clear to yourself and to the child the
origin of your restriction. "It's eight o'clock and time for good
little Muslims to be in bed," might be misinterpreted. There is
nothing in Qur'an or hadith about eight o'clock pm bedtimes
being fard. Saying instead, "I am responsible before Allah for

your health and education, and I have decided that you need an 8:00 bedtime to be up in good form for school."

Don't put Islamic "reasons" on things unrelated to Islam, and when your goal is fulfilling an Islamic injunction, be flexible in realizing that there may be other means to the same goal if the means you have chosen creates opposition. As an example, years ago a mother bought several pairs of polyester double-knit pants for her daughters, liking the convenience of the fabric and the style. She pushed them on her daughters with the explaination that they should dress with Islamic modesty. The daughters grew up thinking that wearing polyester pants, which they detested, was part of Islam, and they became resentful toward Islam as a result.

We need to continually check our motives: Am I making an issue out of this for the sake of Allah or because I like making issues with my children? Is this really important or am I blowing up the matter out of all proportion? Will my making an issue out of this have a beneficial effect or a harmful one? The rule of thumb should be to avoid making issues out of small matters but to save our "fire power" for important matters or issues of principle. Taking time out to consider these questions is important. And central to any change is prayer and seeking guidance from Allah:

> O you who believe, seek help through patience and prayer. Truly, Allah is with the patient. (Qur'an 2:153, 45; 8:46)

> A strong believer is better and dearer to Allah than a weak one. Among all good things, desire what is most beneficial for you. Continue to ask Allah for help and do not stop. If you are afflicted in any way, do not say, "If I had taken this or that step, it would have resulted in such-and-such," but say only,"Allah

decreed it and He did as He willed." The word "if"
opens the doors of evil conduct. *(Muslim)*

Safeguard the commands of Allah and you will find
Him in front of you. Remember Him in prosperity
and He will remember you in adversity. Be sure that
whatever makes you fall into error will not guide
you to the right path and whatever leads you to good
will not deprive you. Remember that the help of
Allah is for those who are patient, and that prosperity follows adversity, and that there is ease after hardship. *(Tirmidhi)*

Even with our firm commitment to seek the right solutions
to problems and implement them in the best way we can, we
are bound to make mistakes, for we are human and this is how
we have been created. We ask Allah to forgive our mistakes,
those we know about and those we don't realize. And once we
realize these errors, we should correct them as best we can.

Sometimes a child is hurt by a parent. Maybe the parent
loses control in anger and slaps him. Or perhaps a parent tells
others about mistakes the child has made and embarrasses him.
Maybe the parent punishes the child for something he didn't do
or did accidentally.

If parents—intentionally or otherwise—do something
which harms or hurts their child, an apology is in order. When
a parent puts away his pride and humbles himself enough to say
"I'm sorry" when he has done something unjust (perhaps following it by some small gift or special act of kindness), the
child will understand that this is correct and appropriate behavior, and will model himself on it. And conversely, if a child is
hurt by a parent but the parent justifies or stubbornly insists
that he was right, the child will learn by this example. Children
have a keen sense of justice, and, as much as adults, they
deserve that justice be done to them. As Muslims, we should

not hesitate to admit our mistakes and ask forgiveness, not only from Allah but from the ones we have harmed. In addition, we should try to make whatever reparation is possible if the situation warrants this.

> O you who believe, stand firmly for justice, witnesses to Allah, and even if is against yourselves, or your parents, or your kin (Qur'an 4:135)

> The one who has wronged his brother concerning his honor or anything else should ask his forgiveness before the Day on which he will have neither dirham nor dinar (that is, neither wealth nor possessions to help him). If he has good deeds, they will be taken from him in proportion to his wrong doings. And if he has no good deeds (in his account), the evil deeds of his companion will be taken and loaded upon him. *(Bukhari, 3.629)*

> The Prophet (S) said, "Do you know who is poor?" They (the companions of the Prophet) said, "Among us, a poor man is one who has neither dirham nor wealth." He (the Prophet) said, "The poor one among my ummah is the one who will come on the Day of Resurrection with prayers and fasts and zakah, but he will have abused others, slandered others, unlawfully taken the wealth of others, and shed the blood of others and beaten others, and his virtues will be credited to the account of one (who suffered at his hand). And if his good deeds fall short of clearing the account, his sins will be entered into (his account) and he will be thrown into Hellfire. *(Muslim, 6251)*

> He who slaps his slave or beats him, the expiation
> for it is that he should set him free. *(Muslim, 4078)*

We have examples in the Prophet (S) and his companions, who publicly admitted making mistakes. We recall the Qur'anic verses, 80:1-10, which came to correct the Prophet (S) when he ignored the questions of a poor blind Muslim to concentrate on his conversation with prominent disbelievers. Again, when a woman reminded the caliph Umar (R), the ruler of vast territories, that he had made a judgment concerning excessive dowry which contradicted a saying of the Prophet (S), he publicly admitted his mistake in the mosque in front of the assembled Muslims.

Being comfortable in admitting mistakes is a good example for our children. We are not perfect, they are not perfect. Allah alone is Perfect. We seek His guidance and try to improve. Likewise, we expect them to seek guidance, make an effort, and try to improve.

Chapter Seven

BROTHERS AND SISTERS

COMPETITION FOR ATTENTION

Each child offers a unique test to his parents, and a parent's relationship with each of his or her children is bound to be different. Accordingly, an only child, middle children, and a last child all present different opportunities and challenges.

Three factors play a major role in determining the relationship of a parent with any one of his or her children: the socioeconomic position of the parent (including the parent's time away from the child for work or social responsibilities), the existence of other children in the family (competition for parents' attention), and the interaction of this child's individual personality with that of his parent (the "chemistry" between the two).

The first factor is usually imposed upon the parent without much chance for alteration. However, the other two factors can be affected by an aware parent who makes a conscious effort to overcome the barriers that may be separating him or her from a positive relationship with a child.

BIRTH ORDER

A great deal has been spoken and written about the importance of birth order. The possible combinations are so multiple and complex that generalities concerning birth order are hard to make.

In the North American nuclear families that have been studied, the first-born usually gets more attention, as well as more pressure, from his parents than do subsequent children. He usually responds to this with a strong desire to live up to their expectations. An only child, who has his parents' undivided attention, may tend to be either selfish and spoiled or a responsible high achiever, depending on circumstances.

Middle children are frequently less noticed by parents. They are displaced by the new baby who is so cute and requires so much attention, at the same time getting hidden in the shadow of the eldest, who gives Mom and Dad their first experiences with kindergarten, the various later stages of school, and with how to raise children in general. The baby of the family frequently receives a different type of attention—indulgence or spoiling. He or she tends to become the least responsible among the siblings in the family. An only girl among several boys is usually reard differently than one reard with several sisters. And the number of years separating children can make a significant impact on their development.

These effects are normal. Allah, the All-Wise, All-Knowing Lord, knows the position of each child in the family, and this position is part of each person's vital statistics, like the color of his eyes or his mental ability. However, when a parent is aware of the importance of birth order, adjustments can be made to improve the balance in the treatment of his or her children.

For example, studies have shown that it is common for the oldest child to be given chores to do for the family. Many parents fail to pass these chores down as younger children grow up. Consequently, the younger ones never have chores, while the older ones are saddled with whatever work was assigned to them from the first year they were able to do any.

These studies become more significant in nuclear families with few children. In large, extended families the effects of parental attention are decreased because the parents' attention is spread further among more children, and because in an extended family, the presence of other adults—grandparents, aunts and uncles, and so on—provides many additional possibilities for adult attention that can counteract and compensate for less attention from of the parents.

PERSONAL CHEMISTRY

It is generally assumed that all parents love their children dearly. However, personality clashes of all sorts can occur even in parent-child relationships. A strict parent and a stubborn child will usually have fights. A gentle, meek parent with a strong, active child may become totally dominated by the child. An energetic, action-oriented parent with a low-key, sensitive, introspective child will have conflicts. All this appears to be a matter of personal "chemistry," or the interrelatedness of the souls which Allah has created:

> Souls are marshalled troops. The similar ones have affinity to each other and the dissimilar ones differ (among themselves). *(Bukhari, 4.552A and Muslim, 6376)*

Although it is usually an unspoken, secret feeling within a parent, the fact is, if we are honest, that most parents have favorites among their children. This is an affair of the heart, difficult to modify. Prophet Muhammad (S) is known to have had a favorite wife, first Khadijah and then later, after her death, A'isha. A parallel situation holds true between parents and their children—and likewise between children and their parents. Usually the affinity is a minor difference, normal, and causes no real problems in the total warm loving family group. Parents need to check themselves occasionally to see that they are not allowing these affinities to blind them to fair treatment of their children.

One child will have a certain way about himself that just speaks to his parent's heart; it is more difficult to be firm with this child, to refuse his requests. Another child may have characteristics that do just the opposite, that irrritate the parent, grate on his or her nerves—a whiny tone of voice or a certain way of smiling that reminds the parent of someone unpleasant in the past. But although the heart cannot be controlled or the personality changed dramatically, our actions *can* be controlled to create an environment in which we can appreciate the best that is in our children—all of them.

For both personality conflicts and birth-order inequalities, some general guidelines come to us from the Qur'an and *hadith*. First of all, it never supports family harmony to play favorites with our children or encourage them to compete with each other for superiority. Fostering the notion of a superior child is a form of self-righteousness and arrogance that can produce only hard feelings in the other children.

> Whenever you speak, speak justly, even if a near relative is concerned. (Qur'an 6:152)

> O you who believe, stand firmly for justice for (the sake of) Allah, and even if it concerns yourselves or parents or relatives, whether one be rich or poor, for Allah is nearer (to you) than either. (Qur'an 4:135)

There is a parallel to this in bothe the following Qur'anic verse and the *hadith* below relating to women:

> Live with them in kindness, for if you dislike them, perhaps you dislike something in which Allah has placed much good. (Qur'an 4:19)

> A believing man must not hate a believing woman,
> for if he dislikes one of her characteristics, he can be
> pleased with another. *(Muslim, 3469)*

So can we be with our children. If one characteristic is particularly bothersome, looking at the child with a positive eye will always turn up something we can view as a blessing. We need to make the effort, whether occasionally or continually, to see each child as a unique individual and appreciate his or her special qualities. Always comparing your middle child to her older sister, for example, does nothing except lock you into a rut. Instead, try comparing her to other children in the neighborhood for a change and see if you don't get a different picture. Or you might try listening to other adults' impressions of the child and reflect on the difference between their impressions of her and your own. This will give you a clue about the realism of your own view and whether getting some sort of advice or help would be in order. If other adults and children seem to reflect the same negative impression you have, then your child has a wider problem. The group may be encouraging the negative image, and more work is needed to improve the environment for the child (see chapter 8 for improving relationships and maybe, depending on the severity of the problem, seeking outside help).

An example: It happens that seven-year-old Siham has a nasty temper that flares with awful name-calling, just like Aunt Mai. But that doesn't mean that she'll grow up to be like her aunt, the hated annoyance of every family reunion; after all, a lot of children have quick tempers and they don't grow up to be Aunt Mais. If her parents let her know of their fear, and broadcast it to others, they will be programming her to fulfill that destiny and follow that role model. Instead of this, they need to concentrate on other characteristics of hers, favorable ones, and compare them favorably to a corresponding role model. Encourage Siham's verbal ability to flower in writing. Reward her when she plays nicely with her baby brother. Find anything good she does when she is not angry and encourage that side of her. In short, try to overlook her bad characteristics and encourage her good ones.

An important rule: one or another undesirable characteristic in a child (or anyone else) should not be taken as a sign that he or she is a *bad person*. This is a very common error with parents. The child is born in fitrah, without sin. With Islamic guidance and the help of Allah, each one will grow up to be a good person. We should therefore be very careful never to put down our child or any other, although we may try to modify their actions.

Parents are often especially challenged in balancing among their children when one child is markedly different from the others. This is but one of the many possible tests from Allah, and it applies equally in the case of a disabled child and one who has been given a superior gift, such as exceptional beauty or mathematical ability. In the case of a handicapped or ill child, whatever the problem may be—blindness, deafness, a limiting or crippling disease, mental retardation—the test for the parent is basically the same: to create an environment in which all the children in the family can feel appreciated and loved, and are able to find useful expression for the gifts or talents given to them by Allah. And whether the disabled individual contributes to the workings of the family or society in the usual sense or not, the mere presence of one whom Allah has afflicted is a source of mercy and blessing for those around him, especially those who love him and take care of him. It is important to remember Allah's saying that,

> He has reard some of you above others in rank in order
> to try you in what He has given you. (Qur'an 6:165)

Often parents are tested by having children of one sex when they prefer the other. Today, many people would rather have sons than daughters, like the Arabs in the time of the Prophet (S) who saw no use in rearing a child who would be of no economic benefit to them and would in any case leave them to go to her husband's house. But the Prophet (S) spoke of the great rewards promised to those who rear daughters, doing so purely for the pleasure of Allah and without hope of any economic benefit:

> The one who is tested by (having) daughters and behaves with goodness, shows them the way of religion, and treats them well, it will be a protection for him on the Day of Resurrection. *(Muslim)*

> The one among you is given three daughters or three sisters, and treats them well, without doubt will enter Paradise. *(Muslim)*

> If anyone cares for three daughters, trains them, marries them, and does good to them, he will go to Paradise. *(Abu Dawud, 5128)*

> Shall I not guide you to the most excellent sadaqah? It is to provide for your daughter when she is sent back to you (after being divorced or widowed) and has no one but you to provide for her. *(Mishkat, 5002,* transmitted by *Ibn Majah)*

> The Prophet's wife A'isha (R) reported that a poor woman came to her together with her two daughters. A'isha (R) gave her three dates. The woman gave a date to each of them, and then she picked up the remaining date and brought it to her mouth to eat it, but her daughters wanted it. She then divided the date that she had intended to eat between them. This kind treatment of hers impressed A'isha (R) and she

mentioned to the Prophet (S) what the woman had
done. At that, he said, "Truly, Allah has assured
Paradise for her because of this (action) of hers, or
He has rescued her from Hellfire." *(Muslim, 6363)*

Once the companion Sa'd bin Abi Waqqas (R) said
to the Prophet (S), "I am rich and have no inheritors
except a daughter. Shall I give two-thirds of my
property in charity?" The Prophet (S) said, "No."
Sa'd (R) asked, "Half?" The Prophet (S) said, "No."
Then he said, "One-third (at most), and (even) one-
third is too great or too much. Surely to leave your
inheritors wealthy is better than to leave them poor,
begging from the people. And you do not spend
anything from your property, seeking Allah's pleasure by it, without being rewarded for it, even for
whatever (food) you put into your wife's mouth."
(Bukhari 2.383; Muwatta)

A word needs to be said about giving to our children. First
of all, we should consider what is necessary and suitable for
each individual child, not merely what we would like him or her
to have. Too much is not necessarily better. Can we be equal
among our children in what we spend on them? Not always,
and not necessarily. Sometimes one child will have unusual
needs or interests which necessitate spending an unequal proportion of the family's income on him or her. However, in the
matter of giving presents, we should be as fair as possible. A
child's keen sense of justice recognizes the fact that there is a
difference between providing for needs and giving gifts.

A companion of the Prophet (S), Nu'man ibn Bashir
(R), reported that his father gave him a gift, but his
mother, Amrah bint Rawahah (R), said that she
would not agree to it unless he made the Messenger

of Allah (S) a witness to it. His father then went to the Messenger of Allah (S) and said, "I have given a gift to my son from Amrah bint Rawahah, but she ordered me to make you as a witness to it, O Messenger of Allah." The Messenger of Allah (S) asked, "Have you given (an equivalent gift) to each one of your sons?" The father replied in the negative. The Messenger of Allah (S) then said, "Fear Allah and be just to your children." In another version, the Prophet (S) asked whether the narrator, Nu'man, had brothers, and upon being told that he had, he asked Nu'man's father, "Have you given all the others like what you gave him?" When the father said that he had not, the Prophet (S) said, "Then it is not just, and I surely cannot bear witness except to what is just. *(Bukhari, 3.760, 3.818; Muslim, 3971;* a similar incident is reported in *Muwatta)*

JEALOUSY

Every child in the world wants to be the focus of his or her parent's attention and love. This creates a sense of rivalry between children which, in a mild form, is natural and to be expected. But when it becomes extreme, it can be devastating and destructive. We recall that the first murder in the world involved two brothers. Although their father was the prophet Adam (S), Cain killed Abel out of jealousy. So it is a given of family life that, even without parents playing favorites, children often have problems living with each other.

We also recall the story of the prophet Joseph (S), recounted in its entirety in the twelfth *surah* of the Qur'an. It is, in truth, a lesson in the terrible effects of envy and jealousy. Among the twelve sons of the prophet Jacob (S), Joseph (S) was the dearest and spiritually closest to his father. Jacob (S) tried to protect the young Joseph (S) from the envy of his brothers, encouraging him not to recount his first vision of his impending prophethood to them. But that did not save him from his brothers' envy. They plotted against him and even considered killing him so that, once he was out of the way, they would become the objects of their father's love.

However, instead of killing Joseph (S), they decided to put him into a well. He was taken out by traveling Egyptians and sold to a high Egyptian official, who treated him as his own son. In accordance with Allah's divine plan, Joseph (S) himself in time became an important official in Egypt. Later he was reunited with his father in a way that proved to his brothers how wrong they had been. One of the lessons that parents can learn from this story is to look for the long-term fruits and rewards of their efforts, and trust in Allah with total trust, even when it appears that the worst has happened to one's child.

Unquestionably the prophets reard their children in the best possible manner. In spite of this, as we have seen, the prophets Adam and Jacob (S), as well as the prophet Noah (S), experienced failure with their children, in two cases out of the three because of envy. And if they could fail, what about us? We must do our best to teach our children how to live with each other, but still this jealousy is part of a child's nature, in which emotions and passions are not under control. And this constitutes a test for us.

> And do not desire that with which Allah has favored some of you over others. . . . And ask from Allah out of His bounty. Truly, Allah is Knower of all things. (Qur'an 4:32)

What is it that children desire, which incites them to jealousy or envy of a sibling? At times it may be envy of possessions or things, but the primary cause of jealousy is desire for a parent's attention, generally the mother's. Too much jealousy among children is generally an indication of unmet needs, of a child who for some reason does not feel loved or that he is getting enough from his mother.

Sometimes when a child, overwhelmed by his jealous feelings, commits aggression or has a tantrum, the best method of quieting him down is to just hold him and reassure him that he too is loved: "Ameena's just a newborn baby, Hafsa, and I *have* to feed her like this because she can't eat any other way. You know, I used to feed *you* that way too when you were a baby, but you can't remember. But I love you just as much as I did when you were that little. (Big hug). Anyway, aren't you glad you're big now and can eat all kinds of nice food?" Parents should usually stress first, the fact that the older child is loved, and, second, the fact that the new child is *his* brother or sister, and as such, he has a relationship of love and caring, not competition and jealousy, with it. "This is *your* baby, too, Ahmad, your very own special brother. You can help me take care of him, and then when he's older, you'll be able to play with him too."

Some people are so thrilled with a new baby that they bubble over with emotional superlatives about how wonderful it is. It might be better to try to express to the older child how you feel he or she is seeing it. "Well, there goes that baby crying again. Babies are a lot of work for Mommy, and they make such a mess, spitting up and needing changing. I'm so glad you are big and can talk, to say what you want. I don't have to guess with you like I do with the baby. And you can help me so much instead of just lying there crying."

Sometimes people really don't think what they are saying to a child when they tell him or her about a new baby. An analogy would be for a husband to say to his wife, "Darling, I love you so much that I went out and married a second wife, to have two of you." This is about what some people say to children, and then they wonder why the children are jealous!

One way of reducing jealousy is to guarantee the child a "rank" in the family, and make the other children respect that rank. Another thing to do is to keep lines of communication as open as possible. Encourage the child to express his feelings if he can, and be understanding of them. Support him in his efforts to come to terms with his jealousy. It is an emotion to deal with like anger, as discussed in the last chapter.

Pointing out the terrible evils of envy, the Prophet (S) said,

> Avoid envy, for envy consumes good deeds just as fire consumes fuel or (he said) grass. *(Abu Dawud, 4885)*

> Seek refuge in Allah from jealousy, which leads to disgrace. *(Mishkat, 2463, transmitted by Ahmad and Baihaqi)*

> One of you has not believed until he likes for his brother what he likes for himself. *(Bukhari, 1.12; Mishkat, 4643)*

> Do not be angry with each other and do not envy each other and do not turn away from each other, and be slaves of Allah, brothers. . . *(Muwatta)*

> When Allah's Messenger was asked who was most excellent, he replied, "The one whose heart is clear of pollution (makhmum al-qalb) and whose tongue is truthful." On being told by those who were listening to him that they understood (the meaning of) "whose tongue is truthful" but not of "makhmum al-qalb," he replied, "The one who is pure, the one who is pure, with no sin, iniquity, deceit, or envy." *(Mishkat, 5221, transmitted by Ibn Majah and Baihaqi)*

RESPECT

Because of the Islamic emphasis on respecting elders, it is common in Muslim families to give titles to relatives indicating rank or relationship within the family. It is also common to require younger brothers and sisters to yield to older ones. This is part of showing respect for others, regardless of their personal merit.

As was discussed ("earlier"), we are not left with the option of deciding for ourselves whether to respect someone or not. We respect a person because he exists, because he is a servant of our Lord. And within the family circle, part of the manifestation of respect is to treat people according to their rank, with respect to age or relationship or both.

Each person occupies a special position in the family and society according to his age, relationship, and status. A woman is a daughter and at the same time a mother, a grandmother, a sister; a man is a father and at the same time a son and a younger or older brother. A child is an older or younger brother or sister. A teacher or professor, a scholar, imam, physician or judge occupy special ranks in society that are to be acknowledged according to the saying of Allah Ta'ala:

> And it is He Who has made you vicegerents of the earth and has reard some of you above others in rank, in order to try you in what He has given you. (Qur'an 6:165)

> . . . We rear some of them above others in rank in order that some may take service from others. (Qur'an 43:32)

In many Muslim languages in which titles are used to denote relationship within the family, a woman is not simply an "aunt" but is a "mother's sister" or a "father's sister," and there are equivalent titles for men. A child may be a "mother's sister's daughter" or "father's sister's daughter" (niece), with the masculine equivalents, and so on. Even outside the family, titles equivalent to "father," "grandfather," "uncle," "mother," "grandmother," "auntie," "brother," and "sister" are often used, even with total strangers, to express respect and relationship-in-Allah. In acknowledgement of these relationships, respect is accorded to elders and compassion and tolerance to younger ones. The Prophet (S) said,

> He does not belong to us who does not show mercy
> to our young ones and respect to our old ones, and
> who does not enjoin the good and forbid the wrong.
> (Mishkat, 4970, transmitted by Tirmidhi)

In some cultures, such distinctions among siblings are carefully maintained. For example, in Turkish, the word "agabey" for older brother and "abla" for older sister are used regardless of how close in age siblings are; likewise in Urdu, "bhai," meaning elder brother, and "apa" or "bajee" for older sister, are used in the same manner, with corresponding respect.

It is a commonplace practice for parents to commend good behavior toward a sibling because of his rank: "Nadia, don't tease Amer. He's still small, so please be gentler with him." "I found your conversation with Hani on the disrespectful side, Housain. Remember, he's your older brother and you want to treat him like one." And this is definitely an effective way of teaching children the compassion toward younger ones and respect for older ones, which are an integral part of Islamic family life.

However, the specific needs and situations of certain children in a family can be factors which may take precedence over rank. The only daughter of a family will need a room of her own, an Islamic requirement, whereas three boys can be asked to share a room. A slow child may need more guidance and certainly more patience from his parents than a quicker one. Likewise, a handicapped child may need extra attention from his parents, although it is best to try to integrate him into the normal stream of life as much as possible, guiding him to max-imize his strengths while minimizing his weakness, and encouraging him to seek the pleasure of Allah, despite his dis-ability, through helping others whenever he can.

Now let us look at a simple example of working to establish rank-oriented respect among our children. A'isha, age sixteen, starts toward the bathroom but Hala, age four, scoots in ahead of her. A'isha tries to order her little sister out but Hala screams for Mommy.

Mommy knows from experience that Hala is only trying to compete with her sister; she doesn't really *need* the bathroom at this moment. Hala has a habit of doing tricks of this kind to try to prove to herself and everyone else that she's just as big and important as her sister; she also gloats over her little victories by such things as making faces at her sister. It's a lot easier in the long run to stop this competition by obliging her to yield to her older sister because she *is* older, except for rare emergen-cies. At the same time, A'isha is old enough to understand the need to be gentle with younger children, so she doesn't take advantage of her privileges.

Daddy drives Fatima, age ten, and Sami, age eight, to school each day. Fatima wants to sit in the front seat of the car and so does Sami. Obviously it's not required that Sami pass his whole life in the back seat just because Fatima happened to be born first. The first time this dispute occurs, Daddy might make Sami yield to Fatima because she's older, or on the other hand he might make Fatima yield to Sami because he's younger. But for the regularly occurring, everyday event, some family rule of sharing the privilege can be instituted.

There's no need to make a rule if there's no dispute in the first place. Disputes usually arise because children want to prove their importance and secure a "special" place in the family. When parents uphold the rights of everyone and make sure that the little ones get their chance too, whenever their turn comes, they are thereby assuring them of their place and giving them a comfortable structure upon which they can depend. Many territorial disputes among children can be resolved by means of this system, fairly and gently applied.

The following hadith is a lesson in practicing the established rules of precedence:

> The Prophet (S) was given something to drink and he drank, and at his right was a boy and at his left were some elderly men. He then said to the boy, "If you permit me, I will pass it to them (first)." He said, "I will not pass along my share from you to anyone, O Messenger of Allah," whereupon he put it (the cup) in the boy's hand. *(Bukhari, 3.774; Muwatta)*

This hadith reminds us that age is not the only criterion for manners and respect. The Islamic custom is that precedence goes to the one seated or standing on the right; for example, the principle of *"al-yameen"* (the right hand) applies when entering a door, saving much discussion over who goes in first. Here we see that the Prophet (S) respected the boy's right to this precedence, regardless of the fact that he was younger than the old people seated on his left. He also gave the boy a chance to show respect for the others present, older as they were, by giving up his right. At the same time, he left the boy free to choose to be the very first to drink from a vessel which the blessed lips of the Prophet had touched, demonstrating his great love for him. And among the choices open to this boy, who can say which would have been the most pleasing to Allah?

Chapter Eight

FAMILY AND COMMUNITY TIES

THE NUCLEAR FAMILY AND THE EXTENDED FAMILY

One of the most significant and disturbing features of present-day Western culture is its effect on family ties, ties which attach individuals to what is established and stable. The enormous changes and upheavals of contemporary society have been brought about through the sacrifice of family ties, which many people today consider to be too stifling. For example, having to consider the opinion of her grandmother and aunts can keep a girl from trying out a daring new dress. Worrying about the reaction of his father can keep a young man working at a steady job instead of taking off on a Yamaha to explore the country.

The only tie that still evokes some respect in Western society is the bond between parent and child, or perhaps more narrowly, mother and child—the so-called nuclear family. While other ties have weakened dramatically, including the tie of marriage, this tie has maintained some degree of strength, although even this is weakened by the overall weakening of the family as an institution. And this tie also loses its social and legal significance as the child approaches the "magical" age of eighteen.

As a cause and likewise as a result of this weakening, mothers are urged by child-rearing authorities to make their children independent from a very early age. From a purely practical point of view, in a society in which the majority of mothers spend eight to ten hours a day outside their homes, this makes perfectly good sense. In order to survive, the child *must* be weaned from his mother physically and emotionally for the simple reason that she usually isn't there for him.

Notwithstanding these factors, the parent or parents of a baby or young child have absolute, unshared authority over all facets of the child's life: what he eats, what he wears, when he sleeps, where he goes, if and when he needs medical attention, and so on. The only authority which can intervene in the parent's absolute control over the child, if the need should arise, is a law enforcement or social service agency, or the child, himself, as the environment allows the child more and more "rights."

In a society in which age enjoys little respect or authority, grandparents may suggest options but parents often have scant regard for this advice. All of the "new and improved methods" of childcare have taken effect so quickly because parents have turned to books and magazines for childcare advice, not to the family elders. However, Islam recognizes strong ties between the child and a large number of extended family members— grandparents, aunts, uncles, cousins of varying degrees, great aunts and uncles, as well as the bond between the child and his "milk mother" and her husband and children. And while the parent-child bond is by far the strongest, the effect of all these other family relationships is to give the child attachments and ties to many individuals besides his parents, who all care about him and contribute to his socialization and upbringing. Allah Ta'ala says,

> Then give the relative his rights, and the needy and
> the wayfarer. That is best for those who seek Allah's
> (Divine) Countenance, and those—they are the suc-
> cessful. (Qur'an 30:38, 17:26)

And the Prophet (S) made clear the importance of the near relatives, saying,

> O people, the one who injures my paternal uncle has injured me, for a man's paternal uncle is the same as his father. *(Mishkat, 6147, transmitted by Tirmidhi)*

> The maternal aunt is like the mother. *(Abu Dawud, 2271 and 2273)*

> A man came to the Prophet (S) and said, "O Messenger of Allah, I have committed a serious sin. Can I do any act of penance?" He asked him if he had a mother, and when he replied that he did not, he asked if he had a maternal aunt. On his replying that he had, he said, "Then do kindness to her." *(Mishkat, 4935, transmitted by Tirmidhi)*

Maintaining family ties is one of the most strongly stressed aspects of Islam. The Arabic term for ties of family relationships is *silat al-rahm, rahm* also being the word for uterus or womb. The letters *r-h-m*, which form the root of these words, are also the root letters of the words *rahman* and *raheem*, meaning mercy, compassion, and beneficence. As we know, *al-Rahman*, the most often mentioned Divine Name of Allah Subhanahu wa Ta'ala among all His divine attributes, relates to His endless mercy, compassion, and beneficence. Thus we can see, through these Arabic terms, how, in the sight of Allah, blood relationships through ties of the womb are intended to be a source of mercy, compassion, kindness, and good for the members of a family.

Concerning this, the Prophet (S) said in two *qudsi* ahadith (that is, ahadith transmitted to the Prophet by divine inspiration, in which Allah Ta'ala speaks about himself):

(The word) "ar-rahm" (the womb) derives from "ar-Rahman" (the Most Merciful), and Allah said, "The one who keeps good relations with you (the womb), I will keep good relations with him, and the one who cuts off relations with you, I will cut off relations with him." *(Bukhari, 8.17 and 8.18)*

Indeed, Allah created the creation and when He had finished with creating it, the womb said, "This is the place of seeking refuge in You from the one who cuts off (the ties of relationship)." He (Allah) said, "Yes. Will you be satisfied if I keep good relations with the one who keeps good relations with you and cut off relations with the one who cuts off relations with you?" And it said, "I do not mind, my Lord!" He (Allah) said, "Then that is (granted) to you. . . " *(Bukhari, 8.16 and 6.354)*

Another hadith states,

Three things will be under the (divine) Throne on the Day of Resurrection: the Qur'an, which will dispute with men, having an outward and an inner meaning; the Trust (given to mankind); and Ties of Relationship, which will say, "O Allah, join those who joined me and cut off those who cut me off." *(Mishkat, 2133; Muslim, 6198)*

Numerous verses of the Qur'an speak about the importance of ties of relationship. Among them are the following,

And it is He who created man from water, and then established relationships of lineage and marriage; and your Lord is All-Powerful. (Qur'an 25:54)

It is not righteousness that you turn your faces toward the East or the West, but rather the righteous is the one who believes in Allah and the Last Day and the angels and the Book and the messengers, and gives his wealth, out of love of Him, for relatives and orphans and the needy and the wayfarer and those who ask and for the freeing of slaves, and establishes the salah and gives the zakah, and the ones who keep their contracts when they make them, and the patient in misfortune and affliction and in times of stress. Those are the ones who are truthful, and those— they are the ones who are mindful of Allah. (Qur'an 2:177).

And worship Allah and do not make anything a partner to Him. And do good to parents and relatives and orphans and the needy, and the neighbor who is of kin and the neighbor who is not of kin, and the companion at your side and the wayfarer and those whom your right hands possess. Truly, Allah does not love the one who is proud, boastful. (Qur'an 4:36)

Indeed, Allah commands justice and goodness and giving to relatives, and He forbids shameful deeds and iniquity and transgression. He advises you, in order that you may be reminded. (Qur'an 16:90)

Then, would you, if you were put in authority, make corruption in the land and cut your ties of relationship? (Qur'an 47:22)

A great many ahadith also deal with this subject, such as the following,

Worship Allah and do not set up anything as partner to Him, and establish the salah and give the zakah,

and keep good relations with your relatives.
(Bukhari, 8.12)

The one who would like to have an expansion of his
provision and a prolonging of his footsteps (on
earth), let him keep good relations with his relatives
(Bukhari, 8.14, 8.15 and 3.281)

The one who believes in Allah and the Last Day
should honor (or be generous) to his guest, and the
one who believes in Allah and the Last Day should
keep good relations with relatives; and the one who
believes in Allah and the Last Day should speak
what is good or keep silent. *(Bukhari, 8.160)*

If you greet all whom you meet, feed the hungry,
care for the well-being of your relatives, and pray at
night when people are asleep, you will enter Paradise
in peace. *(Mishkat, 1907, transmitted by Tirmidhi,
Ibn Majah and Darimi)*

The inhabitants of Paradise are of three types: one
who wields authority and is just and fair; one who is
truthful and has been given power to do good deeds;
and one who is merciful and kind-hearted toward his
relatives and to every pious Muslim, and who does
not stretch out his hand (to take from others) in spite
of having a large family to support. (Muslim, 6853)

A man asked, "Messenger of Allah, to whom should
I show kindness?" He replied, "Your mother, then
your mother, then your mother, and then your father,
and then your relatives in order of relationship."
(Abu Dawud, 5120)

> The Prophet's companion, Abu Dharr (R), reported:
> My friend (the Prophet [S]) ordered me to observe
> seven things. He ordered me to love the poor and be
> near them; he ordered me to think about my inferior
> and not think about my superior; he ordered me to
> join ties of relationship, even when relatives are at a
> distance; he ordered me not to ask anyone for any-
> thing; he ordered me to speak the truth even when it
> is bitter; he ordered me not to fear for Allah's sake the
> reproach anyone may cast upon me; and he ordered
> me to repeat often "There is no might and no power
> except in Allah *(La hawla wa la quwwata illa bil-
> Lah),"* for these words are part of the treasure under
> the Throne. *(Mishkat, 5259, transmitted by Ahmad)*

From all this, the importance in Islam of keeping ties with
members of the larger family unit can be understood. And the
Prophet Muhammad (S) and his companions were extremely
careful about keeping this basic injunction, respecting ties of
relationship as well as they could under often very difficult circumstances. At the same time, new ties of common belief and
life experience were forged among the believers, which took
the place of the blood ties broken by the hostility of the pagans
against their Muslim relatives. These new ties gave rise to a
strong, solid community in which the first generation of
Muslim children was reard; in modern terminology, the believers formed support groups for each other. The examples of this
are numerous and can be studied in early Islamic history.

We now return to ourselves. Only recently have scientists
began to study and document the existence of the phenomenon
called bonding between a mother and her newborn baby and to
verify its tremendous importance, although through simple
observation we have always known that it existed. Bonds of
family relationship, too, are as old as mankind—as old as the
tribe and the clan and the extended family. The roles of rela-

tives such as grandparents, aunts and uncles, nieces and nephews and cousins in the personal security structure of human beings since the beginning of our life on earth have been more profound than anyone can begin to imagine.   We see, however, that modern society, which has given rise to the cutting of so many previously existing bonds, has created a society of loneliness and alienation, while Allah commanded that we respect and maintain our ties to one another.

As Muslims, we know with certainty that Allah knows more about our nature and needs than we can ever know ourselves. Our basic premise, therefore, is that since Allah, our Creator, intends us to have a wide circle of family relationships, such relationships are important and beneficial. It is good for a child to feel the sense of belonging to family, to clan, to nation, as well as to the ummahof Islam. The more loving, supportive relationships he has, the better for him; in addition, the more different kinds of people he knows and is able to relate to, the better for him. One of the primary reasons people in the West have such poor success as marriage partners or as parents is simply because they lack experience and skill in relating to various kinds of people, something which is learned easily and naturally in the extended family setting.

Cutting off Ties with Relatives

> The one who cuts off relations (with elatives) will not enter Paradise. *(Bukhari, 8.13)*

> The joiner (of ties of relationship) is not the one who (merely) returns (the good done to him by his relatives), but rather the joiner is the one who, when a relationship is cut, mends it. *(Bukhari, 8.20)*

> A person said, "O Messenger of Allah, I have relatives with whom I try to have a relationship but they

cut it. I treat them well but they treat me badly. I am
good to them but they are harsh toward me." At this,
he said, "If it is as you say, then you are throwing
hot ashes (on them by being good to them), and
there will always be with you on Allah's behalf one
(an angel) who will keep you dominant over them as
long as you keep to this." *(Muslim, 6204)*

Cutting off ties means refusing to honor a relationship of
kinship with a relative. It could take many forms: disowning
the relative, having no relations with him at all, refusing to
acknowledge his existence, behaving rudely or refusing to
speak to him, and the like. If the relative lives at a distance, it
might take the form of harboring bad feelings to such an extent
as would prevent contact with him if the need or occasion
arose. In reference to our children, it could mean deliberately
allowing them to grow up without knowing or associating with
their relatives, or speaking about them so badly that it would
discourage the young people from forming any relations with
them. In Islam, even being estranged from one's fellow
Muslim for more than three days is prohibited. How then could
a Muslim cut off ties with his relatives when this is such a serious sin in the sight of the Creator? Concerning this, the
Prophet (S) said,

Do not hate one another, do not be jealous of one
another, do not desert one another, and, O worship-
pers of Allah, be brothers. Truly, it is not permissible
for any Muslim to desert (not talk to) his brother
(Muslim) for more than three days (Bukhari, 8.91).
In another version, it is: (After three days pass),
when he meets him and gives three salams and during that time receives no response, the other bears his
sin (Abu Dawud, 4895, and Muslim, 6212 and 6213).
In still another version it is: The one who does so

(keeps apart from his brother for more than three days) and dies will enter Hell. *(Abu Dawud, 4896)*

All of the above furnish us with the Islamic guidelines concerning the awesomeness of breaking relations with family members, and even with friends, while leaving us free to arrange the details that suit our situation. Obviously it is our adult relationships that shape the child's relationships, for a child cannot form ties with his relatives if his parents cut them off or engage in prolonged battles with them. Consequently, if we do not observe our obligations toward our kin, this is not a matter that concerns only ourselves personally but it concerns our children and others as well. Moreover, children have less self-control, wisdom, tact, and understanding than adults. If we cannot keep good ties with our family members, either because we don't feel the need or don't know how, or for any other reason, how can we expect our children to learn and respect their obligations? After all, children learn first from our example, then from our words.

The only workable approach to improving relations with estranged relatives is that we control and improve our own behavior, especially because we set the tone of the relationship with them for our children. Too often, when people see a conflict, they think in terms of "How can I manage to get such-and-such to change?" The answer is, you may not be able to. Sometimes sitting down and talking things over frankly and openly may help—or it may not. Generally, the first and most important, and perhaps the only thing, is to make sure that one's own behavior is correct. In every situation and condition, we must do what is right, what Allah wants of us, without regard to what others do.

> And among mankind is the one who gives his life to seek the pleasure of Allah. And Allah is compassionate to the servants. (Qur'an 2:207)

Then, is the one who pursues the pleasure of Allah like one who earns the wrath of Allah and his abode is Hell; and how evil a destination! (Qur'an 3:162)

And those who join what Allah has commanded to be joined and hold their Lord in awe and fear an evil accounting, and those who are patient in seeking their Lord's Face, and establish the *salah* and spend from what We provide for them, secretly and openly, and turn away evil with good. Those—theirs will be the final Home. (Qur'an 13:22)

Distant or Deceased Relatives

When close relatives are absent due to death or distance, they are relatives nonetheless, a part of a child's family heritage and history. It is important that he be aware of their identities and his connection to them. The Prophet (S) said,

Learn enough of your genealogies to show what ties of relationship you should join, for joining ties of relationship is a means of producing love in a family, increasing wealth, and producing life. *(Mishkat, 4934,* transmitted by *Tirmidhi)*

Probably the easiest way to approach this is to sit with the child over family photo albums and chat a bit about the various people who appear in them, telling stories about absent relatives to give the child some sense of who they were. This gives a child a feeling of identity and having roots, of being part of a larger family with a place among the families of the world. It gives him the message, "I belong" and "This is what I belong to."

Naturally there will be times in the lives of children when they are interested in this information and times when they are not. It is obviously not useful to drill a five-year-old on fourteen generations of family history. One child may know all of his close relatives and how they relate to each other by the age of four or five; another may be eight or nine before it really dawns on him what the words "nephew" and "niece" mean. How much information to give depends on the child and the manner in which it seems most appropriate to implement the goal of creating a warm feeling of family.

There are two restrictions in teaching a child about his family. The first of these is that we must not glory in our family relationships nor glorify our relatives, whether living or dead. Whatever is said of them should be in keeping with facts and truth.

The habit of glorifying family members can depart so far from the truth that the credibility of the person glorifying them may be called into question. For example, in one family, certain members would speak of everything and everyone connected with the family, either closely or casually, in exaggerated terms. In later life, a child of this family realized that she could not really trust the truthfulness of these relatives because their vision of anything connected to themselves was colored with unwarranted family pride.

This kind of false pride in ancestry resembles that of the pre-Islamic period of ignorance, in which boasting about one's forefathers and one's connection with them was a standard practice. Islam abolished all this and taught us that no human being has cause for pride over another.

> And do not puff out your cheek (in pride) at people nor walk insolently upon the earth. Truly, Allah does not like any conceited boaster. (Qur'an 31:18)

> Only those believe in Our Signs who, when they are reminded of them, fall down in prostration and glorify their Lord with praise, and they are not proud. (Qur'an 32:15)

O mankind, be mindful of your Lord and fear a Day when no father will be able to make compensation for his son nor will a son be able to make compensation for his father in the least. (Qur'an 31:3)

Allah has revealed to me that you must be humble so that no one boasts over another or oppresses another. (Abu Dawud, 8477)

Allah Most High has removed from you the pride of the pre-Islamic period and its boasting of ancestors. One is (either) a pious believer or a miserable sinner. You are sons of Adam, and Adam was (created) from dust. Let people cease to boast about their ancestors. They are merely fuel in Hell, and they will certainly be of less account with Allah than the beetle which rolls dung with its nose. *(Abu Dawud, 5097; Mishkat, 4910)*

The Prophet (S) said, "The one who has the weight of a mustard seed of pride in his heart will not enter Paradise." A person said, "Surely one likes his clothing to be fine and his shoes to be fine." He (the Prophet) said, "Truly, Allah is graceful and He loves gracefulness. Pride is disdaining the truth and contempt for people." *(Muslim, 0164)*

The one who fights under the banner of a people who are blind (to good and evil), who is puffed up with family pride and calls (people) to fight for his family honor and supports his relatives (in unjust causes)—if he is killed, he dies as one belonging to the days of jahiliyyah (pre-Islamic ignorance). *(Muslim, 4555)*

The other restriction is not to speak ill of others. In the case of the living, doing so would poison the child's mind against a family member, perhaps before they have even met, and would sow seeds of mistrust, if not hatred, in his heart. And in the case of someone who is no longer living, we should be guided by the Islamic injunctions about insulting the dead.

> Do not abuse the dead, for they have surely reached what they sent on ahead. *(Bukhari, 2.476)*

> The gravest sin is going to lengths in speaking unjustly against a Muslim's honor. *(Abu Dawud, 4859)*

> The one who believes in Allah and the Last Day should honor (or be generous) to his guest, and the one who believes in Allah and the Last Day should join the ties of relationship (with relatives); and the one who believes in Allah and the Last Day should speak what is good or keep silent. *(Bukhari, 8.160, 8.158, 8.48)*

> The Messenger of Allah (S) said to his companions, "Do you know what backbiting is?" They said, "Allah and His Messenger know best." He said, "Backbiting is your talking about your brother in a way he does not like." It was said to him, "What is your view about this if I find what I mentioned in my brother?" He said, "If what you claim is found in him, you have backbitten him, while if that is not in him, it is a slander." *(Muslim, 6265; Muwatta)*

This is a quite difficult rule for people to follow. Somehow the true feelings we may be able to hide in public are harder to hide within the intimacy of the family. For example, Mom may hate her brother. Somehow it doesn't seem wrong to tell her children how mean he was and family tales of the dirty tricks he played when they were little. Even though she might not have cut ties with this brother, she is nursing a grudge against him, keeping resentment in her heart. Those hurts of the past are between two now grown-up people; they may need to be settled between the two individuals concerned, or otherwise forgotten. Time has passed and each has grown and changed.

In any case, the problem doesn't concern the children of the family. Maybe they will never meet their uncle. Maybe he will stop by some day for an hour or two while passing through town, and for that short time be an absolutely delightful uncle, with gifts for all. Or maybe he will change with time and help from Allah, and when Mom sees him again will be a much better person. Or maybe, as is so common, he was never as bad as Mom perceived him, and with time Mom may come to realize this, to appreciate her brother as a person different from herself but as a good person nonetheless.

Reliving those problems and feelings with her children may make the past harder to come to terms with and forgive, and it may also teach her children that holding grudges and resentments is an acceptable thing. Not only will Mom and her children remain cut off from her brother, their uncle, but her brother's children, Mom's nieces and nephews, and her children's cousins, will also be cut off by her poisoned memory.

This discussion does not mean that Mom should describe her brother as an angel to her children. She can be honest. "This is a picture of my brother. We didn't get along very well when we were kids. I haven't seen him in years and don't know what he is like now." This honesty accepts past difficulties, but does not close the door to new, improved relations.

Nearby Relatives

Living near relatives can be a real blessing. The ideal situation for a child is to live in a stable, warm, loving community of his extended family and neighbors. While his bond with his parents is normally the most important relationship for him, he also has the possibility of developing close relationships with aunts, uncles, cousins, neighbors, and probably most important, with his grandparents. Keeping strong family ties provides the minimum basis necessary for forming deeper caring relationships, the ability to love and be loved, to give, to serve, and to have tolerance for varied people and situations.

Examples: Sardar sees his cousin is crying; he runs to see what's wrong and cheer him up. Grandma sends him to bring her a glass of water; he jumps up cheerfully and brings it back, proud of not spilling a drop, to receive Grandma's thanks and feel what a big important job he did. Meanwhile Mom has a break.

Children need a great deal of affection, attention, and a multitude of activities to keep them occupied, contented, and on the right path. In such an ideal situation, the many caring people around the nuclear family are able to take some of the load from the parents—and this sharing is mutual, from both sides. The parents have the ultimate responsibility, but the child is learning from others too. Auntie takes her niece visiting with her and helps teach her manners. Uncle takes his nephew fishing with his cousins, teaches them all about digging up worms for bait, and shares with them the wonder of watching birds building a nest.

A child can and should be expected to help out with chores for his extended family whenever he can be useful, learning to give as well as receive. The child also has a place in family and community celebrations—weddings, births, Eids, and any other festivity that comes up. And without the presence of children, such occasions would be empty and incomplete indeed.

If this is the ideal situation, there is obviously a great deal of difference between it and the realities of the contemporary world. Today, people give little importance to family ties because money, social position, and other uses of their time are more important to them. Some destroy family harmony by fighting over minor problems, backbiting, holding grudges, and mistrusting each other.

When this occurs among Muslims, we recognize that the major cause is a lack of Islamic values being practiced among the Muslim community. Islam is not just praying and fasting, wearing hijab or growing a beard. It is a whole, complete, balanced way of life, practicing a high level of manners and morals following the example of Prophet Muhammad (S), the greatest teacher the world has ever seen and the exemplifier of the Qur'an.

Then how does a concerned Muslim parent rear his children to be good Muslims in this embattled community? How does he manage if his own relatives are not praying or practicing, and perhaps his wife's relatives are non-Muslims, deviating his children from the path of Islam?

It would be so much simpler to cut all ties with these problem people, go off with a few like-minded families, and rear the children away from all the corruption. Or would it? This might be an easy answer but it is not an Islamic answer. Islam is a religion of moderation, not of extremism. We are not escapists, but people who live and work in the imperfect world where Allah (S) placed us.

Such solutions as the above have been tried, many times, in fact. But something always seems to go wrong. The lures of the outside world always manage to creep into the home, even when parents think they have made it safely *dunya*-proof (free of worldy fixation). It's either the TV, or other kids, or the school, or it's the child's own maturing out of the cocoon of his family and his need to be in touch with what's out there. There is no safe place except in the privacy of one's own heart, in one's relationship with and remembrance of Allah.

Inoculation is a more valid concept in social life than quarantining, especially because no sterile quarters exist. It is better for a conscientious parent to introduce his or her child little by little to the outside world, with all its lures, under supervision, than to cut the child off from it altogether, so that he both yearns for what others have and has no armor against it. Sooner or later he must be in the world, either for education or work, and if he has been kept isolated from it, its attractions may take him by storm when he emerges into it, left defenseless because of lack of exposure and the learning of Islamic tools for coping.

A special case—the mother-in-law

In virtually every culture, "mother-in-law" is a bad word, representing an awkward and difficult relationship. Often the problem goes no further than minor friction, at its height for newlyweds and at the coming of the first baby, and calming down thereafter. But in some cases it can amount to a continuously, intolerably eroding relationship and a severe undermining of the younger parents' authority with their children.

Perspective is needed in dealing with the various possible problems that can arise with mothers-in-law. Unfortunately, people tend to react on an emotional level, losing sight of the fact that the mother-in-law is also the mother of one's spouse and the grandmother of one's children. As such, she is probably the most important figure in the Muslim family, given honor and rights by Allah Himself. If a man cannot utter a harsh word to his mother, and his wife chooses to fight with her about her child's clothing, where does that put him? On the other hand, how does a mother rear her child according to her best understanding if "that woman" insists on interfering?

Mom has well-educated ideas about the amount of clothing a child needs, based on the understandings of the society around her. However, Grandma may be convinced that depriving baby of an undershirt under his clothes on a hot day will cause severe colic, and she loves her grandson. When Mom's back is turned, Grandma envelops the baby in a blanket suitable for winter. Mom is sure he'll get heat rash or become dehydrated, and over and above this consideration is the natural emotional reaction of, "He's my baby, not hers!"

Here two problems need to be addressed. The first is the issue of self-control, to avoid blowing up in anger and causing a fight. And here we Muslims have powerful weapons. Through the discipline imposed on us through regular prayer and fasting we learn self-control. If we are able to bear the discipline of fasting for a whole month, we should be able to keep our mouths zipped during a few minutes of intense anger or irritation until we are able to calm down, collect our thoughts, and decide on what it is appropriate to do. And we do this for the sake of Allah, not for any other reason, bearing in mind that the discipline of keeping good relations with our relatives, whether by blood or marriage, and especially with a mother, is just as important in His sight as the discipline of fasting.

The second problem is how to deal with the interference in a constructive, positive way, both treating the mother-in-law kindly and doing what we think is right for our child. And this takes creative thought. It is always necessary to remind ourselves that the mother-in-law is a *mother*. She reard her children with all the love, good-will, and mothering skills she possessed; she gained a lot of knowledge and self-confidence in her own methods, and, whatever her errors, her son grew up to become the father of this child. She loves her grandchildren, and the reason for her interference is that she wants to do the best for this child, according to the understanding she had when she was rearing babies. It is also possible that she may question the knowledgeability or competence of her daughter-in-law, who is younger, lacking in experience, and maybe of a different cultural background.

This is the general case. However, there are as many possibilities as there are people in the world. There is an occasional mother-in-law who acts not out of genuine concern for her grandchild but out of a genuine desire to annoy and put down her daughter-in-law, just because she is the wife of her son whose love she does not accept to share with anyone. Such a case presents a very trying situation for both the husband and the wife, the husband being caught between his love and responsibility for his mother and his wife. After unceasing *du'a* for Allah's help in resolving the situation, perhaps keeping the women at as much distance as is politely possible, while providing his mother with all the care and affection he is able to give, is the best solution for him.

Allah in His endless creativity has instilled in each child a special bond with his mother. Children from adoptive homes, with wonderful adoptive parents, still long to know their real parents, particularly their mothers. Children have been known to idealize mothers who are repulsively ugly, terrible cooks, seriously neglectful, and even quite abusive, just because the mother is the mother. With this, the conflict over who "owns" the baby is, in the long run, a no-contest win for Mom. Even if Grandma smothers the child with love and good things, he knows who his mother is. Nevertheless, the desire to fight and protect one's young is a very strong basic instinct in mothers, and it can remain a difficult issue unless feelings of respect and trust are built between the mother and her mother-in-law.

Both women have rights in Islam, but it takes time for each to prove that she is willing to respect the rights of the other. In some cases, trust is built quickly; in other cases, slowly or not at all. If a young wife makes it a priority to build a good relationship with her mother-in-law, she can usually secure it long before her baby starts walking, and then there will be all those long years ahead for the two women to enjoy watching the child grow up, instead of years of brooding in mistrust or sapping their mutual energies in arguments. There are many ways of managing this situation in a kindly fashion. The secret lies in not betraying negative emotions and in treating Grandma with respect and consideration.

For instance, in the above example in which Grandma has wrapped the baby in too warm a blanket, the following alternatives might be useful:

1. "Oh, do you think he's cold? Well, maybe, but that's a woolen blanket. Here, let me get a lighter one instead."

2. Mom swoops down and picks up baby, blanket and all, saying, "Mommy's little angel, it's time for your nap (or changing, lunch, etcetera").
3. Wait a little while before doing anything, so that moving the baby won't look like a direct reaction to Grandma's act. Then make some excuse to take the baby and leave. Dehydration and heat rash don't develop in a minute.

In the future, to avoid problems, perhaps dressing the baby a bit more warmly in front of his grandmother would be a nice gesture of compromise, and Mom can be clever, making use of cotton sleepers instead of warmer types. Later, either Mom or someone else might hold a purely academic discussion in Grandma's presence about dressing a baby too warmly and the danger of overheating, but not at the time when the situation is occurring. A scientific discussion of the matter may or may not improve the situation, but it is an option to try if a real problem develops. This problem is a mole hill, but it is just from numbers of little mole hills like this that many people build mountains, resulting in years of fighting, resentment, and spiteful behavior.

If a woman makes a major effort to show respect and consideration for her mother-in-law, her mother-in-law will feel it, for respect is what all people—especially mothers—want and expect most. Then, even though each may do small things that upset the other, both will hopefully try to ignore the annoyance or work through it in a polite and constructive manner. This will create a climate of good will and mutual respect to which other family members will respond, and the children will be able to enjoy a deeply loving relationship with their grandmother.

If a mother makes a real effort for the sake of Allah, her reward is due from Allah. Even if her efforts don't result in harmony, she will be rewarded for her intentions and efforts, and her children will treat her well when she is a grandmother. When things become difficult, it may be helpful to recall the orders of Allah Ta'ala concerning this matter:

Be thankful to Me and to your parents. To me is the
(final) goal (Qur'an 31:14)

and the words of His blessed Prophet (S),

Be kind to your parents and your children will be
kind to you. *(Tabarani* and *Hakim)*

A man said, "O Messenger of Allah, what rights can
parents demand from their children?" He said,
"They are your Paradise and your Hell." *(Mishkat,
4941, transmitted by Ibn Majah)*

The Prophet (S) said three times, "Shall I inform you
about the greatest of the major sins?" They said,
"Yes, O Messenger of Allah." He said, "To join others in worship with Allah and to be undutiful to parents." *(Bukhari, 3.822, 9.9* and *9.10)*

Once Abdullah ibn Mas'ood (S) asked the Prophet
(S),"What deed is dearest to Allah?" He said, "The
prayer at its proper time." Ibn Mas'ood (S) then
asked, "Then what?" He said, "Goodness to parents." *(Bukhari, 1.505).*

Other relationships

In some cases, the relationship between the father and his
mother-in-law may be similar. On the whole, however, children
rarely become an issue in such a relationship because men and
women usually don't feel threatened by each other on the issue
of rearing children; if they are going to fight, it is usually about
something else. Grandfathers interfere even less with child-
rearing decisions. Since the emotional tone is lower-keyed,
manners are easier to remember and disputes can generally be
managed more easily.

If Dad is out in the park with his mother-in-law and the kids, for example, he is usually quite ready to let her take charge of them. If he feels she is overly protective, cautioning, "Don't go near the slide! You're too little!" he may say calmly, "We always let them. They're okay." And since he is the man of the house and has the last word, this is less likely to cause offense than the same words said by his wife to *his* mother.

Many men do have various problems with their mother-in-laws, of course, and both a man and his wife can have problems with the parents of either and with their aunts, uncles, cousins, and so on. These may be over issues of principles, specific actions, or the overall relationship. It is complicated, in an extended family, to give due time and attention to everyone's ideas and feelings, and to balance the needs and wants of the various family members.

Yahya, for example, has a sister whose husband has died, leaving her with small children and little means. Her husband's family is not fulfilling its obligation to help her financially with rearing the children. Yahya has an obligation and the desire to help his sister, but he must also balance this with his obligations to his elderly parents, who have many health problems, and to his wife and children. They may all have to make sacrifices for his sister too, but at the same time they must not be allowed to feel neglected.

On a rational level, Yahya's wife might accept that he is doing the right thing and be proud of her good man, but emotionally she may need small extra tokens of his affection, especially if his sister seems to always be on the phone asking for him to come over, and needing help or advice. In turn, Yahya's son might understand that his father is doing good by teaching his cousin to ride a bike, but in his heart he longs for his father to teach him first. The result of all these conflicting demands may result in a high level of stress for Yahya. However, if he carries all these tests for the sake of Allah, with full trust in His wisdom and mercy, he will hopefully be able to achieve balance within himself and among the several people who depend on him.

Improving a Relationship

Even in the best of worlds, people will have some problems in getting along with each other. Islamic values and manners, properly understood and practiced, create an atmosphere in which people try to overlook the minor everyday inconveniences of living with others, not focusing on the little faults we all have but rather concentrating on the good we derive from being together in community, doing the best we can with the circumstances and tests Allah sends us, and looking toward the Day of Judgment in the hope of a blessed outcome.

Of course we are not perfect, and people disagree and quarrel. The following three-point program may be helpful in improving a relationship that is already in difficulty. These three actions are specific, right-now-type efforts to create change in a blocked cycle of arguments and hard feelings between two people. After listing them, we will extend the discussion to include general everyday long-term efforts at self improvement that which lead a person to better relations with everyone. We assume here that, as in most cases, both people have made some mistakes in dealing with each other. But the other person's mistakes are not your concern.

When you want to improve a relationship for the sake of Allah, you improve *yourself* and make *your* behavior the best possible. You cannot force another individual to change and be the way you want—that is up to him or her. If you use these techniques to manipulate another to do or act the way you want, in a power play, remember that all acts are judged by Allah according to intention. Purify your intentions. Use these techniques to correct your behavior, so the responsibility for this poisonous relationship becomes as little your fault as possible, to please Allah, hoping perhaps that the other person will change, but not demanding it as an outcome of your efforts. Nevertheless, Allah can cause the other to improve, if He wills, perhaps in response to your improvement. This is your test.

Avoiding Blocked Issues and Problem Situations

Try to avoid any issue or situation that you know in advance will cause a problem. This can be understood as accepting that you just don't agree on some issues, and moving on to the multitude of other things in life. This will not prevent new problems from arising but will hopefully reduce the number of flare-ups of old problems. Whereas open communication is encouraged, headlong confrontations are ruled out as a means of improving any situation.

Example: Hanan has a long-standing feud with her husband over his lack of help with the house. She thinks he could keep the house in better repair; the bathroom faucet leaks and the kitchen needs painting, among a list of other things. However, when a subject is blocked, it is often best to drop it and talk about something else. Perhaps if Hanan stops nagging, her husband will do the work on his own; his apparent indifference may be a reaction to her constant reproaches about his laziness. A happy family can live anywhere, but Hanan's drive to have a well-maintained house seems to be poisoning this family. The issue is no longer what actually needs doing, but Hanan's nagging and her husband's laziness, weakening the love and respect between husband and wife.

Let Hanan stop mentioning the drippy faucet. Complaining to her mother in front of her husband is also not recommended because she is just insulting him in front of her mother and getting her mother to start nagging him too. In a general discussion with other company, where the conversation gently passes over everyone's pet home improvement plans, Hanan might mention that she and her husband plan to redo the kitchen when they have time, but sly digs at him would be out of line. If her husband does get out his tools and attack the sink, Hanan can be polite and gracious, without exageration or sarcasm. "Thank you dear, I really appreciate your getting that drip stopped." Yelling to the kids, "Hey kids, come see a miracle, a once in a life-time view of your father fixing something!" might fit in a TV sitcom, but not in a Muslim household.

The lesson: It's better to let some things go, and have peace and harmony, than to insist on being right.

> Those who. . . restrain anger and forgive people—
> and Allah loves those who do good. (Qur'an 3:134)

> And the one who is patient and forgives, that surely
> pertains to steadfastness of purpose. (Qur'an 42:43)

> The most hateful man in front of Allah is the one
> who is the most quarrelsome. *(Bukhari, 6.48)*

> He who keeps silence will be safe. *(Mishkat, 4836,*
> transmitted by *Ahmad, Tirmidhi, Darimi and Baihaqi)*

> The one who believes in Allah and the Last Day
> should speak what is good or keep quiet. *(Bukhari,*
> *8.48, 8.158, 8.160, and Muwatta)*

Commenting Favorably About Good Actions

Whenever you are able, try to comment favorably, in front of the person concerned if possible, but elsewhere as well, about something he or she did. For the sake of making peace, it is permissible to exaggerate slightly here.

Example: Hanan can compliment her husband on some of his good qualities: his career, his sense of humor, his trim physique, the time he spends visiting his sick aunt in the hospital. There must be *something* good about him. Some people need to sit down and try to write a list, to remember the good side of one they have been feuding with. Try to find ten good things about the other person. If she *has* been running him down with her mother, or with anyone else, making a specific effort to praise him in front of her will help to make up for the sin of backbiting. It will also signal to her mother that that game is over. Often, other people get interested in encouraging our disputes and can hinder our efforts to improve and change.

Making an effort to speak well of him with others who don't know the problem is important, because often we mentally visualize a person as we describe him, so this works to adjust our internal attitude of him. We are reinforced in this effort by seeing others accept him in the positive light we describe, and perhaps add their own comments on how much they appreciate him. "Yes, I really never told you how much we appreciate your husband's help with Jimmy in soccer, and all his volunteer work for the league. My husband never has time."

The lesson: Try to focus on whatever is positive in a person and ignore whatever isn't.

> A good word and forgiveness are better than charity followed by injury. (Qur'an 2:263)

> Live with them in kindness, for if you dislike them, perhaps you dislike something in which Allah has placed much good. (Qur'an 4:19)

> A believer must not hate a believing woman; if he dislikes one of her characteristics, he can be pleased with another. *(Muslim)* [We assume that this applies to both sexes.]

Lying is allowed only in three cases: falsehood spoken by a man to his wife to please her, falsehood in
war, and falsehood to put things right between people.
(Mishkat, 5033, transmitted by *Ahmad and Trimidhi)*
[Again, we assume that this applies to both.]

The one who has forged (something) in order to put
things right between two persons has not lied.
Another version has: The liar is not the one who puts
things right between people, saying what is good and
increasing good. *(Abu Dawud, 4902)*

A caution is needed about lying to improve relations. First,
remember again that all acts are judged by intentions. Our
intentions are to downplay areas of disagreement and concentrate on the good in others so that we may live together in harmony, to please Allah (SWT). What is allowed are the small
fibs that smooth over reality (see chapter 5, *Tactfulness*). If
your neighbors, Mr. A and Mr. B, are feuding, and you have a
conversation with Mr. A in which he told you that the only
thing Mr. B ever did right in his life was to keep his bratty kids
penned up in his own yard, this converstation could be summarized to Mr. B by saying, "He mentioned how well you look
after your children, not allowing them to run all over the neighborhood like others do."

When Flare-Ups Start, Stop
As soon as you realize you've started another flare-up with
a person, stop. Apologize for what you've done, even though
you feel you're right (that is, apologize for your fighting,
though not necessarily for your position on the issue). When
your aim is to keep peace with someone, it is sometimes wise
to lose a battle to show that peace is more important than this
minor issue.

This is very hard to do because you feel—very strongly, perhaps—that you're right and the other person is wrong, and that by backing down you are giving an undeserving person unjustified power over you. However, letting the person know how important he is to you and how much you want peace with him can be very effective. He must know by now, from past experience, how important to you the issue is for which you're fighting.

Example: Hanan now finds that her husband has assigned their ten-year-old son to mow the lawn, which he had promised to do himself, while he takes a nap. "I don't know how anyone can be so lazy!" Hanan explodes. Forgotten is the love she feels for him and he for her, his good treatment of her, his providing for her, the many years of good times they have shared; the only thing that matters at this moment is her grievance against him. The old, standard argument is cranking up again.

If Hanan can stop and say, "I'm sorry, dear. I lost my temper. I've been trying to work on controlling my temper and I blew it again," that will go some way to defusing the issue. "Excuse me, I'm going upstairs to do something else," would get her out of the scene where she can calm down. If she can say, "Maybe it's good for you to teach our boy to do more around the house," or, "I shouldn't have said that. I know you were up awfully late last night," or "I know you're not getting enough sleep during the week," she might well impress her husband. People tend to cooperate more when they feel respected. At any rate, at the least she will not be guilty of scolding or abusing someone—that someone being her own husband.

> Nor are goodness and evil equal. Repel (evil) with
> what is better, and then will the one between whom
> and you was enmity will become like your warm
> friend. (Qur'an 41:34)

O you who believe, indeed, among your wives and your children are enemies to yourselves, so beware of them. But if you pardon and overlook and forgive, truly, Allah is Most Forgiving, Most Merciful. (Qur'an 64:14) [Again, we assume this applies to both sexes.]

Be mindful of Allah wherever you are; and do good deeds after doing bad ones; the former will wipe out the latter. And behave decently toward people. *(Tirmidhi)*

The lesson: Stop, apologize, collect yourself, and let things cool down before an argument gets heated.

GENERAL SELF-IMPROVEMENT

If this three-point plan can be put into action quickly, to make a recognizable change in a relationship, other efforts are encouraged by Islam to make gradual long-term improvement in each of us, so that we grow closer to Allah (SWT) and live in greater harmony with others.

Trusting in Allah and Du'a

Trust in Allah and constantly ask for His help in all matters. He says,

O you who believe, seek help in patience and salah. Truly, Allah is with the patient. (Qur'an 2:153)

Seek help through Allah and through patience. (Qur'an 7:128)

And do not despair of Allah's soothing mercy; and
no one despairs of Allah's soothing mercy except the
unbelieving people. (Qur'an 12:87)

. . . Do not cut off (your hope) from the mercy of
Allah. . . (Qur'an 39:53)

Example: Maybe in the future, Hanan's husband will earn
more and will be able to afford to pay someone to do the jobs
that need taking care of at home. Maybe Hanan will get used to
his standards and way of doing things, involving herself with so
many other things that she doesn't notice the leaky faucet in the
bathroom any more. Maybe she will learn to do these repairs
herself, or a child or brother will be able to do them. Maybe her
husband will visit a friend who has remodeled his home, will be
impressed, and will want to improve his own home.

Remember that Allah, our Lord, is the master of endless
possibilities, and no one knows when He will open up any or
all of these for His servants. As long as one has life, there is
always room for hope and, yes, expectation of improvement.
We do not need un-Islamic methods for achieving our rights or
our desires, because we pray and trust Allah (SWT). We are
not working alone. Part of our life here is being tested for
patience, and for our ability to grow and learn.

The Lesson: Don't think that you are alone in fighting for
what you believe is right. Trust in Allah, seek His help, and be
patient.

Remember that the help of Allah is for those who
remain patient, and prosperity follows adversity, and
there is ease after hardship. *(Tirmidhi)*

Safeguard Allah's rights, and you will always find
Him with you; if you need something, ask Allah, and

when you need help, beseech Allah alone for that. Bear it in mind that if all the people joined together to grant you some benefit, they would not be able to do so except as Allah has decreed for you, and that if all of them joined together to do you harm, they would not be able to do so except as Allah has decreed for you. The pens have been set aside and the writings of the book of fate have become dry. *(Mishkat, 0062(R), transmitted by Tirmidhi)*

When a man goes out of his house and says, "In the name of Allah; in Allah I trust; there is no might and no power but in Allah," there will be said to him at that time, "You are guided, defended and protected." The devils will go far from him and another devil will say, "How can you deal with a man who has been guided, defended and protected?" *(Abu Dawud, 5076)*

If you trusted in Allah truly, He (Allah) would give you provision as He does for the birds which go out hungry in the morning and come back full in the evening. *(Mishkat, 5299, transmitted by Tirmidhi and Ibn Majah)*

The heart of the son of Adam has a piece in every wadi (valley), and if anyone lets his heart follow all the pieces, Allah will not care in which wadi He destroys him; but to the one who trusts in Allah, He will supply enough for all the pieces. *(Mishkat, 5309, transmitted by Ibn Majah)*

Changing from Negative to Positive Mode

Change your focus. In a way, this is a summary of the three-point program, but nonetheless it deserves a special category all its own. Frequently we get locked into a negative way of looking at things: at people, their behavior, our life situation, our relationships, and our own selves. At best, this results in a coldness, detachment, or sourness in relating to people; you know—the kind of thing which, when it's "on," makes those around us think, "Oh, no, not that again!" At worst, it can lock us into depression, which often is caused by a host of negative factors in our lives which seem to be unchangeable and unmoveable. One at a time we can deal with things, but when they pile up higher and higher on our heads, we are buried under the heap, blaming others, blaming ourselves, feeling guilty and oppressed and horrible about them and ourselves and just about everything.

We often can't change situations, people, or relationships. But there is one thing we *can* change and that is our attitude. Depressed people are people with complaints about everything—about all of life, and especially about Allah. Everything that comes to us comes from Allah, both what we preceive as good and what we preceive as bad. Looking on all this with a negative attitude is actually saying, "Allah has sent me too hard a test. I can't do it. I don't want it. It's unfair."

> On no soul does Allah place a burden greater than it can bear. (Qur'an 2:286)

> Say, nothing shall happen to us but what Allah has decreed, for He is our Patron and in Him shall the faithful trust. (Qur'an 9:51)

> And whoever fears Allah, He will find out a way for him and He will give him provision from where he knows not. (Qur'an 65:3)

> Perchance you hate a thing while it is good for you or love a thing which is bad for you. Allah knows best, you know not. (Qur'an 2:216)

Allah has promised us, and He is the All-Fair and All-Just. We accept what He sends to us and ask His help in finding our way through the difficulties and tests we receive. He knows the people around us and the hardships they are causing us. Yet He put them in front of us. So there is a way of managing and overcoming each difficulty, if we accept the problem posed and start working positively on a constructive solution. And if that doesn't work, we pray and think, and find another possible way of managing an improvement and try that.

> So verily with every difficulty there is relief, verily, with every difficulty there is relief. (Qur'an 94:5-6)

> There is nothing for Man but what he strives for. (Qur'an 65:39)

> Allah does not change a people's lot until they change it themselves. (Qur'an 13:11)

Accept the tests Allah (SWT) has sent you and improve yourself. You stop nagging, and He will help you to have peace and quiet take the place of arguments. You stop seeing faults and instead look for good in the people around you, and in turn He will help them to like you and want to spend time with you. You stop complaining, and all at once you become attuned to all the good things Allah has given you. You stop fighting against what Allah is sending you, and you find His help and mercy at every turn.

One of the most useful tools for making this change is *dhikr*, the remembrance of Allah. This can take the form of recalling all His blessings and favors: life, health, strength and energy (even if limited), good looks, two eyes which are able to see, two ears which are able to hear, a tongue that can speak, two legs on which one is able to walk, two arms and hands with which one can grasp—the list is literally endless. One can be thankful for anything and everything—the blue of the sky, the light of the sun, the comfort of a good bed or easy chair, a kind and trustworthy friend, the homey smell of bread baking in the oven, a houseplant that has just come into flower, and so on, without stopping. And Allah says,

> Therefore, mention the favors of your Lord. (Qur'an 93:11)

This is not merely a "religious" injunction but one which relates to sound emotional and physical health and optimal functioning. Within the human organism, negativity and positivity are programs, just as in a computer, which program the individual for happiness or suffering. When one focuses continually on deficits and negative factors in one's life, a negative biochemical reaction is set up within the brain that affects every part of the organism, often resulting in depression, anxiety, and illness. Conversely, if one focuses on Allah's mercies and favors, all the good in one's life, the body chemistry adapts to the positive input.

Repeated expressions of thankfulness and praise, such as *"Alhamdulillah"* (Praise be to Allah) and *"Subhanallah"* (Glory be to Allah), repeated as many times as one wishes, and a general attitude of optimism and thankfulness to Allah, can make a huge difference. Concerning this, the Prophet (S) said,

> . . .*"Alhamdulillah"* fills the scale (of one's deeds), while *"Subhanallah"* and *"Alhamdulillah"* (in combination) fill up what is between the heavens and the earth. . . *(Muslim, 0432)*

> . . . In every glorification of Allah (saying *"Subhanallah"*) there is a sadaqah, every takbeer (saying *"Allahu Akbar"*) is a sadaqah, every praise of Him (saying *"Alhamdulillah"*) is a sadaqah, every

declaration that He is One (saying "*La ilaha illa-Llah*") is a sadaqah. . . (*Muslim*, 2198)

The dearest words to Allah are four: "*Subhanallah*," "*Alhamdulillah*," "*La ilaha illa-Llah*," and "*Allahu akbar*." There is no harm for you in whatever order you begin (saying them). (*Muslim*, 5329)

Other important *dhikrs* which help to lift one's mood are "*La hawla wa la quwatta illa bil-Lah, al-Ali, al-Adheem*" (There is no power nor might except with Allah, the Most-High, the All-Mighty) and "*Hasbi Allah, wa n'iam al-wakeel*" (Allah is sufficient, and how excellent a trustee!). You may try them. They really work!

I am to a servant of Mine according to his expectation. I am with him when he remembers Me; if he remembers Me in his mind, I also remember him in My mind. If he remembers Me in company, I remember him in a better company. *(Riyad us Saliheen, 1435, Bukhari and Muslim)*

The lesson: Accept what Allah has sent and thank Him.

Keeping Respect
Keep respect for people's personalities, don't put anyone down, and behave with gentleness. No change can ever come about in others' behavior by disrespecting them, making them feel guilty or horrible about themselves, attacking their personalities, or being harsh and rough.

Example: Rasheed is going through an awkward stage. He does everything wrong, bangs himself up, breaks and spills things. Mom reassures him that this stage will pass, but perhaps Rasheed is secretly worried about it—and Mom herself is quite annoyed by it at times. This evening Rasheed spills the milk all over the floor. Instead of Mom's yelling at Rasheed, "You spilled the milk again! I've never seen anyone as clumsy as you," which makes him feel awful about himself, she can either let the incident pass without comment or say casually, "That's all right, Rasheed. We all spill things sometimes, even your dad and me." Or when Nadia forgets to bring her homework home for the second time that week, instead of saying, "What's wrong with you, Nadia—have you got holes in your head? Can't you ever do anything right? This had better not happen again!" Mom says gently, "I think you need to write your assignments in your notebook. I'll try to help you remember things too."

Gentleness, kindness, tolerance, and a good disposition are among the most stressed virtues in Islam, as the following Qur'anic verse and ahadith show:

For it was by mercy from Allah that you (Muhammad) were lenient with them (his companions). And if you had been stern and hard-hearted, they would have dispersed from around you. So pardon them and ask forgiveness for them, and consult with them concerning affairs. . . (3:159)

> Anas bin Malik (R) said: Allah's Messenger (S) had the best disposition among people. . . I served him for nine years but I do not know that he ever said to me, about something which I had done, why I did that or about a thing I had left as to why I had not done that." *(Muslim, 5724)*

> Someone asked the Prophet (S) about virtue and vice. He said, "Virtue is a kind disposition, and vice is what rankles in your heart and what you disapprove of people coming to know about." *(Muslim, 6195).*

A man asked the Prophet (S), "Which (aspect of) faith is most excellent?" He said, "An amiable disposition." *(Mishkat, 0046, transmitted by Ahmad)*

Among the believers who show most the perfect faith are those who have the best disposition and are kindest to their families. *(Mishkat, 3263, transmitted by Tirmidhi)*

Shall I not tell you who is kept away from Hell and from whom Hell is kept away? Everyone who is gentle and kindly, approachable, and of an easy disposition. *(Mishkat, 5084, transmitted by Ahmad and Tirmidhi)*

Truly, Allah is kind and He loves kindness, and He bestows upon kindness that which He does not bestow upon severity and does not bestow upon anything else beside it (kindness). *(Muslim, 6273)*

Show gentleness (or kindness), for if gentleness (or kindness) is found in anything, it beautifies it, and when it is taken out of anything, it damages it. *(Abu Dawud, 4790; Muslim, 6274)*

Allah, the Blessed and Exalted, is kind and loves kindness. He is pleased with it and helps you with it as long as it is not misplaced. *(Muwatta)*

If anyone possesses these three characteristics, Allah will give him an easy death and bring him into His Paradise: gentleness toward the weak, affection toward parents, and kindness to slaves. *(Mishkat, 3364, transmitted by Tirmidhi)*

Equanimity, gentleness, and good behavior are one
twenty-fifth of prophethood. *(Muwatta)*

The one who is deprived of gentleness is deprived of
good. *(Abu Dawud, 4791)*

The Prophet (S) said to one of his Companions,
"You have two characteristics which Allah likes:
gentleness and deliberation. " *(Abu Dawud, 5206)*

The lesson: Gentleness, tolerance, and kindness generate
good feelings and good results; harshness and severity turn
people off and breed negative feelings.

Regaining Your Sense of Humor

When a heavy atmosphere hangs between two people, the
laughter has gone. And any joking is usually sarcastic, to tear
apart the other. As you work at improving a relationship, as the
tension eases, look for ways to return the shared laughter
between you and others. Nothing turns people off more than
individuals who are grim, too serious, taking everything as if it
were of the utmost gravity. Lightheartedness and humor are
not only assets but necessities. The Prophet (S) had a subtle,
gentle sense of humor, and smiled often, people felt happy just
looking at his face and being around him. Turning off attacks
or conflicts with a good-humored remark can make all the difference in the world between confrontation and reconciliation,
especially in situations in which confrontation seems likely.

Example: Mom goes to work early in the morning. The
others are still having breakfast when she leaves, and when she
comes home from work at four o'clock, the litter from breakfast is still there. Fourteen-year-old Maryam comes home at
about the same time. She walks into the kitchen and looks dis-
dainfully at the clutter. "Look at this disgusting mess," Maryam

begins. "I don't see why I have to come home day after a day to a house that looks like this."

Mom's usual response would be to yell, "Well you're one of the people who left it this way! Do you think we have a maid in this house? Why can't you ever do anything to help out around here?" If she can remain calm and think of it in time, she can laugh instead, "Well, I don't know why I should either. Shall we both move out, or both help clean up?" Or she can give Maryam a hug, deflecting her hostility, and say, "Okay, honey, we'll plow into it right now together, and you can tell me how your day at school was."

The lesson: Keep a sense of humor, turn aside hostility with lightness, and don't take anything, including yourself and others, too seriously.

> Repel evil with what is better. We know what ever they allege. (Qur'an 23:96)

> Fear Allah wherever you are; if you follow an evil deed with a good one, you will obliterate it; and deal with people with a good disposition. *(Mishkat, 5083,* transmitted by *Ahmad, Tirmidhi* and *Darimi).*

SEEKING ARBITRATION OR HELP

When a relationship seems totally blocked between two people in the family or in the community, to the extent that by themselves they cannot seem to work out an acceptable relationship, it is commendable to seek arbitration or other forms of help. Parents are the natural arbitrators between their children; otherwise older close relatives are usually preferred to going outside the family for advice in settling disputes. An Islamic scholar or individual of piety of either sex can also be consulted for advice. Whene a Muslim is available for consultation, seeking his help is generally preferable to consulting a non-Muslim advisor, such as a counselor or a psychologist.

The qualities to look for in the one who is consulted are two: that he or she is completely trustworthy and able to keep confidences, and that he or she has the knowledge, understanding and wisdom to be of use in the situation. The consultation should be done discreetly, the aim of the advice being both to protect the rights of all parties affected, including the general protection of the community, and to resolve the conflicts in the relationship. The aim of such consultation is to ensure that future problems are avoided, and rarely to worry over blame, who did what to whom, except for a serious criminal act. Nonetheless, it is important that all the parties be led to assume responsibility for their part in the conflict.

In any conflict situation, there are always two parties, each seeing the situation from diametrically opposed points of view. Generally there is excuse-making, concealing matters that one does not want to make public, whitewashing one's own role in the conflict and fastening the blame on the other person, often by means of exaggeration, either from one or both sides. It is the job of the advisor to sort out all the claims and counter-claims, and to inform them of any Islamic guidelines, any related information from the Qur'an and *sunnah*, and how it applies, to balance the relationship between them.

Allah alone knows the truth, but we hope each side is presenting his or her perception of reality as accurately as possible. The advisor attemps to correct any unbalanced perceptions. A parent may be so worried about her son's guidance that she forgets to balance her concern with the reality that he is an adult, responsible for himself, and that she is capable of making errors of judgment about what is best for him. A man may be so worried about treating his cousin, a new immigrant, with Islamic hospitality, that he neglects his responsibilities to his wife and children for months on end. Both parties will hear the

Islamic position concerning the situation and their behavior, will be told of the gravity of any sin or mistake, and will be introduced to some ways of easing the conflict.

The subject of non-Muslim therapists, counselors. or psychiatrists has already been dealt with at length.

> And if two groups among the believers fight, make peace between them. But if one of them transgresses against the other, fight against the one which has transgressed until it returns to Allah's orders. Then if it returns, make peace between them with justice and fairness. Truly, Allah loves those who are fair. The believers are only brothers, so make peace between your two (contending) brothers, and be mindful of Allah in order that you may be shown mercy. (Qur'an 49:9-10)

> The Prophet heard the voices of some people quarrelling near his gate, so he went to them and said, "I am only a human being and litigants with cases of disputes come to me, and maybe one of them presents his case eloquently in a more convincing and impressive way than the other, and I give my verdict in his favor thinking he is truthful. So if I give a Muslim's right to another (by mistake), then that (property) is a piece of fire which is up to him to take or leave it. (*Bukhari*, vol 9, #295, ch. 31)

> There are six rights of a Muslim upon a Muslim: when you meet him, greet him; when he invites you, respond to him; when he seeks counsel, give him advice; when he sneezes and praises Allah, say to him "Allah have mercy on you"; when he is sick, visit him; and when he dies, follow his funeral. *(Muslim)*

The lesson: If a problem proves, over the long run, to be more than you can handle, get advice or help.

SEPARATING THE WAYS

Sometimes, despite all efforts, conflicts within a family become so severe that separation becomes the best course of action. It may be necessary to agree to disagree and arrange a retreat to a safe distance so that contacts can be limited and controlled.

> And the servants of the Most Merciful are those who walk on the earth in humility, and when the ignorant address them, they say "Peace!" (Qur'an 25:63)

> A person said, "O Messenger of Allah, I have relatives with whom I try to have a relationship, but they cut it. I treat them well, but they treat me badly. I am nice to them, but they are harsh toward me." At this he said, "If it is as you say, then you are throwing hot ashes (on them by being good to them), and there will always be with you on Allah's behalf one (an angel) who will keep you dominant over them as long as you keep to this." *(Muslim, 6204)*

> The joiner (of ties of relationship) is not the one who (merely) returns (the good done to him by his relatives), but rather the joiner is the one who, when a relationship is cut, mends it. *(Bukhari, 8.20)*

> Souls are marshalled troops. The similar ones have affinity to each other and the dissimilar ones differ (among themselves). *(Bukhari, 4.552A and Muslim, 6376)*

Example: Maha's sister is a thoroughly secular, worldly Muslim. She doesn't practice her religion and mocks Maha for doing so. Her children, cousins to Maha's children, follow their mother's outlook, taking pride in their expensive house and clothes, totally wrapped up in their vast numbers of toys, gadgets, and means of entertainment, and using such things to "prove" their superiority. Maha and her sister meet every now and then at family gatherings and on holidays; if their mother and others bring them together, they sometimes see each other more frequently. But Maha's children snub their cousins as their mother snubs Maha. Visits with them always end in bitter feelings.

This is a test from Allah. The early Muslims suffered greatly from such problems, and there is a wealth of material both in the Qur'an and in hadith dealing with it. Maha cannot cut off her relations with these members of her family but she *can* limit contact with them. What is obligatory is to maintain the relationship as a relationship—that is, to remain as sisters to each other, and to be helpful and supportive whenever necessary.

This is an awkward relationship for Maha herself, and even more difficult is teaching her children how to manage in the face of their cousins' bad manners. Politely limiting contact can help keep the world in perspective. Making sure as far as possible that contact occurs when other people are present can dilute the strain when the families do get together, and large gatherings may be easier than small ones. Naturally Maha also needs to provide herself and her children with a social life among friends who will lend support to their values, including as many congenial, practicing families as possible, to provide a positive contrast to her sister's family and their negative examples.

At the same time, Maha must not be self-righteous or allow her children to assume that attitude—that is, she must avoid speaking pridefully about her own "Islamic" qualities, and putting down her sister and her sister's family for their lack of them. When the subject comes up with Maha's children, it might be appropriate to say something like, "I really feel sorry about the way my sister has decided to live her life, and I hope her children will realize that there is another way. But I still remember many good things about her when we were young. I hope one day she'll change and turn to Allah" (or "stop acting like this and become my good sister again"). Such an approach implies that while her sister's actions are wrong, she has a good side and possesses the potential for change; it implies caring, not arrogance. We must make it clear to our children that we are not the judge and that Allah alone knows who will be where on the Day of Judgment.

On the other hand, if Maha complains about her sister all over town, she will, at the very least, be guilty of backbiting, if not slander. Maha could rationalize such behavior by saying that she's warning others about the evil in her sister, but that is a justification for showing how much "better" she is than the sister who snubs her, encouraging people to take sides with her against her sister, and getting things that bother her off her chest. Warnings should be given only when there is a real need, and should be given privately, unless there is a case of serious injustice. Maha may complain to her mother or to a close wise friend who might help mediate or address the problem.

> Whenever you speak, be just, even though it concerns a close relative. (Qur'an 6:154)

As for her sister's children, Maha's nieces and nephews are neither responsible for their parents' values nor, as yet, for their own wrong understanding and behavior. Perhaps Maha and her children are intended to be the means for bringing one of her sister's children to Allah. Conversely, if Maha cut them off, it would end such a possibility and might push them all still further from Allah, and Maha would bear responsibility for that. At the same time, seeing them so often that Maha is unable to keep control of herself and her own children might also turn them away. Islam is the religion of moderation—in such a case, not too close and not too distant. Maha herself is the best judge of the proper distance, which may vary with time and circumstances, always asking Allah for guidance and help.

In dealing with such situations, it is important to remember that a person can always turn to Allah, ask forgiveness for past sins, and reform. This may happen earlier or later, as late as one's last breath. As Allah is endlessly forgiving and merciful, we must also try to forgive others and not hold hard feelings. At the same time, we must not allow ourselves to be pushed into doing what violates our principles.

> Let them forgive and overlook. Would you not like
> that Allah should forgive you? And Allah is Most
> Forgiving, Most Merciful. (Qur'an 24:22)

Maha's example is a common one, but worse threats can come from family than the example of arrogance and disdain for religion. Parents can be torn between their desire to protect their children and their obligation to respect ties, when such ties may be a real burden. If we feel there is just cause, we need to warn our children about people and we can severely limit contact.

> And We have made some of you trials for others;
> will you be patient? And Allah is Seer (of all
> things). (Qur'an 25:20)

Unfortunately, it is often difficult for parents to warn a child in a moderate and meaningful way. This takes tact, thought, follow-up and watchfulness on the part of parents, and even then children may simplify, distort, forget, block out, and/or exaggerate a warning. We do the best we can and know that even if the child doesn't understand much of what is being said just now, in a few months or years matters will be more clear to him or her.

And leave alone those who have taken their religion
as a pastime and amusement, and whom the life of
this world has deceived. . . (Qur'an 6:70)

Allah expands the provision for whomever He wills
and narrows (it for whomever He wills); and they
rejoice in the life of the world, but the life of the
world compared to the Hereafter is nothing but a
temporary comfort. (Qur'an 13:26)

They know the outward appearances of the life of the
world, but they are heedless of the Hereafter.
(Qur'an 30:07)

The lesson: Minimizing contact, without breaking family
ties, may be the most suitable way out of a difficult or destructive relationship.

TIES WITH NON-MUSLIM RELATIVES

O you who believe, do not take your fathers and your
brothers as friends if they prefer unbelief over faith.
(Qur'an 9:23)

O you who believe, do not take not as friends those
who take your religion as a joke and an amusement
from among the ones who were given the Scripture
before you and the unbelievers. And be mindful of
Allah if you are believers. (Qur'an 5:57)

Allah does not forbid you, concerning those who do
not fight you for faith nor drive you out of your
homes, from dealing righteously with them and

being just toward them. Truly, Allah likes those who
are just. (Qur'an 60:8)

Asma bint Abu Bakr reported: During the period of
the peace treaty of the Quraysh with the Messenger
of Allah (S), my mother, accompanied by her father,
came to visit me, and she was an idolater. I consulted the Messenger of Allah (S) and said, "O
Messenger of Allah, my mother has come to me and
she desires (what a mother desires from a daughter).
Shall I keep good relations with her?" He said, "Yes,
keep good relations with her." (Bukhari, 4.407)

There is a difference between being allied with someone,
confiding in him and taking him as a friend and ally to the
exclusion of Muslims, and "dealing righteously," "being just,"
and "keeping good relations." Once this is clear, we are free to
treat our non-Muslim relatives with respect and kindness,
depending on their ability to respect and accept our identity and
practice as Muslims.

When they respect us and our religious choice, our relationship can proceed normally and smoothly. While we put priority
on our religious obligations and our ties with the Muslim community, at the same time we try to smooth over difficulties and
minimize differences, not making issues except in matters of
principle. But when relatives become hostile, we need to adopt
a course like that of Maha and her sister, described above (in
such a case, although Maha's sister is technically a "Muslim,"
her orientation is clearly otherwise, as is shown by her lifestyle
and her hostile behavior to her practicing relatives).

The ahadith about good treatment of parents make no distinction between Muslim and non-Muslim parents (see chapter
4). The examples of the Prophet (S) and the early Muslims support this lack of distinction, except in cases in which the parents (or other relatives) belonged to the enemy side, active in a

war against them. Only when our parents try to force us to act against our religious convictions do we refuse and withdraw to some extent, while not cutting off the tie of relationship and the obligations due from ourselves to them. As Allah Ta'ala says,

> And We have enjoined on man (goodness) to his parents. His mother bore him in weakness upon weakness, and his weaning is in two years, in order that you may be thankful to Me and to your parents. To Me is the (final) return. But if they strive to make you associate with Me anything about which you have no knowledge, do not obey them; and keep company with them in this life with kindness, and follow the path of the one who turn to Me. (Qur'an 31:14)

> And We have enjoined on man goodness to parents. But if they strive to make you associate with Me anything of which you have no knowledge, do not obey them. To Me is the (final) return, whereupon I shall inform you of what you used to do. (Qur'an 29:8)

Since so many diverse life styles are practiced in the Western world, it may be easier for converts in America or Europe to announce their conversion to their families than it would be in more traditional societies. But it can be traumatic to the family nonetheless, and we can proceed with as much empathy and kindness as possible.

Due to the extremely negative image of Islam in this society as a whole, the reaction of families to the conversion may be severe. As a general rule, things may go more easily if a new or intending convert does not drop the news of his or her conversion on the heads of his unsuspecting family like a bomb. Rather it may be led up to gradually and gently, throwing out information and intimations of one's interest long before the actual time of making shahadah. If time does not permit this or there are other constraints, it may be wiser and more tactful in the long-run for some people to keep their acceptance of Islam a secret for a time until their families are mentally prepared for it.

Certainly every new Muslim hopes that the announcement of his or her acceptance of Islam will not be met with hostility but rather with understanding and tolerance. And beyond this, many of us long to be able to communicate our own conviction, sense of fulfillment, and love for Islam to the people who are closest to us. Invariably we hope that they may recognize in it the light which we ourselves have seen. But dropping the news of conversion suddenly on unprepared family members is not a step in this direction; rather it is very likely to create anger and pain, and call all of their upbringing and values into question. Nor does preaching at people work, especially at parents, who seldom are open to accepting advice or new beliefs from their children. So gentleness, moderation, wisdom, and foresight need to be exercised in this regard.

Put yourself in the place of your parents, especially if they are religious, to fully appreciate the pain this step may cause them. We can imagine how we ourselves would feel if a beloved child whom we had brought up as a practicing Muslim appeared one day and announced that he or she had converted to Christianity, Judaism, Buddhism, Hinduism, or anything else. Betrayed, wounded to the quick, rejected, feeling a sense of shame and failure —that would undoubtedly describe our reaction. Recognizing this, then, let us be tender and gentle with our parents when we speak of our new-found faith, not brandishing it over their heads like a weapon with a hint of "Accept this because I have, or else. . ."

What about family members who are not willing to accept our choice once it has been made? Situations differ widely, but the problems are usually greatest in the first few years and die down later, as families grow used to the idea and see the results. Most parents want what is best for their children, and if they see their son or daughter well-settled, peaceful, and happy, living a clean, stable, productive life and possessing the new confidence and special glow that Islam often gives to people, they will gradually unwind. Many of their fears concerning the new religion and its followers will have been tested out and proven to be false over a period of time, and they will have observed and experienced much good as a result of their child's newly-found stability, marriage partner, Muslim friends, and so on.

If the convert's parent or other relative feels very strongly about some religious dogma—for example, a Christian who feels that anyone not accepting Christ as his personal savior is doomed for eternity—the new Muslim will likely have trouble maintaining ties. Closed-minded people rarely change. Even if ties are maintained, there will probably be conflicts over Christian holidays and the like. But we can only do the best we are able. Such a situation is difficult and painful for the whole family. It may help to remember that many of the early Muslims passed through such conflicts and that the Islamic guidelines concerning it are clear.

When reasonably normal contacts can be maintained, the biggest problem is one of education. Most non-Muslims know very little, and often nothing at all, about Islam, or whatever they "know" may be incorrect. When parents of a convert are involved, as a rule they are not prepared to be "taught" by their child, however grown-up—and especially to be taught religion, which normally a parent teaches a child, not vice-versa. As a result, they are often unwilling to learn or to discuss anything concerning their child's newly-adopted religion and way of life. In addition, they may regard his or her having changed from the religion (or culture) of birth to an alien one as an act amounting to treason. It may truly feel like a betrayal of all they have brought up their child to value, whether it be religion or American culture.

Some families, therefore, take the path of avoiding all discussion, treating the Muslim member as if he were just the same as before. This can feel like a real put-down, as if your true identity is not being acknowledged, and can lead to strained or even broken relations. Other relatives may resort to hassling: "Why do you have to dress that weird way? I don't see what dress has to do with religion"; "Why don't you let your kids celebrate birthdays? It gives them a strong sense of identity, self worth, etcetera."; "What's wrong with borrowing money from the bank? After all, everything runs on interest, all over the world. I don't see how you can go along with rules that were made for seventh-century Arabia." And so on; the list is long. These questions are often more statements of disapproval than requests for information. They mean, "Stop that and act normal again."

But time is on the side of change. Gradually, as people live together and share activities and experiences, distorted ideas give place to correct ones, non-acceptance is replaced with tolerance for differences, and indifference is replaced with respect. In most cases, the power of relationship will, in the long run, overcome the hostility or resistance to accepting the new religion and its way of life.

NON-MUSLIM HOLIDAYS

Christmas and Easter

Our life in this society automatically exposes us to a variety of non-Muslim holidays and other occasions. These impinge on both adults and children. Christmas is a particular problem because of the long duration of the pre-Christmas commercialization and the generalized effort to share the party with everyone. All the decorations, music, and razzle-dazzle, which are reinforced by schools as well as by non-Muslim family members, can be very enticing to our children. If the parents are recent converts, used to the emotional appeal and holiday atmosphere of Christmas, there may be a big emotional pull for them too.

As the new convert strengthens his belief in Islam and his spiritual values, the material aspects of Christmas can be phased out gradually. He may find a way to take a limited part in the celebration of the holiday without going deeply into it, accepting family invitations and the like, so long as it does not harm his faith or his children's. Wisdom must simply be used in knowing when enough is enough.

In this vein, many converts continue to give Christmas presents to parents and other near relatives who may be hurt by their rejection of this holiday—and, in the case of Christian relatives, of all it stands for religiously. If grandparents or other family members insist on giving Christmas gifts to a Muslim child, this can be accepted graciously as an act of love. When children are older, they can be told, "Grandma loves you and wanted to share that with you. Christmas isn't our holiday, but we like sharing with Grandma and the family. And pretty soon we'll have Eid, with presents." In this we can be guided by the *ahadith* related to the subject:

> The Messenger of Allah (S) sent a gift to Umar ibn al-Khattab (R), and Umar (R) returned it. The Messenger of Allah (S) said, "Why did you return it?" He said, "O Messenger of Allah, did you not tell us that it is better for us not to take anything from anyone?" The Messenger of Allah (S) said, "That is through asking. Provision which Allah gives you is different from asking." Umar said, "By the one in Whose hand my soul is, I will not ask anything from anyone, and anything that comes to me without my asking for it, I will accept." *(Muwatta)*

> Abdullah ibn Amr slaughtered a sheep and he said, "Have you presented a gift from it to my neighbor, the Jew, for I heard the Messenger of Allah (S) say, '(The angel) Gabriel kept on commending the neigh-

bor to me until I thought he would make him an
heir'?" *(Abu Dawud, 5133)*

And if this applies to a neighbor, one of a different faith,
what about our nearest relatives, on their festive occasions?
The Prophet (S) said,

> Give presents to one another, for a present removes
> enmity from the breast, and a woman should not
> despise even the gift of half a sheep's trotter (to be
> cooked) from her neighbor. *(Mishkat, 3028,* trans-
> mitted by *Tirmidhi; Muwatta; Bukhari, 3.740)*

However, this applies only as long as there are no "strings"
attached to receiving a gift. The Prophet (S) said,

> O people, accept presents so long as they remain
> presents, but when. . .the presents are given for the
> religion of one of you, then leave them alone. *(Abu
> Dawud, 2952)*

More insidious would be accepting to become part of the
Christmas morning gift-opening scene, a tremendously waste-
ful exercise in self-indulgence that makes Muslims feel quite
uneasy. Muslims are not alone in dissociating themselves from
the celebration of a holiday which has become so commercial-
ized and devoid of nearly all higher significance. We can say,
"We respect and love Jesus as one of the greatest of all
prophets, and we don't want to participate in celebrating an
occasion that really has nothing to do with him. After all, no
one really knows what day he was born on, and it's almost certain that it wasn't December 25th." This may have a more tactful effect than more aggressive statements such as, "We have
our own holidays and that's enough for us," "We don't believe
that Jesus was the Son of God or God, so how can we celebrate

his birthday," or, "Christmas is basically a pagan holiday and we don't want to have anything to do with it."

In any case, over time, it will become easier to phase out such practices with gentle discouragement, and will probably be more productive than making issues and hurting people's feelings. It is wiser in the long run not to overreact to the "contamination" of our children. Life needs to be kept in perspective.

An example: Grandma takes the baby to the Mall to have his picture taken with Santa on the afternoon she volunteered to babysit. While from a Muslim's point of view this is disrespectful to his religion, Islam is new to Grandma and this is her first grandchild. She may not be aware that she has done anything out of order; after all, all her friends have such pictures and she has no idea that Muslims don't believe in Santa Claus. How can her son handle this tactfully?

He doesn't have to make it into an issue. First of all, a baby or quite young child wlll be unaware of what happened. The picture can be torn up or left with Grandma. It will fade away. Grandma will gradually adjust as she learns more—gently, Allah willing. Isn't this a better course than a Muslim son's blowing up at his mother and accusing her of disrespecting his religion, especially when she really had no idea of doing anything of the sort (or even if she knew, but thought it just some nonsense of her son). In the long term, for Muslim children whose parents practice Islam in the home, such incidents become very minor, although some children yearn for Santa or a pretty tree for a time. Hopefully, even though we live in a non-Muslim society, we parents will find ways to make Islam so lovely to them that they won't feel they're missing much.

The same observations hold true for the celebration of the other major Christian festival, Easter. This holiday is more spiritual in nature for Christians, but also frequently easier to avoid for a Muslim. We just don't go to the church services. Because of its spiritual nature, schools today do little for this holiday, besides allowing a vacation period. There is usually far less pressure from Christians to share this holiday .

It is often possible to explain for both Christmas and Easter nonobservance, with utmost tact and gentleness, that you are concerned about your children's getting caught in a crossfire of religious values and you feel that it's better for them to participate only in the observances of their own faith, at least while they're young. It can be explained that this is not because you have bad feelings toward Jesus, the holiday, or your relatives, but is simply a measure you feel is correct in order to keep the children from being confused.

Birthdays

The custom of celebrating birthdays was initiated to celebrate the births of the royal and noble children of Europe. During the last century, little by little the celebration of birthdays worked its way down to the middle class, until it became an occasion for all people.

The celebration of birthdays is a controversial subject among Muslims, for it is not and never was an Islamic custom. Some feel that since it is a norm in this culture, there is no harm in observing it and allowing the children to have pride in their being a year older, together with their friends. Others feel that it is an alien and unacceptable practice, that observing it is mere imitation and represents a loss of Islamic identity. In between these two points of view are various shadings. Some families give gifts, even a small token, on a birthday, especially when a child is young. Others have special treats, a cake, or a dinner out with the family. Still others make this an occasion for remembering their own parents, who gave them life and who, if anyone does, deserve to receive thanks and congratulations for this occasion.

But what is the correct Islamic position on this? The answer is that since the celebration of birthdays is a new matter that was not dealt with by the scholars of earlier times, we must simply make certain deductions from the general overall Islamic guidelines.

The idea of congratulating and giving presents to a person because he was born is alien to Islam and in fact makes no sense at all. We did not create ourselves, to deserve congratulations on the event of having added another year (actually, one more day) to our lives. If anyone deserves appreciation on this occasion, it is Allah Ta'ala, Who gave us life for another year, and after that our parents, especially the mother who bore us.

Birthdays, as they are generally celebrated, are an exercise in ego-boosting and self-importance. To a Muslim of right mind, there is something rather odious in the idea of calling people to celebrate an event over which one has no control or say, for the purpose of congratulating him and bringing him gifts—a bit of a throwback to paganism, if you will, and very different from our Islamic celebrations. However, there are no hard-and-fast rules concerning the matter, and each family is free to do whatever is felt to be most suitable. But if birthdays *are* celebrated, it should be done in a correct spirit, in moderation and with thankfulness to Allah Who gave and continued us in this life—an occasion for giving *sadaqah* or doing some other good work, rather than becoming a mere ego trip.

Other holidays

In the observance of Valentine's Day, the Fourth of July, Halloween, Mother's and Father's Day, there is again a wide variation among Muslims, and again, no fixed rules can be given. We can merely suggest that if such holidays are observed, it be done in a way which does not undermine anyone's understanding or practice of Islam.

Valentine's Day, with its commercialization and cheapening of romantic feelings, originated with St. Valentine in the Catholic Church and is thus another example of corrupted ex-religious celebrations. As such, a Muslim can demand exemption of his children from this celebration in schools. The romantic ideas of love are suitable only between husband and wife. Otherwise it is suggested that in the elementary school observance of this holiday, girls be allowed to send Valentine *friendship* cards to girls, and boys to boys. If the school's policy is that everyone must receive a card from everyone else, cards with appropriate messages can be chosen (one could even buy a box of note cards with suitable non-Valentine designs for this purpose).

Although many Muslims observe Mother's and Father's Day, these occasions carry the suggestion that parents are to be appreciated and treated specially only on one particular day out of the whole year, an idea which a Muslim finds totally unacceptable. At the same time, making someone feel special and loved is good, no matter what occasion, and not doing it (especially with non-Muslim mothers and fathers) may be taken as a hurtful slight.

In its origins, Halloween was All Hallow's Eve, the night all the spirits came out of the graves to haunt people. Jack o' lanterns, costumes, and parades were made to scare away the evil lurking, and crosses were drawn on doors and chimneys to protect houses. Evil and Satan have always been associated with this night, inherited by the Church from pagan converts in Europe. In this country, efforts were made to make a clean, safe, fun occasion for children to put on costumes and visit the neighbors for candy. This worked for a number of years, but it has increasingly become a bizarre occasion with definite satanic and occult overtones. This is one holiday that it is unquestionably better for Muslims to avoid having children participate in. Indeed, many Christians are protesting this observance in schools today.

It is suggested that because of all the evil energies being poured forth during this annual event, it is important to keep children indoors that night. It is important to be aware of the following sayings of the Prophet (S):

Cover your utensils and tie up your waterskins, and close your doors and keep your children close to you at night, as the jinn (in another version, devils) spread out at such time and snatch things away. When you go to bed, put out your lights, for the mischief-doer (i.e., the rat) may drag away the wick of the candle and burn the dweller of the house. (*Bukhari,* 4.533)

When it is the darkness or night or evening, stop your children from going out, for the devils are abroad at that time. But when an hour of the night has passed, release them and close the doors and mention Allah's Name, for Satan does not open a closed door. Tie the mouth of your waterskin and mention Allah's Name; cover your containers and utensils and mention Allah's Name; cover them even by placing something across them, and extinguish your lamps. (*Bukhari*, 7.527)

MUSLIM HOLIDAYS

The Two Eids

We now come to our special holidays, the two Islamic festivals, Eid al-Fitr and Eid al-Adha.

While we should celebrate the Eids with our children in a way that doesn't exaggerate them, at the same time, we want them to love our own special occasions, especially to counterbalance the often strong attraction of other holidays. There are no specific rules for the observance of the Eids other than the highly commendable attendance at the Eid prayers, which constitutes a gathering of the whole community. If at all possible, the Eids should be observed as days off from work so that all the family members join in a day-long celebration, congratulating all we meet for successful completion of the fast or the hajj for that year, depending on which of the Eids it is. Muslim holidays should be registered with the local school administration so that children can be excused from school without penalty.

Since the Muslim presence in this country is relatively new, we do not yet have many traditional songs or activities for the Eids as people do in many parts of the Muslim world. Whatever any of us have can be shared, however; there should be singing, playing, and festivity. Our religion does not specify any details on how to celebrate, except the encouragement of making time to be with people and enjoy our time in healthy, wholesome ways.

For example, parents of young children can initiate simple projects, such as making Eid cards or Eid cookies. When children are older, they can help with cleaning and decorating the house, working with their mothers to prepare special foods for the occasion, making decorations of various kinds, and so on. Some communities plan large group picnics when the weather permits. Some make holiday parties for the children of the community with theatrical productions and group games.

This American society is perhaps unique in the world for the enormously extravagant multiple traditions associated with its celebration of Christmas. Whatever we do, we *don't* need to compete with such excesses, but given our particular situation, we do need to do a little extra for our children so that they will love Islamic holidays and not be caught by the lure of the prevailing extravaganza.

With all their lovely traditions and social aspects, the two Eids have always been and will remain primarily religious and spiritual occasions, a time for sharing the happiness and good things Allah has given us. Non-Muslims often suggest sharing all holidays, theirs and ours. Well, theirs may be shareable, but ours have such a strong spiritual aspect, that we cannot share that. How could we share the Eid prayer with them? What would they get out of it? We are celebrating the completion of fasting or hajj, both intensely spiritual experiences. They can appreciate any good meal, perhaps, and the warm, friendly family-oriented parties we have, but what is truly significant is not shareable with someone who has not participated in our community's spiritual effort.

Earlier we discussed the obligatory charities of the two Eids—that is, *zakah al-fitr,* which is to be given on behalf of every Muslim man, woman and child before the salahof Eid al-Fitr, so that the poor as well as the rich are included in the general rejoicing at the end of Ramadan, and the sharing of meat on Eid al-Adha with the poor and needy, as well as with relatives and friends.

Other Occasions

For a Muslim, each Friday *(Jumu'ah)*, our weekly day of congregational worship, is a festive day. Among Muslims in many parts of the world, it is traditional to observe the *Hijra* (the Islamic New Year on the first day of Muharram), marking the Prophet's migration to Madinah. Celebrating the birthday of the Prophet (S) *(Mouloud al-Nabi)* is also common in many parts of the world. Although this was not done by the early Muslims, there is nothing in it contrary to religion; in fact, since it constitutes an outpouring of love for the blessed Prophet (S) and a reminder of his life and mission, in this time its observance may be important for the building of our faith. *Lailat al-Me'raj,* commemorating the night of the Prophet's ascension to Heaven, and *Lailat al-Qadr,* the Night of Power, commemorating the first revelation of the Qur'an to the holy Prophet (S) in the cave of Hira, are considered special, holy nights of the Islamic year, which are observed by many Muslims who stay awake to pray during the night.

As for other, more mundane occasions, it is traditional among Muslims, if Allah blesses one with something good— one gets a promotion, passes an important test, gets married, has a baby, or some calamity is averted—to give charity as a gesture of thankfulness. One may also celebrate by inviting others to a meal, and it is especially recommended to remember the poor at these times.

Whatever events we are celebrating, it is best to keep the occasion simple so that the expense and effort will not be too great on the host and hostess (potlucks are a great invention!), and so that a larger number of people can be invited, especially for weddings. Trying to outdo others, or at least come up to their level, when one cannot afford it is an unacceptable and foolish practice. One should do what is easy and possible, not becoming bankrupt or wiped out with exhaustion in order to put on an extravagant show for others. Guests who are invited to these celebrations are not expected to bring gifts, for the host is showing kindness to his guests because he values them and wants to share his happiness with them, not expecting anything in return. However, bringing a gift (or food) as a spontaneous act is a way of showing that one cares, and it is always appreciated.

Children, as we all know, love parties and celebrations and outings with friends. Islam has neither institutionalized nor forbidden any such traditions. Therefore we are free in this regard, and we can be creative according to our needs and means, evolving our own special family traditions. Some families celebrate the child's first recitation or memorization of the Qur'an with a Qur'an or *"Bismillah"* party. Creating celebrations around children's special achievements or significant personal or family occasions helps to bond families, but these must not be allowed to become an exercise in self-congratulations and showing-off. Humbleness and modesty are prime Islamic virtues, which often contrast sharply to the showing-off and boasting which is so common in the society around us.

As a person celebrates his joyous occasions with his family and community, so the community pitches in to help him during hard times, visiting or calling to lighten the time for someone sick in bed, offering condolences and helping out with food for a death in the family, caring for widows, divorced or destitute people and orphans, and so much more. And the children participate in this as well as the adults.

THE CHILD AND THE MUSLIM COMMUNITY

The Muslim community is an extension of the family. Since few parents living in America have close extended families of Muslim relatives to support them in rearing their children, the Muslim community must fill the void. Likewise, if the parents are gone, the Muslim community has responsibility for orphans as well.

> The believing men and women are protectors of one another. They enjoin what is right and forbid what is wrong, and establish the *salah* and pay the *zakah* and obey Allah and His Messenger. (Qur'an 9:71)

> Indeed, this *ummah* of yours is one single *ummah*. (Qur'an 21:92, 23:52)

> The believers are brothers (to one another). (Qur'an 49:10)

The Prophet (S) said,

> I and the one who looks after an orphan will be like this in Paradise," and he showed his middle and index fingers and separated them slightly. (*Bukhari*, 7.224, *Muslim* 7108, *Muwatta*)

> "If anyone strokes an orphan's head, doing it only for the sake of Allah, he will have blessings for every hair over which his hand passes; and if anyone treats well an orphan girl or boy under his care, he and I

will be like these two in Paradise," and he put two of his fingers together. (*Mishkat*, 4974, transmitted by *Ahmad* and *Tirmidhi*)

The best house among the Muslims is one in which there is an orphan who is well-treated, and the worst house among the Muslims is one in which there is an orphan who is badly treated. (*Mishkat*, 4973, transmitted by *Ibn Majah*)

The one who exerts himself for a widow and for a poor person is like a fighter in the cause of Allah or one who fasts during the day and stays awake (praying) in the night. (*Bukhari*, 8.35 and 8.36)

You see the believers in their mercy and their love and their sympathy (for one other) resembling one body, for if any part of the body has a complaint, the whole body shares with it the sleeplessness and fever. (*Bukhari*, 8.40)

In a collective fashion, Muslims look out for other Muslim children and sometimes act like a concerned relative when the parent is not around. If an adult sees Usama throwing rocks in a dangerous fashion, it is commendable for him to do whatever is suitable to prevent harm and teach Usama not to do it again. If, on the other hand, he sees Usama helping his little brother in the park, he might commend him for the kind deed and praise his good nature, rewarding Usama with recognition for the good he has done and encouraging him to do more.

Those who do not show mercy to our young ones and do not realize the right of our elders are not from us. (*Abu Dawud*, 4925)

> He who is deprived of gentleness is deprived of good. (*Abu Dawud*, 4791)

> If anyone possesses these three characteristics Allah will give him an easy death and bring him into His Paradise: gentleness toward the weak, affection towards parents, and kindness to slaves. (*Mishkat*, 3364, transmitted by *Tirmidhi*)

> Shall I not tell you who is kept away from Hell and from whom Hell is kept away? Everyone who is gentle and kindly, approachable, and of an easy disposition. (*Mishkat*, 4084, transmitted by *Tirmidhi*)

An important aspect of training children is to discourage their misbehavior away from home. Parents often feel embarrassed when a child acts up in public, so any support for the child in doing this undermines their authority. For example, if Mommy is trying to get little Safiyah to stop climbing on the furniture in the home of a friend, Mommy's authority is undermined if the hostess says, out of politeness, "That's ok, I don't mind."

Mommy is trying to teach Safiyah acceptable behavior and respect for other people's property, an important lesson. Since obedience to parents is fard (obligatory), a considerate bystander will always support the parent's authority. "Okay Safiyah, quickly, quickly, listen to Mommy."

How that authority is expressed is another matter. If the parent's rule or method of discipline seems out of line, a private discussion with the parent is the most tactful way to bring about meaningful change rather than a headlong, confrontational challenging of parental authority in front of the child. When more serious problems are discovered, we seek the method of least disruptive intervention if the child needs protection from the parent.

SERVICE

As we have seen, Muslim children are expected to treat others respectfully, particularly older people. In addition, they can be encouraged to be considerate, caring, and helpful whenever they can. Since Islamic life is both group- and individual-oriented, service and concern for others' needs is an essential principle which should be introduced at an early age.

> No youth will honor an old man because of his years without Allah's appointing someone to honor him when he is old. *(Mishkat, 4971,* transmitted by *Tirmidhi)*

> He does not belong to us who does not show mercy to our young ones and respect to our old ones, and who does not enjoin the good and forbid the wrong. *(Mishkat, 4970,* transmitted by *Tirmidhi)*

> A companion asked A'isha (S), "What did the Prophet use to do in his house?" She replied, "He used to keep himself busy serving his family, and when it was the time for salah, he would go to it." *(Bukhari, 1.644)*

CONCLUSION

In Islam, we do not segregate children out of the world of adults, for our children are an integral part of our world as adults, both in our families and our community. Some have played important roles in Islamic history. Many more have played important roles in teaching Islamic lessons to the adults in their lives.

Our children are born pure and free of sin, but they lack knowledge and experience. After all, they have only recently arrived in this world. Little by little they grow in their ability to exercise self-control, both physical and mental. Physically they grow into abilities from finally being able to reach the door knob and tying their own shoes, to riding a tricycle, then a bicycle, and finally driving a car. Mentally they grow by learning such matters as waiting to be served their meal without crying and negotiating taking turns with others instead of grabbing and fighting. They need our responsible guidance to grow in the best direction.

From the Qur'an and ahadith we know that Allah recognizes and takes into account the complexity of rearing children, and we pray that His leniency is greater for those of us who are rearing our children in this extemely difficult time. He has given us general guidelines concerning our responsibility, our goals as parents, and a sense of the overall environment best suited to the family's well-being. The techniques we have discussed here stress moderate, positive-reinforcement training with a minor note of punishment, reflecting Allah's promise of a scale of justice weighted heavily in favor of mercy.

Parenting is not a minor, insignificant matter, but a tremendously important, time-consuming task for which there is, justifiably, the promise of great reward. It is hoped that more and more Muslim parents will educate themselves about how children develop, take note of their children's unique personalities and abilities, and try to find the best way to rear them accordingly.

Children are a trust from Allah, both a test and a joy. We will be judged according to our intentions and efforts as parents, and we pray that we may be able to make Allah Ta'ala pleased with us and with them.

Bibliography

The Holy Qur'an
Collections of *Hadith:*
   Sahih Bukhari
   Sahih Muslim
   Abu Dawud
   Mishkat al-Masabih
   Al-Muwatta
   Riyadh-us-Saleheen

Abd al-Ati, H. *The Family Structure in Islam,* American Trust Publications, Plainfield, IN., 1977.

Aims and Objectives of Islamic Education, chapters 4 and 6. Hodder and Stoughton, U.K., 1980.

Al-Ghazali, M. *The Muslim's Character.* International Islamic Federation of Student Organizations, Kuwait, 1983.

Bransford, J., and Stein, B. *Behavior Therapy.* Harcourt Brace Jovanovich, N. Y., 1987.

The Ideal Problem Solver. W. H. Freeman & Co., N. Y., 1984.

Crary, E. *Without Spanking or Spoiling.* Parenting Press, Seattle, Wa., 1979.

Al-Dhahabi. *The Major Sins.* Dar al-Fikr, Beirut, 1993.

Dobson, J. *The Strong Willed Child, Birth Through Adolescence.* Tyndale House Publishers, Wheaton, Ill. 1987.

Elkadi, A.. "Muhammad as a Family Man." *Al-Ittihad,* vol. 19, No.1. The Muslim Students Association, Plainfield, In., Jan-March 1982, pp. 49-61.

Faber, A., and Mazlish, E. *Siblings Without Rivalry.* W. W. Norton & Co., N. Y., 1987.

Frost, R., and Moore, S. *The Little Boy Book.* pub. by Ballantine Books, Clarkson N. Potter, Crown, N.Y. 1986.

Ghazali, Imam. *Ihya Uloom al-Din.* (Arabic).

Gibbs, Nancy. "Bringing Up Father," *Time* Magazine, June 28, 1993, p. 53-61.

Gordon, T. *P.E.T., Parent Effectiveness Training.* New American Library Pub., 1975.

Hubaiti, A. "The Prophet and Children," *Journal of the Muslim World League,* Makka, Saudi Arabia, July 1979, pp 25-29.

Ilg, F., and Ames, L. *Child Behavior from Birth to Ten.* Harper & Row, N. Y., 1955.

Joomaye, M. H. "The Muslim Woman: Backbone of the Family." *The Muslim World League Journal*, Makka, Saudi Arabia, Vol. 13, No. 2, Oct.-Nov. 1985, pp. 38-42.

Leman, K. *Making Children Mind Without Losing Yours.* Power Books, Old Tappan, N.J., 1984.

Lewis, D. *How to Be a Gifted Parent.* Berkley Books, N. Y., N. Y., 1979

McDermott, J. *The Complete Book on Sibling Rivalry.* Putnam Publishing Group, N. Y., 1980.

The Parents' Manual, prepared by the Women's Committee of the MSA, published by American Trust Publications, 1992.

Qurashi, M. Y. "Tips on Child Socialization for a Minority Family," *Al-Ittihad.* The Muslim Students Association, Maryland, Oct.-Dec, 1981, pp, 3-13.

Spock, B. *Raising Children in a Difficult Time.* W. W. Norton and Co., N. Y., 1974.

Index